Poetry and the Public

JOSEPH HARRINGTON

Poetry and the Public

The Social Form of Modern U.S. Poetics

Wesleyan University Press, Middletown, Connecticut

Published by Wesleyan University Press,
Middletown, CT 06459
© 2002 Joseph Harrington
All rights reserved
ISBN 0-8195-6537-7 cloth
ISBN 0-8195-6538-5 paper
Printed in the United States of America
Design and composition by Julie Allred,
B. Williams & Associates
Cataloging-in-Publication Data appear
at the end of the book

5 4 3 2 1

For my father, John F. Harrington,
and in memory of my mother,
Elizabeth Peoples Harrington

Contents

ACKNOWLEDGMENTS *ix*

INTRODUCTION. Poetry as Social Form *1*

ONE. Poetry and the Reading Public: Poetic Debates in the Popular Press, 1910–1940 *21*

TWO. High Modernism in Polite Society, or, Allen Tate's Conservative Liberalism *57*

THREE. The Modernist as Liberal: Wallace Stevens and the Poetics of Private Insurance *81*

FOUR. Publicity, Sabotage, and Arturo Giovannitti's "Poetry of Syndicalism" *105*

FIVE. Poetry as Crossing: The Newspaper Verse of Anise (Anna Louise Strong) *127*

SIX. Poetry and Its Publics in the 1990s *159*

NOTES *187*

BIBLIOGRAPHY *205*

INDEX *219*

Acknowledgments

I am indebted to many people, none more so than Susan Schweik, whose belief in this project has sustained my own. The late James E. B. Breslin, Frederick Dolan, Alan Golding, and an anonymous reviewer for Wesleyan University Press also read and critiqued various drafts of the manuscript, and I am deeply grateful for their contributions. I owe many thanks for their insightful and useful comments to those colleagues who have read and critiqued one or more versions of one or more chapters, especially Kate Garrett, Eric Peterson, Meredith Miller, Heather Findlay, Catherine Porter, Marjorie Perloff, Anna Neill, Byron Caminero-Santangelo, Dorice Elliott, and Kathryn Conrad—as well as to all those other folks at Berkeley, the University of Kansas, and elsewhere who egged me on or, in some cases, reined me in. I appreciate all the librarians and information specialists who have assisted me in the research for this book; special thanks to Karyl Winn and the staff of the University of Washington Libraries' Manuscripts, Special Collections, University Archives Division who helped me make the most of a limited amount of time. And many thanks to Suzanna Tamminen, editor-in-chief at Wesleyan, who not only saw value in the manuscript originally, but also shepherded a neophyte author through the process of getting a book into print.

I am grateful to the University of Kansas for a Hall Center for the Humanities Research Fellowship, which allowed me to complete this manuscript, as well as for a Faculty Travel Grant to view the papers of

Anna Louise Strong at the University of Washington Library and for two summers of General Research Fund Grants. I also wish to thank the Huntington Library for a Mayers Fellowship and the University of California, Berkeley, for the Doreen B. Townsend Center for the Humanities Fellowship that allowed me to get this project going.

Portions of chapters 1 and 6 have appeared in *American Literary History,* and an earlier version of chapter 3 appeared in *American Literature.* Thanks very much to Gordon Hutner and Cathy Davidson for making those chapters stronger.

The support of my parents (to whom this book is dedicated) in completing the book goes far beyond bringing the author into being, and cannot be described, let alone repaid. And I am quite sure I would not have made it over the finish line without the continuous encouragement and understanding of my partner, MariaAna Garza. "El amor es grande."

Wesleyan University Press and the author gratefully acknowledge permission to reprint from the following sources:

Excerpts from "Aeneas at New York," "Causerie," "Eclogue of the Liberal and the Poet," "Ode to Our Young Pro-consuls of the Air," "To the Lacedemonians," "The Swimmers" from *Collected Poems, 1919–1976* by Allen Tate. Copyright © 1977 by Allen Tate. Reprinted by permission of Farrar, Straus and Giroux, LLC. Essays of Allen Tate reprinted by permission of Helen H. Tate. Excerpts from *Opus Posthumous* by Wallace Stevens Copyright © 1957 by Elsie Stevens and Holly Stevens. Reprinted by permission of Alfred A. Knopf, a division of Random House, Inc. Excerpts from *Collected Poems* by Wallace Stevens. Copyright © 1954 by Wallace Stevens. Reprinted by permission of Alfred A. Knopf, a division of Random House, Inc.

INTRODUCTION

Poetry as Social Form

Quick: who's better, Itzak Perlman or the Rolling Stones?

If this question sounds like a non sequitur, it is because the grounds for such a comparison are too broad. Both may produce music (indeed, Perlman can play the Stones, the Stones can incorporate "classical" music), but beyond that, the style of music each plays is so distant from the other that such a comparison begins to look meaningless out of any historical context. Likewise, asking whether T. S. Eliot is better than James Whitcomb Riley begs the same questions—it would depend upon whether one wanted a modernist long poem or humorous, rhyming newspaper verse. Comparing them is comparing apples and oranges—unless we are posing the *historical* question of who read each, and what the relations were between the two types of poetry in the 1910s, 1920s, or 1990s.

Nonetheless, it is precisely this sort of comparison that remains fundamental to poetry studies, along with the implicit question, "Is it any good?" Or, said another way, why should we care about *bad* poetry? Despite exciting alternatives to and critiques of this procedure, the overall tendency of poetry studies in the United States (more so than other fields of criticism) has remained evaluative and canonical. And the twentieth-century canon has remained high modernist: even if they're treated historically, when it comes to books of criticism, especially, at the turn of the twentieth century, it's still Pound, Eliot, Williams, Stevens, and maybe Moore, H.D., or Frost. Not only does this picture continue to marginalize other interesting poets, it presents a reified, inaccurate picture of poetry, including "modernist" poetry, of the period. It is difficult to avoid the legacy of New Criticism in explaining the persistence of this canon, though it has become passé to critique the New Critics—largely because their attitudes have been challenged and decentered from most fields of literary studies. But not so in their original metier, poetry scholarship. The story of the early twentieth century is that of modernism, and modernism is defined, axiomatically, by very familiar names.

"New Life for Modernism," proclaims a headline of a recent article in the *Chronicle of Higher Education*. The article reports on the founding convention of the Modernist Studies Association: "[S]cholars of modernism, who, after years of being associated with the fusty and retrograde, suddenly found themselves energized and optimistic" (Heller A21). Modernism's stock was up, in other words. "[T]hey were Fascist, they were sexist," Michael Coyle admits of the canonical high modernists. "But the work is still astounding," he continues. "How do you deal with that?" (A21). Modernism: can't live with it, but, doggone it, can't live without it. "By no means have scholars of literature given up on the canonical modernist authors" (A22), the article continues, but it's alright, because scholars "are no longer willing to cordon off the most prominent modernists from other movements going on in literature and culture" (A21) Indeed, a picture of Langston Hughes is accompanied by a caption describing him as "one of the recent additions [!] to the modernist canon" (A21). The companion article, "Beyond the Usual Suspects: Scholars Expand the Modernist Canon," begins by heralding the entry into the canon of such obscure writers as H.D. and Wyndham Lewis.

I, however, am inclined to view this glass as half empty; if new writers eke their way into the penumbra of the modern poetry canon, it is only when they can be considered modern*ist* writers. The study of non-modernist modern poetry is not visible, let alone taken as interesting or valuable. So I must concur with conference participant Seth Moglen: "We're mostly talking about the same half-dozen figures as we have for the last 35 years." Poetry studies may be marginal, but within poetry studies, modernism's stock has never been down.

Accordingly, high modernism of the 1920s comes to stand in for the period from 1900 to 1950. If, however, we choose to think *historically* about aesthetic judgment—which is, after all, the only way our own standards are formed—we find that, in the 1910s, for instance, the very meaning of poetry was in considerable flux prior to "the modernist era." "Poetry," before the culture wars of the 1930s, the subsequent Cold War, and high modernist/New Critical hegemony, described not a genre with a consensus definition, but a crossing point, an indeterminate and contested space in which new ways of writing emerged. To understand modernism as already central, dominant, or unified prior to World War II is quite to misunderstand the literary-historical milieu and to read it through the desires and anxieties of later eras. Poetry was not a static art form; nor was it viewed by all or most readers and writers as either an idealized repository of tradition or pure autotelic form. But ironically, because modernism was later hypostatized by postwar academic critics, only by dethroning the academic modernist canon and canons of taste it presupposes can we begin to write literary histories of the conflicted and unstable moment that allowed for the category "modernism" to arise in the first place.

Consequently, I am more interested in the history of poetry reading than in evaluating individual poems or poets. In *Sensational Designs: The Cultural Work of American Fiction, 1790–1860* (1985), Jane Tompkins took aim at the perennial question, "Is it any good?" She concluded that, "while the *term* 'literary excellence' or 'literary value' remains constant over time, its *meaning*—what literary excellence turns out to be in each case—does not" (192). Likewise, formulations and reformulations of poetry issue from its changing meaning and valuation in respect to other cultural forms. For students of fiction, this notion is nothing new.[1] But as the canon becomes more open and the question of quality less central in the study of fiction, the way poetry has been constructed in this country (especially in the academy) continues to make the demand for evaluation unavoidable.[2] Christopher Beach is correct in saying that what he calls the "institutional model, rather than the 'aesthetic' model of canonicity . . . has come to hold sway in most academic discussions of the literary canon" (10). What is remarkable, though, is the relative lack of such discussions with regard to early-twentieth-century poetry, especially when compared to other fields of literary study.

Rather than evaluating the textual form of poems (in practice, their canonicity), or taking their greatness for granted, I propose to approach the question historically; like Mark Van Wienen, I would change the question "Is it any good?" to "Good for what?" (24). Likewise, Susan Schweik finds "the question of bad poetry" to be "productively unanswerable." She proposes "to take up the *question* of the question . . . to trace the social processes of valuation at the time when and the sites where these poems were first produced and read . . .—their historical otherness" (12–13). Rather than praising or burying any poet, I, too, am more interested in finding out why their contemporaries did so; why given poems were written and published when and where they were; how poets, critics, and audiences understood the art of poetry; and how and why those judgments have changed. Consequently, for the purposes of this project, a textualist analysis of works already designated as literary, or of the ways such texts reflect a historical reality assumed to exist elsewhere, is of more value as illustration than as model.

I will focus, instead, on what I would call the social form of the genre of poetry. The social form includes the historical meaning of the genre; the institutional production of the "poetic" (by publishers or critics, for instance); the interpretations, reception, judgments, and uses to which readers subject poems; the identity of the poetry audience (whether represented statistically or rhetorically); the text's physical context of presentation or publication; and the roles and meanings of different poems and types of poetry as points within larger social relationships. I do not mean to suggest that "social form" is a novel concept or a novel coinage. Instead, I seek to link the two in order to provide a name for an extant orientation to literary studies—one that differs substantially from the usual conception of textual analysis in literary criticism and history.[3]

One implication of a social-formalist point of view is that "poetry" is not reducible to "poems." That is, I take as a premise that genres do not inhere in texts in any ontological sense. However, unlike Coleridge (who made the poem/poetry distinction long ago), I do not see "poetry" as having any transcendent independent existence, either. I understand genre descriptively (an understanding that changes over time) rather than normatively—as it is, rather than as I or anyone else thinks it ought to be (an approach that also changes over time, as it happens). In both 1922 and 2002, quite a few readers would say that "The Waste Land" isn't true poetry because it doesn't adhere to those features they identify with poetry; this is the circular nature of the "inherent" notion of genre. Poetry is not simply a value-neutral, universal taxonomic or analytic category; it is an interpretive cue and an evaluative epithet that shapes uses and judgments of texts. Indeed, poetry is not determined by poems but overdetermines them; accordingly, poets, critics, publishers, and readers have vied for the power to define what poetry "must be"— whether through critical debate, pedagogy, or through the presentation context and distribution of texts.

Bereft of inherent properties, the conversation called poetry instead stages literary ideologies. Tzvetan Todorov cites Friedrich Schlegel as saying, "A definition of poetry can only determine what this must be, not what it has been or is in reality; otherwise, it would be expressed in its briefest form: poetry is what has been called poetry at any time, in any place" (11). In other words, the meaning of "poetry" would be "merely" historical, and therefore indeterminate, unless a normative meaning were assigned to it. "It is because genres exist as an institution," Todorov continues, "that they function as 'horizons of expectation' for readers and as 'models of writing' for authors" (18). Tony Bennett expands upon this notion, writing that genres exist as "modes of sociality" (110). To understand these modes within a given period,

account must be taken of the organization of the system of generic differences—conceived as a differentiated field of social uses—prevailing at that time in terms of its influence on both textual strategies and contexts of reception. Furthermore, account must also be taken of the specific institutional frameworks conditioning the deployment of literary texts in order to assess the regions of sociality to which, at the time, they were concretely connected and within which they operated—as parts of technologies of self-formation, nation-formation or class-formation, for instance, or as combinations of these. (110–11)

I quote Bennett at length because here he delineates some important aspects of what I am calling social form, with respect to literary genres. Bennett regards literary works as practices, as institutions or parts of institutions, and as points in larger social relationships. According to this conception of genre, one may discover "poetry" in prose, in poems about "poetry," or anywhere else that reader-writers have at once declared, defined, theorized, and altered both poetic theories and poetic texts in relation to one another in a given time and place. Accordingly, this book will deal not only with poems, but with prose about poetry.

Clearly, a number of important works have dealt, at least in part, with one or another aspect of noncanonical modern poetry or of the social form of poetry.[4] In particular, readers are sure to see the influence of Cary Nelson's *Repression and Recovery: Modern American Poetry and the Politics of Cultural Memory, 1910–1945* (1989) on the pages that follow. Indeed, it was this book that first introduced me to Anna Louise Strong and Arturo Giovannitti. By the same token, my placing two modernists prior to two radical labor poets is, in a sense, repression before recovery. This procedure will seem blunt to some. And it necessarily is—precisely because the New Critical arguments and maneuvering in the 1930s and 1940s were so bluntly political. Allen Tate, John Crowe Ransom, and their allies were not interested in judging a poem on its own terms; they were interested in setting the terms themselves and institutionalizing them. Not only are the public pronouncements of writers like Tate and Ransom often extraordinarily blunt (and intentionally provocative), but the New Critics' internal correspondence, as it were, reveals "the conniving of all sorts of things—editorships, teaching posts, speaking dates, prizes and fellowships, book projects, book reviews; it also included, often, the conniving of the appearance that no conniving had taken place" (Hammer, review 166). Where there is a conflict between incommensurate aesthetic premises, I must agree with Nelson that a cultural-political war of position, rather than a neutral or universal standard of taste, prevails in determining visibility and influence. What Nelson wrote in the late 1980s is still largely true of modern poetry studies in the 2000s: "[L]iterary history is often implicitly construed as a centuries-long competition to enter the official canon and be taught in literature classes, a concern that was often not central to writers or to their audiences" (6). This competition is, as I have suggested, a matter of ongoing and acute concern to modern poetry critics today, however. Moreover, "literary history is generally addicted to narrative presentations that ignore diversity when it cannot be fitted into a coherent historical sequence" (7). Thus the official story of modern poetry told today is generally the story of canonical modernist poetry; it really begins after World War I, and it is in decline by the 1930s. My presentation obviously differs from this official account—because, as Nelson puts it, "The full range of modern poetries is so great that it cannot be persuasively narrativized in any unitary way" (7). By focussing on the 1910s and the 1930s and reversing them chronologically, by juxtaposing modernists and "repressed" poets, by first documenting the "poetry wars" of the period in some detail, and by applying a variety of theoretical tools and approaches, I obviously intend (like Nelson) to challenge any "consistent, uncontradictory presentation" (7) of the historical development of modern poetry as being grossly inadequate, not to mention dull.

Nelson's book was intended as a broad overview of many previously invisible poets and was intended to break the ground for more specific studies like this one (or his own on Edwin Rolfe); my treatments of Giovannitti and Strong, for instance, are more focused and extensive than was possible in Nelson's more encompassing book. In addition, *Repression and Recovery* is more interested in describing the textual form of many different books and magazines than in exploring the social form of a few, which is my task here. Nelson does not focus on poets' theorization of the social work they understood their poetry as doing or the reception those poems actually received from critics and other readers. Nelson does mention in passing some of the debates *Poetry and the Public* details: "Poems designed for a mass audience were sometimes faulted for their naivete, while complex modernist experiments were sometimes castigated for ignoring the needs of a mass audience" (25). This is information we assume we already know, but it seems to me that, in order to understand "the history of the genre in our own culture" (43) or "the varied cultural roles for literariness" (41), we must look in detail at specifics — at the language in which these arguments were couched, as well as the underlying reasons they were made in the first place.

Likewise, Maria Damon's canon-questioning *The Dark End of the Street: Margins in American Vanguard Poetry* (1993) served as a vanguard itself for the sort of study I have undertaken. In particular, by placing the unpublished writing of teenagers in South Boston alongside Robert Lowell's, her approach anticipates my own. But my understanding of the word "poetry" is quite different. Damon would emphasize the inherent "*differences* between poetry and other forms of cultural or institutional discourse" (10), since "[p]oetry as a form of discourse has been marginalized — specifically feminized and exiled — by the founders of the philosophical system that dominates the West" (7). This is largely because poetry allows for subjective discourse. However, as I hope to show, the social role of poetry is constantly a point of contention and is frequently revised. Poets have been subjectivists or objectivists; poetry can just as easily serve conservative social functions as progressive ones. To downplay this fact is to reinstantiate, rather than to deconstruct, "the neat dualisms that have informed the Western value system" (16) — such as those between poetry and prose, masculine and feminine, subjective and objective, or between "the West" and the rest. In other words, I see no a priori essence to poetry.

Christopher Beach's more recent *Poetic Culture: Contemporary Culture*

Between Community and Institution (1999) also makes a valuable contribution to social-formalist criticism of U.S. poetries. Like Beach, I see "the study of poetry within a sociocultural context" as being "a useful counterbalance to the critical methods that have until now been brought to bear on poets and poetic texts" (2). This tack will necessarily require "new critical methods that allow us to examine poetry beyond the limits of the accepted contemporary canon, and beyond the terms in which canonical poetry has been discussed and evaluated" (3). I largely share these premises, even though my focus and approach are different. Most obviously, *Poetic Culture* focuses on the late twentieth century; the current study, by contrast, focuses on the first part of the century. Beach finds much of his own method in Pierre Bourdieu's notion of cultural capital and in the twin axes of "community" and "institution"; by contrast, I tend to think about poetics more in terms of political philosophy, especially public-sphere theory. In any event, although my project is very different in some respects, the reader may be justified in regarding it as engaged in much the same project as Beach's.

Finally, Mark Van Wienen's groundbreaking study of World War I poetry, *Partisans and Poets: The Political Work of American Poetry in the Great War* (1997), diverges sharply from most studies of modern poetry by "making poetry the primary media [*sic*] for analyzing American culture during the Great War" (38). Thus the book happily avoids—completely—the more predictable pattern of studying canonical modernist poets in the "context" of history while continually genuflecting toward evaluative criticism. Van Wienen gives the reader a taste of the social form of poetry before and during the war by presenting poetry as part of the vivid texture of life in the period, as when he quotes one commentator's remark that "[e]very prairie schoolhouse in America was an outpost of English literature, hardly less potent to inspire recruits when the time came than the British drum-beat itself" (277n). However, Van Wienen concedes, "poetry is only one of many possible sites for articulating ideological resistance, enunciating alternative subject positions, and politicizing the masses according to those positions" (33–34). This unobjectionable statement begs the question of why one would use poetry in particular as a means of assessing U.S. political culture. If the Industrial Workers of the World's propaganda "stickerettes offer a tangible link between poetic language and advertising slogans" (100), then the question "how can politics and partisanship not be central categories of 'poetic' understanding?" (38) begs the further questions, What was "poetic," what wasn't, how did it get that way, and why does it matter?

These are questions I propose to address. Despite the very useful work of Nelson, Damon, Beach, Van Wienen and others,[5] no one has attempted an account of the social form of the genre per se, that is, the history of the construction of poetry as a category in the United States. Yet such a study is necessary to provide a rationale and a historical framework for the new cultural criticism of U.S. poetry. The common objection to such criticism, of course, is that "nobody reads poetry." Everybody says this—even poetry readers. But if poetry seems to be beside the point of American culture (or even American literature) today, such was not always the case. Discussions among U.S. writers of the early twentieth century indicate a widespread conviction of the popularity of poetry and its centrality to literary and cultural-political conflicts. What quite explicitly has been at issue is the social meaning of that genre, which means that, at certain moments in U.S. history, the stakes were surprisingly high. *Poetry and the Public* centers around an important time of crisis and transformation, in the United States, of the meaning of poetry as a genre—namely, that occurring roughly from 1910 to 1940. This is a particularly good vantage point from which to survey the theoretical issues outlined above. As in the early nineteenth century, this period saw an intensification of struggles over the meaning of America and of democracy during a moment of concentrated economic and military crises, and a consequent contest to redefine poetry and art generally. So just what, historically speaking, was poetry, in the context of U.S. cultures in the early twentieth century? And what could it (have) become?

In attempting to answer these questions, I have found that American poets and critics tended to define poetry with reference to "the public," in all its senses—to the reading public, to the public sphere, to public norms, to public service, to publication, publicity, popularity. U.S. poets and critics have had a marked tendency to regard poetry as either an alternative to or refuge from the public, as a vehicle or mode for participating in and engaging with the public, or as a way of negotiating or problematizing the separation of public and private spheres. On the one hand, poetic theorists as diverse as William Cullen Bryant in the 1820s, Arthur Davison Ficke and Allen Tate in the early twentieth century, and New Critics in the latter half of the twentieth century attempted to configure poetry as both the domain of a private universal subject and, at the same time, as a means of delineating or composing a cultural consensus in the public sphere. On the other hand, critics and poets from controversialist Philip Freneau in the 1770s to the newspaper poets of the early twentieth century understood poetry to engage and intervene in public life; the same could be said of genteel critics such as Robert Underwood Johnson, activist poets in the 1930s, or performance poets (such as Sekou Sundiata, Patricia Smith, or Joy Harjo) in the 1990s. This second understanding of poetry often dissents from consensus and joins in debate and the shaping of public opinion—and, as a result, has been largely ignored in academic accounts of American poetry.

In saying this, I do not mean to imply that I think public and private are, in fact, reified categories. Indeed, Jürgen Habermas thinks the legitimacy of this separation of spheres had collapsed effectively by the 1920s. It is my assumption throughout that "public" and "private" are, like the term "poetry," categories of understanding that are constructed historically, through discourse (speaking, writing, symbols), especially in debate. Indeed, the story of this book is largely the history of attempts to establish, reestablish, rearticulate, or dissolve the terms "public" and "private," or the distinction between them, via poetics. For instance, I argue that although we can detect a strong desire in both Wallace Stevens and Allen Tate for a clear distinction between public and private, their own writings reveal that they despair of maintaining such a distinction in the twentieth century. Likewise, although Arturo Giovannitti and Anna Louise Strong produced politically charged writings directed toward "the public," they in fact invoked aspects of the inward-looking, private subject of nineteenth-century bourgeois poetry. It is precisely this complication of public and private that makes their work interesting to me.

My own notion of the public is perhaps influenced by Ernesto Laclau and Chantal Mouffe more than anyone. In the "original forms of democratic thought," they write in *Hegemony and Socialist Strategy: Towards a Radical Democratic Politics*, the "public/private distinction constituted the separation between a space in which differences were erased through the universal equivalence of citizens, and a plurality of private spaces in which the full force of those differences was maintained." Under the force of social movements from the mid–nineteenth century to the late twentieth, however, "the overdetermination of effects linked to the democratic revolution begins to displace the line of demarcation between the public and the private and to *politicize* social relations" (181). Thus we increasingly are confronted with "a new situation" in the twentieth century, "characterized by the essential instability of political spaces, in which the very identity of the forces in struggle is submitted to constant shifts, and calls for an incessant process of redefinition" (151). Thus the apparent formal political unity of what Habermas calls the classical or bourgeois public sphere gives way to "the plurality and indeterminacy of the social" (152), in which "the site of power becomes an empty space" (186). All of this means conflict rather than consensus, and it is the instantiation of these large social conflicts of the early twentieth century within the much smaller (though symbolically deep) pond of poetry that I seek to depict. Moreover, if the "distinctions public/private, civil society/political society are only the result of a certain type of hegemonic articulation" (185), that articulation is, at the same time, very important indeed. What is interesting historically are the continued attempts by liberal thinkers to retain or reconstitute the separation of spheres, even nostalgically. It is this desire for a clear public/private distinction that I find in the writings of Tate and Stevens, even though both recognize the belatedness of that desire.

As will be evident, my understanding of "publicness"[6] is also informed by critiques of Habermas by Nancy Fraser and Carole Pateman, and by Oskar Negt's and Alexander Kluge's notion of different, overlapping, competing publics. Indeed, my understanding of a "poetry scene" is an amalgam of these ideas: an empty space that is not defined in advance, in which many different (and fluid) types of poetries and poetry communities compete to determine the meaning of poetry (which they never do, once and for all), and in which any clear distinction between public and private has dissolved—except (and this is crucial) in the discourse employed by some of the contestants in this struggle. Accordingly, the distinction I draw between "academic" and "popular" poetries is intended as a distinction between historically defined institutions and one which is not, by the same token, hard and fast. Nonetheless, the sometimes dismissive comments by academic intellectuals about popular poets or bitter comments about academia by poets outside the university do suggest some (contingent and historical) interpretive value in these categories.

Indeed, in the early twentieth century, a broad cross-section of U.S. poets and critics argued for what I will call the "populist" position, namely, that poetry is (or ought to be) a popular art form—either in terms of the number of readers or by way of some inherent connection to "the people." Freneau and Bryant, genteel and newspaper poets, communists and New Poets, beats and the Poetry Societies of America all share one thing in common: they all, in one way or another and to a greater or lesser extent, agreed that poetry possesses an intrinsic or potential duty toward or power among reading (or listening) publics. Accordingly, they all became suspect in the eyes of the institutionally ascendant modernist critics. It is only under the institutional influence of "high modernist" poetics that the poem comes to seem more important than either the poet or the public; the modernist poet therefore renounces the ethical duty toward an audience, or anyone else.[7] While these same divisions can be found in much European poetry and poetics, they are especially important in a nation sensitive about its cultural heritage (or lack thereof), uneasy about its multiple and pluralistic identity, and with a self-image (and, in some cases, image abroad) as the original and quintessential liberal-democratic society. "Poetry," as a category of judgment and understanding, becomes an important term in the resolving or exacerbating of these conflicts and anxieties.

But in order to understand the conflict between popular and modernist poetics, we must first understand the broader social-historical origins of the modernist revolt itself. In recent years, high modernism has come under attack as an expression of fascist tendencies.[8] However, I argue that high modernist poetry and poetic theory represent a resurgence of the ideas of *classical* liberalism of the late eighteenth and early nineteenth centuries in reaction *against* the emergent *social* liberalism of the late nineteenth and early twentieth centuries. This newer liberalism, which grew up at the same time as the modernist poets themselves, emphasized a more democratic and egalitarian form of polity with a more activist state; social liberals, such as John Dewey, Walter Rauschenberg, and (the early) Walter Lippmann, emphasized solidarity, interdependence, and a conception of freedom as the "positive" ability to do things. This value system is expressed in the popular definition of poetry by its relation to (and responsibility toward) the public. By contrast, many of the modernist poets of the 1910s to 1930s invoke a libertarian language of the "negative" freedom of the individual (especially the exceptional one) from coercion, as well as a strong split between public and private spheres (especially between political controversy and high art)—all consistent themes in classical liberal philosophy from Locke through the Enlightenment through the early Mill. Americanists from V. L. Parrington to Sacvan Bercovitch have examined the U.S. novel in light of the nation's liberal-democratic traditions; however, no study has attempted to understand the development of modern American poetry by examining the history of liberal thought.[9]

As shall become apparent, each of the strands I have described bears the trace of the other. In the moments of indeterminacy represented by the shifts in U.S. poetry between 1910 and 1940, what emerge are hybrids or "crossings" in the cultural understandings of poetry and in the textual forms that had existed previously. Consequently, this is a story of impurities, a historical example of the breakdown of boundaries that begins as soon as any binaries—public/private, poetry/prose, Victorian/modernist, bourgeois/proletarian—are established. This was a period of poetic heterogeneity: poetic theories from the 1920s, for instance, carry some traces of the dominant poetics of the nineteenth century intact, while they intensify, diminish, or revise others. Moreover, with the insight provided by an examination of the meanings of poetry in the early twentieth century, one can recognize similar alterations occurring in the tension between dominant institutional and minority poetry practices in the 1990s.

I divide the discussion of the early twentieth century poetry into two sections, the first dealing with the reemergence, in intensified form, of a privatized notion of poetry, the second with an alternative self-consciously "public" poetics that vied with the first for institutional authority. Accordingly, the first half of the book is taken up with a revisionist account of the long rise of high modernist poetry and with a discussion of the poetic theories and practices of two key figures—Wallace Stevens and Allen Tate—in the 1930s.

Having traced the institutional development of canonical modernist poetics and the dichotomy that it posited between poetry and the public, I then turn, in the second half of the book, to alternative attempts by poets to mediate "poetry" and "the public"—attempts that implicitly refute some of the basic premises of the dominant poetics examined in the first section. These new poetries emerged in the 1910s, the same decade that saw the emergence of modernism, and a decade in which dichotomies between poetry and the public, form and function, were not yet as clear for readers as they would seem in subsequent decades. Rather, many styles and philosophies competed for the allegiance of writers and readers or combined in hybrid forms that would later seem suspect. In this section, I pay special attention to the examples of Arturo Giovannitti and Anna Louise Strong, poets of the radical labor movement in the years before the codification of high modernism. The contexts of two broad, internally diverse artistic (and political) tendencies during two decades provide a frame for a discussion of the ways in which poetry can function within a given historical moment and social space, as well as the ways that the same poetry is influenced by, transgresses, and points beyond that context.

Obviously, this presentation is not chronological, and this may puzzle some readers. However, it seems to me that presenting high modernism last would confuse even more—precisely because it has defined the way we think about poetry in the academy. Without problematizing that way of thinking first, then, radical poets of the 1910s can simply be dismissed as bad (hence, uninteresting) poets—bad from a *post*-1910s high modernist point of view, that is. In other words, unless we can critically examine standards of taste constructed in the 1930s and 1940s, our impression of poetry of the 1910s can only be anachronistic.

Moreover, my method in each chapter is different. If we are to take a broader view of literature, as I am suggesting, and specifically of the relation between different *notions of* literature (without reaching that level of generality that is a "night in which all cows are black"), it seems to me that we need to employ a variety of ways of reading, not just one. Part of the intervention I want this book to make is to present several models for social-formalist analysis: reception studies, historical analyses of poetic theory, debates about poetry in the popular press, studies of the material contexts of publication, interview research, reportage. In these chapters, I attempt to develop and apply several approaches that are appropriate to different types of texts and that elucidate a number of aspects of poetry's relation to the idea of publicness. Chapter 1 examines a broad array of articles *about* poetry in the popular press and literary journals—the paratext, if you like—and the way that this conversation affected the institutional form of the genre. Chapters 2 and 3 read poets reading their own work (with an eye to shaping its reception) and then reads their readings in light of contemporaneous changes in political and economic theory. Chapters 4 and 5 examine the ways reception and presentation context shape the meanings of literary texts; here I offer an argument about the ways such texts respond to and manipulate those contexts or combine with other forms and modes of political culture. Chapter 6 examines academic literary criticism in order to make an argument about the effects of genre on discipline and about the interaction between a general reading public and an academic one; the second part of the chapter uses first-person reportage and interviews to analyze "social locations" for poetry that exceed the bounds of a written text.

Through these different facets, however, a coherent picture appears. Chapter 1 outlines debates, found in popular magazines of the 1900s and 1910s, concerning the social functions of poetry and its effects upon the audience. Poetry appeared less as a type of text than as an *influence,* at once spiritual and practical, that could either change or reproduce the social order, and that served as a counterweight to the negative effects of modernity. This was a poetry, self-consciously oriented toward a public, that was meant to serve a public, often social, function. This notion would be little challenged until the 1910s and remained dominant even after that. This chapter then examines the effort, by modernist poets and pro-modernist critics, to redefine poetry, in the debates in the popular press in the 1920s and 1930s, in terms of a materialist and "intransitive" poetics. Poetry, for these writers, came to be defined largely by its opposition to "the public": poetry was not to participate in the public sphere nor to constitute public speech, and, perhaps more importantly, neither was it to orient itself toward a reading public (indeed, pro-modernists declared the death of the poetry *reader*). Thus high modernism opposed both popular and political poetries as well as the insurgent populist and leftist cultural politics they represented. Yet anthologies and criticism, as well as films like *Mr. Deeds Goes to Town* (1934) and poetry programs on the radio in the 1930s, all indicate the persistence of the popular notion of poetry, even as modernism gained more influence.

In order to understand the origins of this antipopular position, I use the poetics of Allen Tate and Wallace Stevens as extended case studies; these two poets were outspoken and influential representatives of the self-consciously traditionalist and abstract strains, respectively, of modernist poetry. Chapter 2 examines the paradoxical coexistence of Allen

Tate's "disinterested" value-neutral notion of the poem as object with his strongly stated normative program for culture and poetry's role therein. Rather than accept Tate's self-description as "reactionary," I read this conflict as corresponding to a similar fundamental split within classical liberalism—one that is in fact intensified under the pressure of political radicalisms in the twentieth century. Chapter 3 examines Stevens's long poem "Owl's Clover" (1936), which, like Tate's articles and poems in the liberal *New Republic* and other periodicals, responds to attacks against modernism by such critics as Stanley Burnshaw of the *New Masses* and populist popularizers of American poetry such as Louis Untermeyer and William Rose Benet. Seen in this light, Stevens's abstractness, I argue, is not a symptom of aestheticist escapism, but rather an example of a modernist desire to use poetry actively and imaginatively to control a public world beyond the self that had come to seem beyond salvation or coherence. As the century wore on, the public realm increasingly took on the aspect of a hostile space and a threat to the integrity of the individual subject of classical liberalism; this notion of the public represents a radical departure from nineteenth-century attempts to bind an unstable liberal society together through the influence of poetry and of "culture" generally.

The second half of the book highlights little-known episodes in U.S. literary history, and it introduces two fascinating poets of the 1910s. Anna Louise Strong and Arturo Giovannitti, both poets and activists widely known in their day, crossed formalist modernist techniques with a functional genteel poetics. The results appeared within unusual presentation contexts to create hybrid textual forms written, in different ways, to intervene in specific historical moments or interact with specific audiences. While the same could be said of many now-forgotten poets from this period, these two writers produced work that brings the theoretical issues and political stakes into especially clear focus. And although this attempt at "turning" the pervasive notion of poetry was, if anything, less successful than Tate's or Stevens's, it provides a concentrated sense of the many competing types and notions of poetry that existed in the 1910s, the many potential directions American poetry might have taken at the time, and the possibilities for poetry vis-à-vis publics then and now.

Giovannitti used his celebrity as a jailed syndicalist strike leader to code his poems in ways that sabotaged received canons of taste. In chapter 4, I suggest that the various "publication" sites of Giovannitti's poems —in the *Atlantic* as opposed to IWW propaganda, or in a slender volume from a small press versus oratory in the midst of a strike—alter the poems' social meanings from "rebellious" literary innovation to seditious political speech. In chapter 5, I show that Strong's "Ragged Verse," which ran daily in the Seattle *Union Record* from 1918 to 1921 under the byline Anise, combined aspects of modernist, genteel, and popular poetic traditions, along with elements of features and editorial journalism and outright political propaganda. This hybridization produced a new modality for writing. Such a "crossing" allowed the author to use a previously feminized genre to gain access to a masculinized social sphere.

Chapter 6 charts the course of the issues already discussed into the late twentieth century. The first part of the chapter accounts for the implicit equation of American literature with American fiction for most of the postwar history of the former as an academic field. In the 1980s and 1990s, as studies of the American novel became more historical, and as "documentary" texts became the object of critical scholarship, the tendency to exclude poetry from American literature became only more pronounced. I account for this predilection by tracing the social form of poetry in the academy. But it is precisely poetry's social form that makes it important for cultural history, and an examination of that form will require new methodologies and a cognitive remapping of both poetry studies and the literatures of the Americas as fields of scholarship. In the second part of chapter 6, I explore the poetries of the 1990s, specifically those that hybridized poetry with other cultural forms and physical media, that refused to separate the poetic sphere from the public, or that linked the expressive subject and the poetic community. In particular, this section examines two social sites for poetry, one old, one new: the community-based writing workshop and the poetry slam. These are two sites for the continued existence of popular, transitive, and agonistic poetries outside the academy.

Poetry and the Public relates textual form to institutional meaning and operates on the premise that "poetry," as a *conversation,* may be found dispersed throughout many textual and institutional sites, not simply in texts already recognizable as poems. In these respects, the social-formalist approach I have pursued here may help critics theorize the way that genre, criticism, literary text, political philosophy, and cultural authority define themselves relationally. Accordingly, this book brings together several different approaches to cultural critique and uses the protean social forms of poetry as an index of the place of the literary in the United States.

[E]very author, as far as he is great and at the same time *original*, has had the task of *creating* the taste by which he is to be enjoyed.
—*William Wordsworth, "Essay Supplementary to the Preface of 1815"*

[W]e have not defined the hostility or inertia that is against us. We have not recognized with any Voltairian clearness the nature of this opposition, and we have not realized to what an extent a renaissance is a thing made—a thing made by conscious propaganda.
—*Ezra Pound, "The Renaissance" (1915)*

CHAPTER ONE

Poetry and the Reading Public: Poetic Debates in the Popular Press, 1910–1940

Within a social-formalist framework, it becomes apparent that not only do styles change within a genre, but the meaning of a genre changes; such changes are precipitated by what Antonio Gramsci called a "war of position" within a society. What Louis Untermeyer said of Amy Lowell in 1936—that she "had made poetry a fighting word" (*Modern* 189)—could be said generally of poets and critics in the United States throughout the earlier part of this century. Much of this fight took place in articles in the periodical press, from *Ladies' Home Journal* at one end of the circulation figures to *Poetry*, that big little magazine, on the other.[1] Genteel, popular, and avant-garde tendencies at one moment converged and in the next clashed in the ongoing effort to claim the right to write Poetry.

All of these tendencies were sometimes present in the work of the same poet. For instance, Vachel Lindsay's notion of the poetic was rather genteel, his writing was considered innovative in the 1910s, and he enjoyed a large degree of popularity. I therefore demur with Lawrence Rainey's identification of "avant-garde, elite bourgeois, and popular cultures" (196), since "cultures" seems too strong here. Not only do these tendencies overlap, but it is not clear that we can identify them with particular socioeconomic classes (e.g., "bourgeois"). The debates I describe, though resulting in cultural hierarchies, represent not expressions of sociologically defined class interests, but rather discursive fantasy constructions of class and culture. Thus they have more to do with symbolic than economic capital.

That being said, although Pierre Bourdieu's book *Distinction* deals with French culture in the 1960s, his division of tastes into "legitimate," "middle-brow" and "popular" (16) could apply to poets and poetry critics in the early twentieth-century United States. Legitimate taste is established, Bourdieu holds, as the result of a struggle between those "who offer products directly adjusted to the dominant taste" and those whose "products must produce their own markets" (317)—or must, as Wordsworth says, "create the taste by which [they are] to be enjoyed." Of these categories of "objects offered for consumers' choice, there are none more classifying than legitimate works of art, which, while distinctive in general, enable the production of distinctions ad infinitum by playing on divisions and sub-divisions into genres, periods, styles, authors, etc." (Bourdieu 16). With the accession of New Criticism in the U.S. academy, the preeminent genres had become discursive and meditative poetry, the period style and authors a handful of metaphysical poets and high modernists. The taste had been created, the market share prepared, and popular audiences and authors extirpated from literary history as well as excluded from legitimate and legitimizing institutions. Yet this configuration resulted from a forty-year-long process. As a result, poetry possessed one set of meanings within U.S. culture in 1910 and quite another in 1940.

Both "legitimate" and "middlebrow" critics, for their part, busied themselves with "teaching others the legitimate life-style by a symbolic action" (365)—in this case, a proper understanding of poetry's value. *Women's Home Companion* assured its readers in 1911 that poetry books outclassed etiquette books, because "the girl who loves and understands poetry has immensely the advantage of the girl who does not" (McCall 30)—presumably, by demonstrating breeding, culture, and sensibility better even than do the rules of etiquette. High modernists assumed a stance of enraged enmity and contempt toward such uses of the art. While modernists attempted to position their work as a more legitimate literature than the traditional and established poetry of the turn of the century, they also attempted to gain and maintain an elite status by distinguishing themselves from amateurs and from popular poetry. Yet in both the old poetics and the new, readers were to be acculturated but also disciplined into the appropriate regime of poetry. Within these debates in the early twentieth century, poetry, which would be marginalized within American studies in the latter part of the twentieth century, became a central term in struggles over the meaning of culture in a modernizing United States.

Such a disciplinary clash of cultural premises is narrated in the 1890 story "A Poetess," by Mary E. Wilkins (later Freeman). The title character, Betsey Dole, writes poems to satisfy the desires, needs, and customs of individuals in her community. Mrs. Caxton, Betsey's neighbor, asks her to write the obituary poem for a recently deceased son. In so doing, the neighbor specifies the contents she wishes the poem to contain: "You could mention how—handsome he was, and good, and I never had to punish him but once in his life, and how pleased he was with his little new suit, and what a sufferer he was, and—how we hope he is at rest—in a better land" (199). In other words, Mrs. Caxton orders a poem to fit a specific social purpose—in this case, to serve as a memento as well as a means of consolation and sympathy. And the poem fits the bill; upon delivery, Mrs. Caxton exclaims, "It's jest as comfortin' as it can be, and you worked that in about his new suit so nice" (201).

These functions serve not just the individual but also a community of readers bound by sentiment and convention. That community shares an aesthetic in which poetry represents a social medium. Thus the poem's presentation context becomes just as important as its textual contents in determining its "value": "'I've been thinkin',' said [Mrs. Caxton], keeping her mouth steady with an effort, 'that it would be real pretty to have —some lines printed on some sheets of white paper with a neat black border. I'd like to send some to my folks, and one to the Perkinses in Brigham, and there's a good many others I thought would value 'em'" (199). This finished product will be, Betsey realizes, suitable for framing. When Mrs. Caxton places this order, Betsey's "face took on unconsciously lines of grief so like the other woman's that she looked like her for the minute" (199). As Willis Buckingham concludes from his study of Emily Dickinson's reception in the 1890s, "[P]oetry reading, though taking place in solitude, joined itself to other social activities, especially communion between like-minded persons" (165). The text of the poem drops out; what is important is the women's image of the poem as both a thing of value and a mode of sympathy among family and friends. The words on the page are so predictable that the narrator does not bother to repeat them: "It seemed as if one, given the premises of herself and the room, could easily deduce what she would write, and read without seeing those lines wherein flowers rhymed sweetly with vernal bowers, home with beyond the tomb, and heaven with even" (200). Betsey, as town "poetess," is not composing an original expressive art work but performing an office for the quick and the dead—an office that she performs precisely by adhering to convention.

When Mrs. Caxton prints up the poem as promised, "Betsey flushed and smiled. It was to her as if her poem had been approved and accepted by one of the great magazines. She had the pride and self-wonderment of recognized genius" (201). "Magazines" represents a realm, for both Betsey Dole and Mrs. Caxton, beyond the ken of the townspeople. For them, poetry circulates by hand, or through the newspaper; for Betsey, local approval and acceptance by the community—face-to-face "recognition"—count for more than having a byline in literary periodicals. Consequently, when Mrs. Caxton tells Betsey that the town minister "said that you had never wrote anything that could be called poetry, an' it was a dreadful waste of time" (202), Betsey is cut to the quick. The minister writes poetry himself, "an' has had some printed in a magazine"; for him, "*it was in dreadful bad taste to have it printed an' sent round that way*" (202). The minister's sentence carries out a certain immediate violence on the poetess: "She sat looking at Mrs. Caxton as a victim whom the first blow had not killed might look at her executioner" and "[h]er back was as stiff as if she was bound to a stake" (202). At this point, the judgment of taste from a male authority becomes a powerful utterance; what can and can't be called poetry forms the substance of the "sentence" being pronounced. Betsey, having been convinced that, contrary to her neighbors' impression, "there wa'n't any use in it" for her to write poetry, falls into a depression that exacerbates her consumption and thereby leads to her death.

Betsey wrote because there was use in her poems. Now, it's no use: you can't fight city hall—or the meeting hall, it would seem. The grounds of judgment shift so abruptly for Betsey Dole that the social context that gives her art value is destroyed. The "use" of poetry changes from its use value for the townspeople to its use as a marker of distinction that must be recognized by legitimate culture as legitimate and as sequestered from autoproduction and decentralized circulation. The figurative and emotional violence that ensues—what one might call a "violence of taste"—results from the obliteration of the premise of Betsey's poetics. The very speaking of the minister's critique breaks the chain of sympathy the poem depends upon and reinforces.

In fact, what is and isn't poetry is the minister's word against Betsey's: neither she nor the reader ever learns the minister's reasons. Before Betsey's death, the minister visits her. He is "a young man—a country boy who had worked his way through a country college" (204); though he represents largely the same socioeconomic background as the town poetess, his education has acculturated him into elite aesthetic norms. Poems in magazines, emanating from the cultural center of Boston, are "worth something," poems on cards produced in rural New England are not, even if the audience for the latter is all around him. His utterance creates an authority of its own, one underwritten not by arguments, but by the aura associated with higher education, the church, and literary magazines. The sentence sticks. In Betsey's dying breath, she says to the young man, "[B]ut I've been thinkin'—if you would jest write a few —lines about me—afterward—I've been thinkin' that—mebbe my— dyin' was goin' to make me—a good subject for—poetry, if I never wrote none" (204). As town poet, Betsey enjoys standing in the community and serves a function for it. Producing poetry is, for her, agency. Yet at the last, Betsey places herself in the position of aesthetic object—*materia poetica,* not poet. Likewise, Betsey's poems become objects of judgment rather than cultural events that possess social significance.

More than a clash between highbrow and lowbrow poetries, this conflict is between two different versions of sacralization. For the minister, religious utterance and art-writing form separate discourses to be understood in different ways. Betsey, on the other hand, is performing a posthumous service comparable to preaching a funeral sermon: the "scribbling woman" enjoys an informal ritual authority that challenges the minister's hieratic role as both cleric and critic.[2] When her locally based social authority runs up against the minister's universalist aesthetic authority, two types of value collide. Betsey's, based on sympathy and coded as feminine, loses out. This imagined clash of premises partakes of Wilkins's own nostalgic fantasies of region and class. In 1890, this narrative represents a backward glance: Betsey, as the narrator describes her, "looked like the very genius of gentle, old-fashioned, sentimental poetry" (200). Thus the story, while celebrating a poetry of "the people," also enacts its supposed demise and reconstitution. Likewise, the rise of the regionalism of Wilkins and other women writers around the turn of the century coincided with the widespread defense of a popular poetry against highbrow or cosmopolitan models.

Yet while genteel critics in the 1890s and 1900s attempted to maintain and control elite standards of aesthetic judgment and the means of literary production and distribution, their notion of poetry as a means of moral and emotional development was never far removed from the popular conception embodied in Betsey Dole. From the early nineteenth century onward, U.S. critics had understood poetry in terms of the personality of the poet and in terms of poetry's effects on the reader. By the late 1920s, however, modernist poets and the original New Critics writing in the *New Republic,* the *Nation,* or the *Literary Review* attempted (in reviews, poems, and essays) to change the focus of debate to the textual "form" and "content" of poems. For many traditionalist and populist critics, the modernism of writers like Allen Tate and Ezra Pound represented a sudden withdrawal of the "soul" of poetry that left only the "form" of the text (to use Emerson's terms). Walter Michaels relates that "in what may constitute the ne plus ultra of the materialist aesthetic in poetry, [William Carlos Williams] is even reported to have *weighed* his poems" (38). If traditional, conventional poetry, was, for Wilkins, something that could be read without seeing, then cubist, visual, and objectivist poetries, perhaps the most radical forms of the new textualism, suggested the possibility that poetry could be seen without reading.

The number of periodical articles on poetry skyrocketed between 1900 and 1914; many of those articles claimed that the size of the audience was increasing, too. Readers enjoyed their favorite poems not only in books but in other presentation contexts as well: David Perkins relates that Joyce Kilmer's "Trees" "produced royalties of $1,500 per year from a motto-card publisher" (318). Perkins claims that "[b]y the end of the decade from two to three times as many volumes of some significance were appearing as at the beginning" (317), and he accepts the existence of "an increased public for poetry" and "larger sales" (318). James D. Hart, in his list of best-selling volumes in U.S. history, records seven books of poetry between 1909 and 1919—more than for any decade after the Civil War.

However, the salient point for the social construction of poetry is to be found not in a statistical representations of the audience, but in the *rhetoric* of popularity. Here the audience becomes a "phantom public," a hypothetical entity or nonentity that served as the site of ideological combat. Magazine writers could thus explain this putative rage for poetry in the 1910s not by reference to the avant-garde rebellion of the same decade but by citing a desire for a more conservative poetics.[3] For example, in 1916, Joyce Kilmer opined that the stress occasioned by the onset of the Great War had led to a boom in poetry sales: "[B]ooks of verse are selling by the thousand and even by the ten thousand" (181). This expansion of the market for poetry was, Kilmer suggested, an indication of "the 'spiritual awakening' of the American people" (181).

Lovers of poetry in the 1910s hailed its ability to beget spiritual sensibility, to expand one's sympathies, to refine one's sense of beauty, truth, or morality, to instill values, to build character, as well as simply to console or to entertain. Genteel critic Robert Underwood Johnson wrote in 1916 that poetry "has the power to help transform the world through the purity of its principles"; it "transmits from generation to generation the essential values of life. . . . even in this time of shifting standards," he continued, "poetry has been and is to be the largest contributing factor in the creation of great men" (179). The point here is not so much that poetry teaches or edifies, but that it directly produces changes in character and in culture. Poetry not only communicates; rather, it transmits values, creates personality, transforms the world. Arthur Davison Ficke already had sounded this utilitarian note in 1911 in the *North American Review*. Noting that "just now there appear to be more writers of verse than there have been at any time in the history of literature" (429), Ficke explains that poetry can create a pleasant imaginary world to which "the tired or baffled mind may resort for consolation and forgetfulness" (432), or poetry can engage in the more active task of "scrutinizing of valuations, the expansion and clarifying of purposes, the widening of sympathies" (441).

In each of these formulations, poetry supplies a function beyond its form. This practical effect on the reading public resides, paradoxically, in poetry's idealizing influence. Poetry in these descriptions becomes not a classification of texts, but an immaterial cure or tonic that uses the text as a sort of conduit. Poetry is at once spiritual, practical, and virtually detextualized. According to Madeline Alston, writing in 1918, poetry "is a necessity, like fresh air and sunshine, and it is the *necessity* of poetry and of the cultivation of the poetic spirit that requires recognition if we are to save our children from the asphyxia of materialism" (485). The *Literary Digest* reported that poets were classified as part of an "essential industry" during World War I and so were legally protected from the draft, because poetry "has had a very genuine effect in uplifting the hearts or stiffening the courage of thousands of readers" during the conflict ("Legal Status" 27). A 1916 review averred that "in times of stress and sorrow, even the most practical people turn to the poets for the renewal of strength with which to combat the ills and misfortunes of life" ("Substance" 114). If the Great War or the "second industrial revolution" induced asphyxia, the poetry industry provided the antidote.

The most-read poets of the nineteenth century had espoused some version of this poetics. As early as 1825, William Cullen Bryant made his "Lectures on Poetry" manifestos of a practical-ideal poetic philosophy. Bryant anticipates Alston's declaration of the need for poetry, saying, "Well, when we are persuaded to part with our hearth-fires, and to refuse the fruits which sunshine and showers have ripened for our sustenance, let us give up poetry" (20). In his second lecture, "On the Value and Uses of Poetry," he affirms that it "delights in inspiring compassion, the parent of all kind offices," as well as "sentiments of fortitude and magnanimity, the fountain of disinterested sacrifices" (17). The numinous breath of Poetry inspires virtuous sentiments and dispositions; these states of mind issue forth in concrete, useful offices and toils.

For a genteel critic like Ficke, as for Bryant before him, poetry's function in the individual's life dovetailed with its function in the life of society: "Great poetry is a trumpet to the spirit, a voice in the night. Our society in its search for happiness is marching to-day in a disordered mob along divergent paths largely because of the lack of such guidance" (439). The poet for Ficke—as for the Whitman of "Democratic Vistas" —binds an unstable individualist liberal society together. And Ficke links the poet's function as pastor to the poet's acknowledgment of a public: "[T]he poets exist for the people, not the people for the poets, and . . . any sane ideal of the poet's function must shrink from the conception of a poetry which makes no honest attempt to reach the majority of even the distinctly intellectual portion of mankind" (435). Ficke cites Edwin Markham and his genteel-populist anthem "The Man with the Hoe" as a case in point (438). Markham's poem, after its 1899 appearance in the *San Francisco Examiner,* enjoyed numerous reprintings in newspapers, magazines, and anthologies around the world.

In the 1910s, the pervasiveness of this traditional poetics coincided with a large-scale movement for social reforms and a struggle over the meaning of democracy. In 1914, one writer in the *Independent* articulated a connection between a traditional poetic theory and a Progressivist or "social-liberal" agenda: "The reason why people are taking more interest in poetry is because poetry is taking more interest in people." That interest manifests itself, among other ways, in an accessible "social" poetry that "deals with daily toil and the common lot, with the workingman and the submerged tenth, with the overburdened child and the suffering wife" ("New Poetry" 342). Charles Wharton Stork of the University of Pennsylvania explained how the practical, spiritual, and social aspects of poetry followed one from another: "There should, however, be no antagonism toward the old poetry of beauty, which has in fact a great practical value. By beauty the mind of man is freed from the clash and oppression of the present so that he may examine himself and learn to look beyond himself. Thus he will learn to care less for money and more for the things of the spirit. Also they who have seen ideal beauty can hardly be satisfied with moral ugliness and social injustice" (283). Because "the old poetry of beauty" causes readers to free their souls from competition, getting and spending, such poetry ameliorates the social ill-effects of individualism and capitalism. Personal moral transformation leads immediately to a collective social transformation.

John Drinkwater also linked a reformist social-liberal agenda with poetry when he told Americans that poetry promoted social justice, not by sermonizing, but by actually producing a "radical quickening of the spirit which is the only effective cure for injustice of all kinds" (102). Once poetry "begets spiritual activity in its hearers," they recognize that injustice "is loathsome, and crush it" (103). In 1914, Christabel Abbott of the New York State Normal School wrote that "[i]n some poor homes there is so much discontent with the present and worry for the future that it is not a soil in which much poetic thought germinates" (555). Abbott's solution to this Wordsworthian observation is a "poetic" education: "The world is full of people who have not the power to lift themselves out of their present condition. The more the real poetic spirit of faith, hope and inspiration we can put into the school children, the better, in after life, can they lift themselves" (560). If aesthetic and political radicalism could be conflated, so too could upward mobility and poetic uplift. This was a poetry understood to provide a "practical value" through its "public" function.

At the same time, socialist poets' "genteel, idealized notion of the poetic," the dominant notion in the 1910s, was not, as Cary Nelson holds, a "symptom of cultural restriction" (55), but was rather an idealization of their cause and embodiment of their hopes for human liberation. Radical poet Max Eastman explicitly joined poetic uplift to economic and political uprising. Not only did poetry, in Eastman's formulation, stir the emotions, it also formed part of an inheritance of beauty that capital denied workers. "Among the poor," Eastman wrote, "it is unattainable . . . and so poetry appears not to belong there at all, but to be almost an exclusive pleasure of those whom we call cultivated. . . . They who cherish hopes of poetry, will, therefore, do well to favor in their day every assault of labor upon the monopoly of leisure by a few" ("Why All" 1060).

If highbrow critics from Bryant to Johnson to Eastman presented poetry as social, functional, and audience-oriented, purveyors of more popular verse agreed. For instance, Walt Mason of Emporia, Kansas, reputed to be the richest poet in America in 1914, crowed, "The modern newspaper poets are doing more to brighten the world and make it a good place to live in than all the extinct poets in the Hall of Fame or

Westminster Abbey ever did" ("Kansas" 341). Mason says so because newspaper poets produce optimism "for the people who really need the influence of optimism—the breadwinners, the weary, and heavy-laden." Mason, himself a syndicated poet, imagines newspaper poetry as circulating among a public that uses it: "A man sees in the newspaper a clever rime full of hope and encouragement, and he cuts it out and shows it to his friends, and carries it in his pocket-book, and takes it home and reads it to his family, and his wife pastes it in the scrap-book for future reference. That sort of poetry is doing more good than all the highbrow stuff on the shelves" (341–42).

Many articles from the early 1910s mention such informal "home uses" of poetry. In 1913, a reader of the *Dial* asked, "Where are the lovers of verse?" and answered, "they are everywhere. . . . the doubter might try to discover the home without its scrap-book of verse" (A.W.P. 308). The clipping of newspaper verse for scrapbooks remained a common practice well into the twentieth century: a librarian in Denver, for instance, reported in 1924 that some children brought "time-worn scrapbooks" to the library's "poetry circle" (McClung 455). For the Bard of Emporia, newspaper poetry in such day-to-day use confronts, as its opposite number, less-accessible literature in books, "[h]igh-brow stuff on the shelves" (341).

Moreover, for popular writers, no contradiction existed between poetry's exalted status and its commodification. Mason boasts (with a wink), "My lowest price for a rime is $15, except where I sell in car-load lots" (340). Mason's work sells because he knows his audience, knows that "the Tired Business Man . . . is one of the chief consumers of literature, and anything that makes the Tired Business Man more tired is going to fall flat" (341). Likewise, the *Bellman* of Minneapolis reported that Alfred Noyes, the more highbrow yet immensely popular British poet, confessed to a similar sentiment, if in somewhat more delicate terms: "[A] poet, if he is to receive the pecuniary recognition to which he is entitled, must adopt the business methods that are applied to any other profession, not excluding, let us whisper it, the sweet uses of advertising" ("Poetry and Profits"). Unlike T. S. Eliot or the American Fugitives/Agrarians, who distanced themselves from the market in order to accrue cultural legitimacy (Hammer, *Hart Crane* 10–26), for poets of the *arrière-garde*, the sales of poetry indicated its power to fulfill its social function.

This social role also implied a "solidaristic," rather than individualist, cultural politics. It is no accident that Ficke chose "The Man with the Hoe" as an exemplar of a "sane ideal of poetry's function." The publishers of Mason's book *Rippling Rhymes* devote a page to a statement by William Jennings Bryan, who testifies that "the rhythm is perfect and the philosophy that runs through his lines is illumined by an irresistible humor" (n. pag.): the publishers of Mason's folksy newspaper verse calculated that its potential audience would esteem the word of a populist icon. Similarly, Francis Gummere's *Democracy and Poetry* made quite a splash with reviewers in 1911. The *Dial* summarized the book's thesis, saying "the consent of rhythm and the power of human sympathy" makes poetry a fundamentally "democratic" and "social-centripetal" art; "[i]n poetic justice, the democratic ideal of the people found its best expression" (Northup 525).

Some writers even understood the "New Poetry" of the 1910s in terms of a populist or collectivist conception of "democracy." Although critics considered E. A. Robinson, Robert Frost, Amy Lowell, Carl Sandburg, and Sara Teasdale as rather daring because they dealt with "unpoetic" material or sentiments via Imagistic or Whitmanesque free verse, these poets, who dealt with themes close to hand, impressed many of the periodical writers as more approachable than either genteel or early modernist writing. Marguerite Wilkinson, in her 1918 "Poets of the People" series for *Touchstone* magazine, praised "the poets who are doing the best work of the modern or Georgian type, using simple diction, democratic themes and unhampered, organic rhythms" (71). Louis Untermeyer also prized these "democratic" traits in the Chicago and New England school poets: "This democracy is twofold: a democracy of the spirit and a democracy of speech. . . . it intensifies what is their inherent Americanism; it charges their varied art with a native significance" (*New Era* 11).

And if Mason linked poetry to both entertainment and populism, so did Vachel Lindsay, whose "higher vaudeville" poetry performances drew packed houses throughout the country. This "democratic" poetic was, of course, often quite intolerant and chauvinistic. Mason's remarks celebrate what Ezra Pound saw as a tyranny of the cultural majority. And as Untermeyer's remarks suggest (and as Lindsay's *oeuvre* makes plain), this populist poetics was never far from nativism. This intolerance emerged, in part, as a backlash against belittling sneers at popular tastes, such as Mencken's jabs at the "booboisie." Moreover, this nationalistic populism was not entirely divorced at the time from left egalitarian tendencies. In the 1910s, Untermeyer was also an editor of *The Masses*.

This confluence of popular poetics and Progressivist or populist politics is not surprising, given that popular notions of poetry presented it as transitive and therefore naturally social or political (even if the politics espoused varied widely, and often became muddled). Bryant, in his day, drew upon this idiom as he defended his poetics against charges of sentimentalism arising from the formalists of his day. "I know that some critics have made poetry to consist solely in the exercise of the imagination," he wrote. "They distinguish poetry from pathos. . . . I do not know by what authority these gentlemen take the term poetry from the people, and thus limit its meaning" ("Lectures on Poetry" 8). Likewise, in the late 1910s, a University of Illinois professor, in a letter to the editor of the *Nation,* would reject modernist contempt for Alfred Noyes and defend the tastes of both popular and elite genteel audiences by linking the two: "Being at present an eligible witness from the great Middle West whence the magazine *Poetry* arises, I wish to offer my testimony that hereabouts, as elsewhere, the old poetry is still what is wanted by the two kinds of readers that alone count in the long run; the great mass of the plain people, and the great mass of the truly cultivated—the readers and teachers of literature" (Alden 387).

This use of the authority of "the plain people" and of a unitary notion of the heartland was not inconsistent with the views of "the truly cultivated" in the East. By 1918, *Art World* would invoke a utilitarian vocabulary to defend poetry as a means of social solidarity: "Every Rationalist [*sic*] is opposed to Modernism" because "mere craftsmanship" that ignores the "exalting of our emotions . . . becomes socially disintegrating because no longer True nor Good nor Beautiful" (Arbiter 509). Even Imagist Amy Lowell confirmed the secondary importance of the poetic text itself, writing that "poetry is chiefly vision, its words merely serving to wing it forth to other minds" (117). Behind Lowell's remark lies an old fear that formalism would undercut poetry's essentially social raison d'être.

But the very organicism of the notion of "the People" invoked by populist poets and critics belies the nature of the debate in which they were engaged. No longer could a unitary notion of people or citizenry be taken for granted. The very diversity of publics (in literature as in politics) meant that the classical public sphere (itself a hegemonic articulation, to use Laclau and Mouffe's terms) had been displaced by a political society defined by conflicting premises and values.

By the mid-1920s, critics and poets allied with an insurgent high modernism had moved beyond the little magazines and were attempting to make an impact in the monthlies and weeklies that purveyed apologies for the established poetry. These pro-modernists attempted to create a taste for modernism by redefining poetry. In 1925, for instance, Archibald MacLeish, writing in the same *North American Review* that fourteen years before had provided a forum for Ficke, complained that "[t]he difficulty is obviously to make people understand that a poem is, in no mystical manner of speaking, a sensuous object, as real, as sensible as the bronze inkwell there on the desk" (512). Poetry was no longer to be understood as an ethereal, detextualized influence. "Poetry," for MacLeish, had become "a poem," the poem had become the text, and the text, a material object. MacLeish presents Amy Lowell's own wingèd words as exemplary of this new "objective" poetic.

MacLeish attempts to change the terms of the debate. He gripes about "the misuse of poetry for mere communication, mere expression, [in which] so many elderly Wordsworths exhibit their moral excellence in the anthologies" (512). Yet the genteel critics MacLeish attacks also rejected the idea of poetry as *mere* communication. No longer are discussions of poetry to concern its good or deleterious effects; for MacLeish, the debate will now deal with the poetic text as object versus the poetic text as means of "communicating elevated thoughts" (512). In 1926, MacLeish would write, in his poem "Ars Poetica," "A poem should not mean / But be." His prose remarks of the same period suggest that a poem should not *do,* either. That MacLeish would reverse his position as dramatically as he did by the late 1930s serves to emphasize just how polarized and fundamental this conflict became within the literary world by the 1930s.

In the 1930s, Allen Tate would likewise substitute a textualist critique of the *content* of *poems* for a more popular/populist preoccupation with the *effects* of *poetry.* Tate fuses the old foe with the new, the "practical" Victorian view of poetry with the "proletarian" view that art and propaganda are of a piece. Tate, writing in the *New Republic* in 1934, dismisses "the crude optimism of a Victorian like Tennyson, a moral outlook that has almost vanished from poetry, surviving today as direct political and social propaganda" (237). Instead, for Tate "the creative intention removes [statements in a genuine work of art] from the domain of practicality. . . . The stanza is neither true nor false; it is an object that exists" ("Three Types: III" 239). It follows for Tate that "poetry finds its true usefulness in its perfect inutility" (240). In other words, Tate not only argues against both the old and the new "practical" ideas of poetry, he also argues for that which "Poetry" is and ought to be—an object of judgment that embodies, as Kant puts it, "purposiveness without purpose." Poetry becomes material, inutilitarian, and intransitive.[4]

Tate declares that the school of social poetics "so ably represented by Mr. [Edmund] Wilson is the heresy that I am opposing throughout these essays" on the history of poetics ("Three Types: II" 181–82). And Tate critiques this poetic "heresy" precisely by identifying its *failure* to find a social role for poetry: "Yet, the Seven Deadly Sins being now a little threadbare, our new allegorists are quite clear in their recognition that the arts, more especially poetry, have no specific function in society. The arts offer to society a most pusillanimous instrument for the realization of its will. The better the art, one must add, the more pusillanimous. For art aims at nothing outside itself and, in the words of Schopenhauer, 'is everywhere at its goal' " (182).[5] What Tate calls "a poetry of the will" ("Three Types: III" 237) is contemptible *because* it makes nothing happen. That is, if the functionalist poetics falls short on aesthetic grounds, the political poetics collapses, in part, because it is not functional.[6]

But if the leftist poetics of the 1930s can conceive of "no specific function in society" for "social" poetry, such was not the case for a previous generation of poets and critics who saw all poetry as "social." The older poetics constructed "poetry" as addressed to a reading public and serving a public function (and, hence, as positing a public sphere). Tate acknowledges the rhetorical power of such a premise by asserting its absence from "public" poetry of the 1930s. In this way, the high modernist objectification of poetry renders it impractical; its impracticality desocializes it; and the desocialization of poetry depoliticizes it. Thus, "Poetry" and "Politics" (of whatever sort) necessarily become separate and competing, rather than overlapping, discourses.

In the 1930s John Crowe Ransom also argued against both the poetics of uplift and the poetics of revolution at the same time; he thereby merged an argument against a popular functional notion of poetry with an argument against "public speech," 1930s style. Ransom, like Tate, argued that art is not political because it is not practical: "The aesthetic forms are a technique of restraint, not of efficiency. They do not butter our bread, and they delay the eating of it" (446). He then shifts, in the same paragraph, from restraint versus efficacy to form versus politics: "The formal tradition in art has a validity more than political, and the latter I am content to waive" ("Poem Nearly" 447). Ransom, like Tate, affirmed the "validity" of one political-aesthetic "solution" in the act of waiving another, and a populist antiformalism bore as much credit as the Communists. Ransom would similarly describe Wallace Stevens's "Sea Surface Full of Clouds": "That it has not been studied by a multitude of persons [Ransom is writing in 1935] is due to a simple consideration which strikes us at once: the poem has no moral, political, religious, or sociological values. It is not about *res publica,* the public thing" ("Poets without Laurels" 506).

For Ransom, those who look for moral or religious value in poetry are on a par with those who look for political or sociological value: he lumps both together under the banner of a demotic, debased version of the republic of letters concerned with "the public thing." As Langdon Hammer points out, this is also typical of Tate and Cleanth Brooks, who tend to "lump their various enemies—liberals like MacLeish and Van Wyck Brooks, *Saturday Review* pundits, Marxist critics" alike into a unified bloc.[7] The combined threat, in the 1930s, of a demotic poetry and a Marxist poetry would exacerbate what Andreas Huyssen identifies as modernists' "fear of the masses in this age of declining liberalism" (196).

On the face of it, this way of thinking is completely absurd: genteel critics saw the usefulness of poetry as lying in its capacity to soothe the savage beast, while revolutionary poets saw poetry as a means of awakening the slumbering masses. But it is this lumping of all notions of utility in opposition to aesthetic autonomy that marks the crucial rhetorical intervention of modernist critics in shaping the social form of poetry— particularly when their version of poetry, having failed to find a "general public," became institutionalized in the academy. Ransom and Tate thereby linked two senses of "the public"—as reading public and as public sphere—and, ironically, confirmed the legitimacy of those concepts even as they opposed them both to poetry.

Consequently, writers who championed a high modernist cultural politics asserted the death of the audience (as, indeed, they still do). Tate wrote in 1929 that "[s]hortly after 1920 a popular agitation for poetry, the most successful and sensational in our history, came to a close." "[T]he genie withdrew into his bottle" because the promoters of popular poetry withdrew: "Mr. [Louis] Untermeyer leaves no successor, and the popular defense of poetry has lost its effectiveness" ("American Poetry" 78). This is good, since the old poetry was "simple, untutored, and crude" (80); for Tate, as for Wilkins's parson, "it was in terrible bad taste" and "there wa'n't any use in it." In the 1933 essay "Poetry and Politics," Tate asserted that "the popular prestige of poetry has declined. It may be a good omen. The rewards of a quick career have less endurance than disciplined craftsmanship" (310). The poet-critic's textual formalism presumes the decline of the audience: disciplined craftsmanship and popularity are implicitly at odds. In fact, on this logic, in order for such craftsmanship to come to the fore, the popular prestige of poetry *must* decline—or at least be posited as declining. In 1935, Ransom defined modernist poets as "those whom a small company of adept readers enjoys, perhaps enormously, but the general public detests; those in whose hands poetry as a living art has lost its public support" ("Poets without Laurels" 503). As early as 1923, the *New Republic* lamented that "[s]ix million people go daily to the movies. . . . At most a few dozen gather together here and there at the same time to listen to poetry or to talk about it" (Hill 10). The article goes on to explain that "[p]oetry itself supplies a sufficient explanation for its own neglect. Men and women read, after all, something that is useful to them. . . . In poetry they doubtless look for a similar usefulness. And it must be confessed that modern poetry disappoints them" (10). The *American Mercury* echoed these sentiments in 1924, declaring that "the mass even of educated people refuses to read verse. It was evidently a serious mistake to tell men and women that poetry would improve them. Perhaps when this fallacy is forgotten, the mass of men will appreciate good poetry again" (McClure 106).

This hypothesis, in effect, answers Bryant's challenge to formalists: it provided the rationale for a poetry premised upon a small audience (or none) and for an aesthetic that held, as Pound had in the 1910s, that "[t]he artist is not dependent upon the multitude of his listeners. Humanity is the rich effluvium, it is the waste and the manure and the soil, and from it grows the tree of the arts" ("Audience" 29). Harry Scherman, founder of the Book-of-the-Month Club, described the book market in the 1920s by saying: "[W]e had known as part of our established experience that you could sell individual books which might be called 'use books,' like *Power of Will* or *American Gardening,* things of that kind where there would be a broad market" (quoted in Radway, "Mail-Order" 518). Scherman faced the challenge of providing a motive to buy a book that did not have an apparent use: "You had to set up some kind of authority so that the subscriber would feel there was some reason for buying a group of books" (519). Critics had "set up" volumes of poetry as "use books" for prewar audiences; while they wouldn't make you rich, readers knew what they were for. As new authorities told the reader that poetry had neither uses nor users, the reasons for reading poetry came into question.

Ridding poetry of social and political functions itself served a social function for the autonomous New Critical intelligence—a function that operated in the act of making itself vanish. As Tate writes, "There have, of course, been groups, like the Fugitives of Tennessee who did not advertise themselves at all. These poets started with open minds—that is, with the simple aim of writing poetry" ("American Poetry" 80). Of course, these sentences are published in a major literary magazine in the 1920s by one of the leading Fugitive poets in an essay that holds the Fugitives as superior to popular Midwestern poetry of the 1910s. Thus Tate advertises the superiority of his poetics by declaring its lack of intent to advertise. He and his colleagues don't want to make up anyone's mind, they just want to write. Of course, Tate's "simple aim" means, in this case, making "[t]he chief emphasis . . . form and style" and, unlike the poets of the 1910s, taking "only that minimum of public interest that one feels in one's arms and legs" (81). Tate's essay thereby publicizes a new social status for art.[8] This demarcation of a private poetic sphere appealed to a liberal like the (pre–Popular Front) MacLeish of the 1920s, just as its elitist implications appealed to Tate's "aristocratic" pretensions.

In the 1930s, poetry populists and popularizers grew increasingly defensive in response to this modernist offensive. If modernists located inauthenticity in convention, middlebrow critics felt the same way about what they saw as modernist affectation or snobbishness. The audience-as-manure theory did not escape the watchful eye of William Rose Benet, poetry editor of that outpost of "middlebrow" taste, the *Saturday Review of Literature,* who fulminated that "[i]f poetry is to establish no immediate—yes, and emotional—contact with the people, but simply to bombinate *in vacuo,* one can see no reason for its being" ("Poetry and Modern Life"). *Time* magazine reported in 1938, "Twentieth-Century poets have had a hard time trying to make their 20th-Century words make sense, but that was their responsibility" ("Nine and Two" 41). Inaccessibility and formalism once again appeared as moral failings and social threats. Conversely, the *Literary Digest* would "suggest that when 'Trees' and 'If,' for instance, sell in the millions as cards, wall-mottoes, calendars and desk blotters, the Herd doesn't show up as so terribly dumb" (Braley 41). Such outbursts responded to patronizing, often misogynist, put-downs like Ransom's gibe that Edna St. Vincent Millay was "the best of the poets who are 'popular' and loved by Circles, Leagues, Lyceums, and Round Tables; perhaps as good a combination as we can ever expect of the 'literary' poet and the poet who is loyal to the 'human interest' of the common reader" ("Poet as Woman" 783). Indeed, such organizations have provided "the common reader" with a forum for poetry writing and reading from the 1910s to this day. "A Page for Poets," "Conducted by Henry Goddard Leach, President, Poetry Society of America" in the 1937 *Forum,* would "iterate and reiterate that we are all poets, yes, even you, though you may not be able to write two consecutive lines with rhythm and rhyme" (Stone 144). The absence of poetry clubs from academic literary histories both masks and marks the incompleteness of the modernist victory over this belief.

Nonetheless, some writers feared that the avant-garde was in fact scaring off the public. Thus Elizabeth Drew would recall in 1940 that in the preceding decades the poet's "audience became a narrow literary coterie . . . out of all contact with the solid body of contemporary cultivated society" (271). The decline of poetry was also accepted by the curmudgeonly H. L. Mencken, who speculated (patronizingly, as usual):

Why poetry should thus go on the rocks is a somewhat mysterious matter, for the American people are naturally poetical, as Rotary and Kiwanis so brilliantly demonstrate. . . . In the last heyday of the craft—say in 1915 or thereabout—they bought poetry so copiously that a new volume of it often outsold the latest pornographic novel. If sound goods were on the wharves today they would buy again, even at the cost of missing payments on their radios. But nothing is offered that they can get their teeth into. They ask for something to make their hearts leap, and all they get is something that puzzles and scares them. (152)

Both fans and foes of Eliot and company sounded this note: people don't read poetry anymore because it isn't addressed to them. In response, the *Christian Science Monitor* pleaded that "[i]n these times, we, the people, need what poetry offers" (Ritchey 15), and Louis Untermeyer iterated this position in a 1935 edition of the *Rotarian,* the Rotary Club's official organ: "Today . . . is the very time when poetry is most valuable. Never before in America have we needed it so desperately; never before is its healing and revitalizing power so definite" ("Poetry and the Common Man" 46).[9]

As early as 1925, an article significantly entitled "Let Us Go Back to Poetry" appeared in *Good Housekeeping*. This article, by another regionalist author, Indiana novelist and naturalist Gene Stratton-Porter, speaks to both the persistence of popular notions of the poetic and the anxiety felt by people who held those notions in the wake of the promotional campaign of Pound and others. "Poetry" for Stratton-Porter signifies more than a category of texts; it represents a culture. She pictures this culture as traditional, rural, pious, conservative, and one that makes poetry reading and writing aspects of daily life. It is a culture, like Betsey Dole's, in which women have a modicum of cultural authority. Stratton-Porter, who was born in 1864, tells the reader that "I have no reason to believe that my childhood home differed essentially from the majority of other homes of that period" (35), and her article pitches the remembered practical results of poetry reading in childhood and youth: "[O]ur sympathies quickened; our sense of humor developed . . . our memories were given rigorous training; our ears were tuned." Poetry, in the author's family, merged with religion, song, oratory, pedagogy, child rearing, politics, and patriotism. These experiences lead Stratton-Porter to declare that poetry "must have some excuse for being" (196), because "[a] product that benefits only the producer is not worthy" (197). Ultimately that excuse for being is poetry's ability to help Americans "to hold together as a nation" (198). As in nineteenth-century theory, poetry is developmental and integrative and thus serves a crucial social function in the development and maintenance of nationhood.

But for Stratton-Porter, the mid-1920s have brought a libertinage to both poetry and the rest of American culture: "[M]any modern poets, in an effort to discard 'shackles,' have also discarded common sense and delicacy" (195). This new poetry is the bellwether of a broader degeneration: "[T]he banishing . . . of poetry and home-made music from our homes . . . has left the door wide open for insidious moving pictures, for machine-made jazz music, and cubist painting, all tending toward moral laxity" (198). Poetry has been displaced by new forms of entertainment as well as by the new aesthetic; popular culture and morals merge with modern art to form a mortal menace to an essentially integrative, ethical literary form. Moreover, the acceleration of life, "the rush of progress," Stratton-Porter declares, has led "most men" into a pattern of getting and spending "without stopping to revel in beauty." The result is that "the man who has striven . . . very often through nerve-strain has contracted disease which tortures him" (35). Cubists who celebrate this rapidity become guilty of contributing to social disintegration when they could be culturing (or curing) minds. Modern(ist) culture, on Stratton-Porter's account, is sheer torture. She pleads with whomever will listen to make it stop.

More than competing media or aesthetics, the issue for Stratton-Porter is the disappearing social role of poetry. Urbanization and atomization, the dispersion of the extended family and devaluation of the domestic, the mediation of relationships by mass culture, and the acceleration of life together form a united front against "the old poetry." People, in this vision, have lost control of art either to the culture industry or to an abstruse and disillusioned cabal of aesthetes. No longer do people write, recite, and memorize poetry for themselves; poetry has lost its place, and people have lost their desire for poetry. Betsey Dole is dead. So too, for that matter, was Stratton-Porter: "Let Us Go Back to Poetry" was published posthumously by one year.

As in Freeman's 1890 story, representations of the rivalry between these poetries continued to evoke violent metaphors in the 1910s, 1920s, and 1930s. For instance, in 1913 Pound wrote Harriet Monroe, "[S]o far as I personally am concerned the public can go to the devil. It is the function of the public to prevent the artist's expression by hook or by crook. . . . we're in such a beautiful position to save the public's soul by punching its face that it seems a crime not to do so" (*Letters* 13). The public be damned, the public be saved. Pound's statement expresses a rejection of a transitive, social, or audience-oriented notion of poetry, a fear of and constitution of "the public" as an Other that threatens the artist "by hook or by crook." But Pound's words also evince a desire both to transform and to define the public, to make it safe for poetry as Pound sees it. This goal was to be accomplished by a blow, a literary coup that was at once coup d'état and renaissance—a crossing that Pound would later map onto Fascist Italy. A confusion over the textual form of poetry, what George Steiner calls a "modal difficulty," was contiguous with a confusion over the social form of poetry, which, in turn, indicated much larger cultural-political "difficulties."

In 1929, in "How to Read," Pound praised poetry that "contained an invention, a definite contribution to the art of verbal expression" as opposed to "a nice poem or a poem Aunt Hepsy liked" (*Essays* 17). Traditionalist critics were happy to respond in kind. John Crowe Ransom reported in 1935 that "[a] Pulitzer committeeman, I hear, says about some modernist poet whose book is up for judgment: 'He will never get the award except over my dead body.' The violence of the remark seems to exceed the occasion, but it is not exceptional" ("Poets without Laurels" 504). Meanwhile, purveyors of "popular" or "democratic" notions of poetry for their part took exception to pronouncements by representatives of "legitimate" culture, whether the graying academic critics of the Gilded Age or younger representatives of the then-recently-christened New Criticism.

If the fight between different versions of poetry seems violent, like a "culture war," to invoke an overused phrase (one thinks of culturally conservative full professors who say they're being "lynched" by their "P.C." undergraduates), it's not because there are too many poetries floating around. Rather, the conflict over poetry is expressed through symbolic violence to the extent that each poetry claims universality for itself. Such universality excludes rather than encompasses regional or gender differences, as we have seen. Universalist discourses express particularities of a particularly volatile kind. The universalist ideal, as Carole Pateman suggests, "also hides the figure of the armed man in the shadows behind the civil individual" (51), another avatar of the subject of aesthetic judgment. But it is not only, as Pateman suggests, the failure of the social contract to deliver equality that necessitates the guards. It is also, by the same token, the need for a cultural consensus—one that corresponds to and validates the fantasy of universal judgment and values— that requires the denial of dissensus. This demand for consensus stems from and expresses what Chantal Mouffe describes as the "evasion of the political" (2), the failure to own up to the differences and antagonisms inherent in social life, the demand for and expectation of agreement that both Pound's and Stratton-Porter's comments evince. Given the zero-sum terms of the conflict, it can only degenerate into a confrontation between different types or levels of institutional authority. Or one can turn to that old liberal standby, the appeal to self-evidence. As Tate concludes his essay "Three Types of Poetry": "Let us not argue about it. It is here for those who have eyes to see" (240). In "Poetry and Politics," he declares that in "propagandist art" "[w]e get neither art nor politics; we get heresy" (310). In Tate's orthodoxy, by contrast, "to discuss poetry we assume in it certain features that seem to give us reasonable assurance that we know what we are talking about" (308). Indeed, the hermeneutic circle described here would seem to depend upon a near-religious faith for its power—and, by implication, to present the grounds for holy wars.

This row between popular and elite literary cultures had become an established institution in its own right by the time *Mr. Deeds Goes to Town* in Frank Capra's 1934 film. Longfellow Deeds, a small-town poet, has made a comfortable income by penning inspirational verses for greeting cards. His housekeeper reads aloud a Mother's Day poem, prefacing it with the remark, "He got $25 for this one: 'When you've nowhere to turn and you're filled with doubt / Don't stand in midstream hesitatin.' / For you know that your mother's heart cries out: / "I'm waiting my boy, I'm waiting."' Isn't that beautiful? Isn't that a lovely sentiment?" The porter at the railroad station describes Deeds as a "fine fellow—very democratic." Deeds's poems reach a wide audience ("Longfellow's famous," the housekeeper says); they also adorn a welcome sign to the town, Mandrake Falls, Vermont. Deeds is thoroughly a part of the life of the community; not only does he write verses, he also owns the tallow works, plays tuba in the town band, and serves in the volunteer fire department. As his name indicates, Longfellow Deeds represents a widespread, conventional, moral, traditional poetic taste. In the movie's representation, as in Stratton-Porter's or Wilkins's, this poetics is associated with small-town or rural life, a nostalgic, populist, utopian imagined community peopled by a respectable, salt-of-the-earth lower-middle class with low cultural capital (the utterly destitute displaced farmers Deeds helps in New York are nowhere to be seen in Vermont). The character of Deeds, like popular newspaper poets such as James Whitcomb Riley and Bliss Carman at the turn of the century, gave, as Angela Sorby notes, a "mostly white, middle-class audience . . . access to and distanced them from the popular" at once (201). But, although the "nostalgic longing" evoked by Deeds's verses is "a form of social and cultural distancing" (207), he is the protagonist and the character with which Capra invites us to identify. Like Riley, "he perform[s] social distinctions—genially, but with a startling undercurrent of aggression" (Sorby 198). By the end of the film, Mr. Deeds's giving away his inherited fortune to finance family farms cinches the connection between popular poetry, populism, and an agrarian community, and it is a constellation of values that the first-generation American Capra idealizes.

When Deeds, played by Gary Cooper, does go to town to come into possession of his newfound wealth, he decides he wants to spot some literary stars. Capra accomplishes the transition with a shot of a flashing sign: TULLIO'S: EAT WITH THE LITERATI. At this point, the film suggests a connection between an elite poetry and the more popular versions: "Brookfield, the poet" and other "literati" serve as objects of admiration for Deeds. The Tullio's sign also suggests that the literati, for Capra, are every bit as commodified as Longfellow Deeds's greeting-card mottoes. The waiter tells Deeds that the famous poets are "at that round table over there"—not unlike the one at the Algonquin Hotel, we may assume. As soon as the writers invite Deeds to their table, viewers become aware of a great divide between legitimate and mass poetics. The big-city poets, who don't see their own audience as composed of people like Longfellow Deeds, begin to bait him. "Tell us, Mr. Deeds," one begins, "how do you go about writing your poems? We craftsmen are very interested in one another's—methods." When the poet Morrow says that his publishers have been complaining about his "dashing them off," Deeds replies that "your readers don't complain, Mr. Morrow." For Deeds, the audience reception counts for more than the process or the product of composition. The invitation to discuss technique is lost on Deeds, who replies, "Well, I, ah—I write mine on order. The people I work for just tell me what they want, and I go to work and write it." Like Betsey Dole, Mr. Deeds writes for occasions and in response to requests, and he also writes for money. In other words, he is not acculturated to an ideology of poetry as a space apart from the market and, by the same token, from social norms or expectations.

When one writer asks Deeds to recite a Mother's Day poem, Brookfield seconds the request, saying, "Exactly! Give us one that wrings the Great American Heart!" At this point, "Longfella" gets wise to the sophisticates' contempt for him, for the sentimental poetics he represents, and for the culture he comes from. Deeds shoots back: "I think your poems are swell, Mr. Brookfield, but I'm disappointed in you. . . . I guess maybe it *is* comical to write poems for postcards, but a lot of people think they're good. Anyway, it's the best I can do. . . . I guess I found out that all famous people aren't big people." Deeds, the naive artist, responds to scorn of his work by invoking the size and response of his audience, and the person of the author outweighs the impersonal excellence of the work. If famous people are not big people, fame is undeserved. "The best I can do" counts for more than Matthew Arnold's definition of culture as "the acquainting ourselves with the best that has been known or said in the world." Poetry serves not as an object of contemplation or discrimination, but as a medium for social relationships. When those relationships go bad in this scene and Deeds's words meet with laughter, dialogue gives way to fisticuffs as the rural poet "mops up the floor" with the urbanites. If in the 1930s the figure of the poet had come to look rather like Leslie Howard's deracinated Alan Squier in "The Petrified Forest," an American "once removed" in a waste land of lowbrow culture, Deeds presents a defensive counterimage.[10] Squier views the yokels in the Arizona desert with detached irony, and he must die in the end; Cooper, in the person of Deeds, meets the violence of taste as discipline with the violence of physical force. If Tate's and Ransom's poetics propounded one sort of cultural reaction (self-styled), Capra's vision of poetry embodied another sort.

Indeed, the very pervasiveness of laments over poetry's supposed decline, and of accusations that modernists were the responsible party, indicate the at-best-mixed results of the modernists' campaign of conscious propaganda. If the *Nation* and the *Dial* turned renegade, the *Saturday Review* and *Women's Home Companion* did not. In 1928, *Ladies' Home Journal*, whose circulation outstripped that of more literary periodicals, published a feature page entitled "Can You Name These Modern Poets?" As the answer key revealed, the unsigned photographs and verse excerpts included those of Millay, Markham, Mason, and Frost, along with those perennial favorites Lindsay, Teasdale and Edgar Lee Masters.

Again, in 1938, "Do You Know Your Poetry?" featured first lines by Kipling, Longfellow, Shelley, and Felicia Dorothea Hemans. For the *Journal*, these poets (rather than Eliot or Donne) represented the canon that every literate American knew. Nor did the status of poetry as both unabashed commodity and cultural capital simply evaporate. The *Literary Digest* of the 1930s was fond of crowing over the sales of popular poets and declared that Mason and other newspaper poets continued to reach over a million subscribers (Braley 41). If "The Waste Land" (1922) rocked the literary world, Kalil Gibran's *The Prophet* (1923) made an impact on a wider audience, which bought three million copies between its initial publication and 1970 (Nye 134). In 1935, Harcourt, Brace and Company published both Eliot's *Murder in the Cathedral* and Louis Untermeyer's *Selected Poems and Parodies*. If the *New Republic, Poetry,* and the *Sewanee Review* published poetry in 1935, so did the *Daily Worker,* the *Nashville Christian Advocate,* and the *Saturday Evening Post;* and that (in)famous institution *Best Loved Poems of the American People* saw the light of day in 1936.

Yes, we may ask, but is it *poetry?* If U.S. academics today are inclined to think not, the culture wars of the 1930s may have informed their answer. If, as Andreas Huyssen claims, a feminized "[m]ass culture has always been the hidden subtext of the modernist project" (191), mass poetry was a double threat to modernist poetics. "The autonomy of the modernist art work," Huyssen writes, "is always the result of a resistance . . . to the seductive lure of mass culture, abstention from the pleasure of trying to please a larger audience" (198). For literary high modernism in the United States, poetry constituted the most autonomous form of literature, an alternative to the public, the popular, the feminized, and the mass. A mass poetry threatened to vitiate a fortification of cultural boundaries based on generic boundaries.

Nonetheless, radio listeners of the 1930s heard the debut of numerous local and nationally syndicated poetry shows such as Ted Malone's "Between the Bookends" and "Pilgrimage of Poetry" (about the houses of famous poets) or "Tony Wons's Scrapbook." Making payments on a radio did not, as Mencken suggested, necessarily mean missing poetry: the "home scrapbook of verse" was now a scrapbook of the air, and popular poetry was mass poetry. Harriet Monroe declared that "[p]oetry is a vocal art; radio will bring back its audience" (35). But, to her horror, the great audiences were not listening to great poetry: "[T]he poets of quality and standing are not being broadcast, while numerous impossibles are reading their maudlin verses to invisible audiences of millions" (32). The popular audience that modernists had attempted to disappear had returned—in invisible form, as a mass audience—to haunt "poets of quality" with "impossible" verse.[11]

This mixed outcome suggests the improbability of modernist/New Critical attempts to crack the "prepared taste" by arguing against the audience. Tate and Ransom attempted to prepare a degree of popularity by arguing that popularity is bad; they argued against public art in public debates. The public, who didn't matter, mattered very much; but high modernism's and New Criticism's rejection of the public insured their status as minority movements within the literary debates in the periodical press. MacLeish fled this status by producing an ever more public poetry printed in inexpensive editions, illustrated with W.P.A. photographs, or broadcast as radio verse plays—projects that earned him the scorn of his former allies. Conversely, by 1940, Tate and Ransom had abandoned the popular press for academic quarterlies sympathetic to them or of their own design.

It was a short step thence to the universities. If the debates in mass-circulation periodicals did not provide an institutional base for a subcultural poetics with hegemonic ambitions, then the academy could be made to serve that purpose. As Mark Jancovich relates, "By 1937, then, the group [Agrarian/New Critics] had come to regard the departments of English as the best location for the development and distribution of their social and cultural criticism" (80).[12] In that year, Ransom asserted that a work of art, particularly poetry, "calls for public discussion" ("Criticism, Inc." 597), but "the university teacher of literature . . . should be the very professional we need to take charge of the critical activity" (587). Ransom thereby transfers the site of "public" literary debate to the university—that is, outside of the forum of popular periodicals. Poetry—real poetry—would be wrested away from "amateurs"; in the process, it would be wrested from much of the popularity it enjoyed.[13] High modernism would cease to be a ragtag assortment of insurgents battling the old guard; rather, it would soon be installed as the Party of the Institutional Revolution, with the academy, not the publishing industry, as its home. As *Saturday Review* founder Henry Seidel Canby set about making literary selections for the Book of the Month Club, Tate and Ransom schemed to take over the Modern Language Association (Jancovich 80).[14]

Thus poetry would come to bear very different meanings inside and outside the academy. As Frank Ninkovich points out, when these conceptions clashed in the 1949 controversy over the award of the Library of Congress's Bollingen Prize to Pound, a concentrated symbolic struggle ensued between two broad cultural-political alignments. The struggle to determine modern American culture was once again played out in the exalted realm of poetry. The champions of the poem as autonomous aesthetic object were winning out in the English departments, but not elsewhere. The demagogic congressmen who attacked Pound (and modernism generally) from the floor of the House found a sympathetic public, and the Library of Congress handed Princeton the politically hot rock of the Bollingen Award.

Large audiences inside and outside universities continued to reject modernism and its heirs and to head in a very different direction. By 1962, with the New Criticism at its institutional zenith, *Time* magazine reported that "[i]n the 16 years since World War II, more poems have been composed in the U.S. . . . than were written in ten centuries between Beowulf and the Bomb" ("Poetry in English" 92). These poems were not all products of university workshops and journals: "[S]ales of poetry on records are tuned to unprecedented volume. U.S. poetry buffs have bought 50,000 platters of Robert Frost reading Robert Frost, 400,000 of the late Dylan Thomas reading Dylan Thomas. And poetry readings have been box office in the U.S." (92). One reason for the popularity of readings was the popularity of Beat poetry. Yet "on the entirely tenable theory that a beard does not make a bard, the leading literary periodicals (*Partisan Review, Kenyon Review, Hudson Review, Sewanee Review*) have firmly refused to print action poetry" (93). The younger poetry publics appeared to be on one track, the quarterlies founded or favored by the first New Critics on quite another. Yet *Time* could find little to applaud in that quarter either: "'The level of technique in verse,' says poet Auden, 'is probably higher today than ever before.' But with all their skill, most contemporary poets seem to have little to say." The article closes in terms that echo the *Saturday Review* of the 1930s: cause for hope lies in "a growing number of talented poets" who "seem aware that readers outnumber poets, and seem willing to write something that might interest them" (95).

Indeed, "the modernist tradition" never seized the public imagination as had earlier, more congenial poets such as Frost—understandably, given modernist disdain of "the public" and all it represented. So when Frank Lentricchia, in his celebration of modernist resistance to commodity culture, claims that 1929 saw a "literary revolution won, modernism fully in place and Ezra Pound its widely hailed entrepreneur and guru," we may wonder where he is looking. When Lentricchia states that "Frost's side lost" to Pound's, we soon learn *where:* "[O]ur chief accounts of modernist poetic history find [Frost] anomalous at best, a poet of the twentieth century but not a 'modern' poet" (84). This is literary history of literary histories ("our chief accounts") that gives primacy to academic tastes. While Pound's side certainly won in the academy, Frost could hardly be said to have lost in terms of general readership or popular esteem.[15] Literary critics who, like Lentricchia, narrate this victory of high modernism have reduced the checkered history of modern poetry to its institutional form in the academy today.

In fact, even the publicists of an inutilitarian poetics in the 1920s and 1930s admitted that poetry carries a trace of social utility. Ransom praised "Sea Surface Full of Clouds" because "[t]he poem has a calculated complexity, and its technical competence is so high that to study it, if you do that sort of thing, is to be happy." But for that very reason, "it has not been studied by a multitude of persons" ("Poets without Laurels" 506). It is precisely the poem's impenetrability by the public that makes it the sort of text that yields happiness for those who "do that sort of thing." New Critics are few in number because most people look for a more obvious use value in poetry; or, put another way, the Stevens poem is useful only to the few.[16] Stevens himself would go a bit further: poetry, the expression of "the imagination pressing back against the pressure of reality" in "the sound of its words, helps us to live our lives" (*Necessary* 36). When Tate argues that poetry is "a focus of repose for the will-driven intellect that constantly shakes the equilibrium of persons and societies" ("Three Types: III" 240), his "intellect" shares with Walt Mason's tired businessman the desire to find refuge in poetry from the stresses of modernity.

Years earlier, I. A. Richards, in "Science and Poetry" (1925), had assured readers of the *Atlantic Monthly* that "to a suitable reader [of poetry] . . . the words will reproduce in his mind a similar play of instincts putting him for the while into a similar situation and leading to the same response" as that experienced by the poet (488). Richards preached mental equilibrium through poetry imagined as "a League of Nations for the moral ordering of the impulses—a new order based on conciliation, not on attempted suppression" (490); this effect was to be achieved, paradoxically, by relinquishing "the desire to be effective" (487). Once again, for both Tate and Richards, poetry's practicality lay in its countering the mental ill-effects of a "practical" modern society (one that had produced both the October Revolution and Verdun). Here the practicality of poetry was reconstituted at a "higher" level, where its cultural aims were sublimated; Richards is interested only in "a suitable reader."

Despite Richards's disavowal of efficacy in literature, literature, for him, produces a result ("the moral ordering of the impulses"). Cleanth Brooks, who considered Richards an ally, recognized this point and felt the need to recuperate it. He wrote Allen Tate in 1934 that Richards's statement " 'it is never what a poem *says* that matters, but what it *is*' comes close to your statement that 'the stanza is neither true nor false; it is an object that exists'" (Vinh 19). Brooks allowed, "I do not like Richards' utilitarianism"; "but," he suggested, Richards "has made it rather broad. He gives poetry a 'use,' it is true, but all of us who regard poetry as valuable also give it a use." Brooks understands this as "a value or use which would include contemplation" (Vinh 19). Tate, perhaps sensing the applicability of Brooks's statement to himself ("all of us . . . give it a use"), would have none of it; for him, Richards "would say . . . the poem has 'value'—a strictly pragmatic value—because it orders our minds, or something like that" (Vinh 22).

From this point of view, Richards's orientation (and, by implication, Brooks's) is not far removed from that of the more lowbrow Robert Haven Schauffler, author of another 1925 *Good Housekeeping* article, "The Poetry Cure: A Novel Remedy for Weary Hearts." In it, Schauffler tells us that "Poetry affords us a respite in which we may gather renewed strength for the old struggle to adapt ourselves to reality" (37). Schauffler has developed "a working science of poetic medicine" via "a compact medicine chest of verse in anthology form" (37), and he prescribes different poems as specifics for different ailments. For instance, Schauffler prescribes a Wordsworth sonnet as a cure for insomnia. The author recommends "The Man with the Hoe" as an antidote to "[h]ardening of the heart" (256). Likewise, a poem can counter neurasthenia through the mechanism of escape: "The poet's subconscious mind invents a poem whose argument provides a dream-solution of his—and your—mental or spiritual ailment" (253). Thus W. H. Davies's poem "Leisure" can aid "sufferers from the strenuous life of cities"; after reading "Kublai Khan," "almost any reader can hear the milk of paradise purling deliciously down the cobbled ways of Hoboken" (253). Poetry appears destined to make an "appeal to our common sense as a reducer of doctors' bills and an uplifter of salaries" (258). Bryant had prescribed the poems of nature's haunts or hearthside for "a world whose inhabitants are perpetually complaining of its labors, fatigues, and miseries" ("Lectures" 15). Over a century later, poetry continued to be seen as a practical art form, either in a very specific, therapeutic role or as a more general object of contemplation and source of repose or happiness.

As I will argue in the following chapters, despite modernist poets' and critics' renunciation of publicness and efficacy, they continually found themselves drawn into public debates, specifically with an eye to positing or controlling the effects of poetry on a reading public. Richards preached mental equilibrium through exposure to a sort of literary snapshot of psychologically "ordered impulses." Tate's and Ransom's ideal readers found repose in techno-aesthetic perfection. All three evince a concern with the effects of poetry, with its relation to reader and writer, and all are in tension with a notion of a purely autotelic or intransitive work of art.

But why did the modernist effort to shift the social form of poetry arise in the first place? In the next two chapters, I will suggest a reading of poetic modernism in the context of U.S. political culture. Canonical poetic modernism in the United States, I would argue, hews rather closely to classical liberal conceptions of separation of spheres, the role of community, and to a liberal metaphysics of the self. As T. J. Jackson Lears suggests, by the 1890s, liberalism had come under attack from militarists, neo-Catholics, and the Arts and Crafts movement, among others. The legacy of mid-nineteenth-century liberalism mutated into social liberalism and various forms of populism, progressivism, and the social gospel, which find echoes in popular poetics of the era. As the twentieth century slouched forward, classical liberalism had to compete not only with a newer, more collectivist social liberalism, but with communism and fascism as well. In the following chapters, I will suggest that modernist poetics in the United States from the 1910s through the 1940s, rather than being an antiliberal reaction, as is usually supposed, can be read as a classical liberal response to these challenges. This is even the case with a poet and theorist who may seem to be the unlikeliest of candidates—Allen Tate.

We are a band of brothers
And native to the soil
Fighting for our liberty
With treasure, blood, and toil.
And when our rights were threatened,
The cry rose near and far,
"*Hoorah!* for the Bonnie Blue Flag
That bears a single star!"
—*"The Bonnie Blue Flag,"*
Confederate anthem

"'Liberty and union
now and forever'"
—*From "Marriage," by*
Marianne Moore. Moore's note:
"Daniel Webster (statue
with inscription, Central Park,
New York City)"

CHAPTER TWO

High Modernism in Polite Society, or, Allen Tate's Conservative Liberalism

At the nadir of the Depression and the zenith of leftist influence on the arts in the United States, Allen Tate summed up his own *ars poetica* by stating that "poetry finds its usefulness in its perfect inutility" ("Three Types of Poetry: III," 1934). Tate (like the early Ezra Pound or T. S. Eliot) here associates art, and poetry especially, with a technical expertise exercised by free and disinterested individuals. He envisions the artist as a self-possessed and -contained subject who can adopt a disinterested universal perspective from which political authority can be critiqued. But, according to Tate, the artist must, by the same token, be protected from incursions of the "interest and power" inherent not only in public authority (as in the form of censorship) but in "the public" in all its senses. Mark Jancovich sums up this position nicely: writers "should engage with society through a critical investigation of that society. They should not be limited to the role of an apologist for particular economic or political positions. This independence also required a specific social and material base" apart from the market (49). The content or the aim of the poet's art are, from this point of view, therefore less important than his[1] freedom to say what he wishes and the quality with which he says it. In other words, the art's usefulness lies neither in what it communicates nor in its effects, but rather in its (and by virtue of its) apparent inutility, not to mention individuality. In this sense, art, like the cultivation of the self, becomes part of the project of what Kant calls *autotely*. Tate and other high modernist poet-critics, like their professed New Critic admirers in the 1950s, believed that only by asserting this value-neutral integrity of the poem could the autonomy of the artist be preserved.

But in spite of Tate's equation of poetry with disinterested craftsmanship and insistence on the poet as free agent, he and his Fugitive/Agrarian colleagues had very definite opinions, early and late, about political and social organization and the poet's role therein. Both their literary and their social criticism extol (in various ways and to different degrees) orthodox religion, a unitary culture, traditional societies, and what today we might call a communitarian political philosophy. Tate, for instance, frankly rejected the new social liberalism represented by John Dewey, Walter Lippman, and Herbert Croly and celebrated a putative agrarian squirearchy in the antebellum South. If Tate engaged in "a critical investigation" of his society, he saw solutions to its problems in earlier societies—ones that tolerated very little critique indeed.[2]

Langdon Hammer notes a similar "Janus-faced" quality of modernism within Tate's work. In the 1920s, the poet embraced "a modernism that challenged the traditional, identity-defining authority of religion, family, and region, and that approved the artist's freedom to respond to the demands and potential of the aesthetic medium itself." By the 1930s, Tate was "moving toward the conservative anticapitalist politics of the Southern Agrarian movement," which considered itself "a *remnant* community, dedicated to the marginal but enduring values of premodern cultures," to the " 'organic' form in both society and art" (*Hart Crane* xi–xii). In other words, Tate is first antiauthoritarian (in the 1920s), then authoritarian (in the 1930s).

In fact, Tate wants artistic freedom but regrets the very liberalism of which it is a historical part. Indeed, I will argue, these competing desires coexist throughout Tate's career; moreover, this tension is symptomatic of a larger one within high modernism, and the same tension exists in the history of liberal political philosophy. Tate's version of modernism, and, by extension, his colleagues', is (in spite of itself) a *classical* liberal reaction against *twentieth-century* "social" liberalism.

When Tate uses the word "liberal," its meaning reflects the semantic shift in the use of that word from the eighteenth to the twentieth century. "Liberal," by 1934, meant social liberal, the sort of liberal who, following what James Kloppenberg calls the *via media* between socialism and laissez-faire capitalism, wants the state to assume responsibility for promoting positive rights. The "new" social liberals such as Herbert Croly or John Dewey reacted against the "old" libertarian liberal philosophy and embraced a conception of liberalism more centered around "positive freedom," equality, and social solidarity than around negative liberties and individualism. Michael Levenson traces this shift in L. T. Hobhouse's influential book *Liberalism* (1911), which paints it as a progressive narrative

> "[T]oward social amelioration and democratic government," . . . [with] two major phases. The first, "older liberalism" worked to endow the individual with civil, economic and political freedom [and was a] negative activity, devoted to the removal of constraints, sure in the belief that once individuals were allowed to develop freely, an "ethical harmony" would ensue.
>
> According to Hobhouse, Bentham initiated a second phase in which the highest value attached not to the individual but to the community and its collective will. . . . This commitment has led to the positive aspect of the liberal movement: the regulation of behavior, the intervention in markets, the exercise of legal restraints and . . . state paternalism. (87)

For Hobhouse, there is no contradiction between "a commitment to social reform and an unremitting respect for personal liberty" (88). These newer liberal philosophers reacted against a long line of what J. G. Merquior defines as "conservative liberals from about 1830 to 1930" who "were generally intent on *slowing the democratization* of liberal politics" (97). I would locate poet-critics such as Tate, John Crowe Ransom, and Cleanth Brooks in that "conservative liberal" tradition. It is the *newer* meaning of the word "liberal" that John Crowe Ransom uses when he attributes to the "blandishments of such fine words as 'Progressive, Liberal, and Forward-Looking'" the "Deracination of our Western life" (Twelve Southerners 6).

The new social liberalism is countered, in both Tate and Ransom, by an older, pessimistic liberalism—elements of which are found in both Locke and Jefferson—that preserves liberty by establishing limits and boundaries (as between public authority and individual rights). Originally, according to Sheldon Wolin, "liberalism emerged as a post-revolutionary reaction," and "a philosophy of sobriety, born in fear, nourished by disenchantment, and prone to believe that the human condition was and was likely to remain one of pain and anxiety" (293–94). Hence it had no truck with "grandiose schemes of social reconstruction projected during the French Revolution" (297). In other words, Tate's and Ransom's liberalism is that of the 1790s rather than the 1930s.

As we shall see, however, this older, classical liberalism is pulled in different directions by its dual emphases on the value of individual autonomy on the one hand and the desire for cultural consensus on the other. It is precisely due to this conflict in classical liberalism that the high modernist poetics of Tate and his contemporaries appears Janus-faced—or even contradictory.

During the 1930s, Tate became increasingly suspicious, not to say paranoid, of the public as a threat to the creative integrity of the poet and of poetry. For Tate, a factional "politics" threatened to subsume poetry and rob it of any independent imaginative existence. By the beginning of World War II, he would warn Cleanth Brooks that Archibald MacLeish, Van Wyck Brooks, and the Donovan Committee were engaged in "a conspiracy . . . to suppress critical thought in the United States" and "to discredit all the good writing of the past twenty years" (Vinh 83). In the preface to his self-consciously titled *Reactionary Essays on Poetry and Ideas* (1936), Tate complained that "[w]e are trying to make a fine art respectable by showing that after all it is only a branch of politics." The problem here is that "[b]oth politics and poetry, having ceased to be arts, are cut off from their common center of energy" (x). Now, as part of the modern condition, these two forms of "art," rather than being merely branches sprouting from the trunk of the same organic society, have become competing, equivalent, symmetrical discourses that attempt to cancel each other out: "For a political poetry, or a poetical politics, of whatever denomination is a society of two members living on each other's washing. They devour each other in the end. It is the heresy of spiritual cannibalism" (x). Accordingly, when one attempts to transgress the boundary between the poetic and the political, poet and politician are reduced to the common level of cannibals who "devour each other in the end."[3] Though this separation of spheres is a Fall from an original organic society, the separation must be maintained to avoid catastrophic results.

Tate enacts this breakdown in the poem "Eclogue of the Liberal and the Poet" (1938). In this "dramatic" poem, the language of the Poet and that of the Liberal become matter and antimatter that destroy each other. The poem begins with a tone of high seriousness:

LIBERAL
    In that place, shepherd, all the men are dead.
POET
    Yes, look at the water grim and black
    Where immense Europa rears her head,
    Her face pinched and her breasts slack. (*Poems* 91)

The Poet then asks, "Shall I turn to the road that goes America?" [*sic*]. Shortly thereafter, the decidedly unpoetic voice of the Liberal intervenes:

POET
    But what about her face and the tasked
    Wonders of her air and soil, her big belly
    That Putnam writes about under the sun?[4]

LIBERAL
>   I don't know Put, I don't know his Nelly—
>   I'd name her that if she'd name it fun
>   But you know she hasn't any name,
>   Nowhere you touch her she's the same.

POET
>   What, shepherd, are we talking about?

LIBERAL
>   You started it, shepherd.

POET
>   Shepherd, I didn't. (92)

The Poet's incipient pastoral (including its allusions, apostrophe, and rhyme scheme) is quashed by the Liberal, who speaks a sort of burlesque of poetry while making it clear that he knows neither the allusion nor the specificity of names, but only "fun." The Liberal, in other words, stands in for a culture without a unified culture or history: "Nowhere you touch her [America] she's the same." The intrusion of the Liberal's voice, in fact, derails the poem, as its diction disintegrates. It continues:

LIBERAL
>   You did; you saw the poetical face of Europe.

POET
>   You said it was no place for men to be.

LIBERAL
>   I meant seawater; you thought I meant hope.

POET
>   Hell, I reckon you think I am a dope.

LIBERAL
>   I didn't say that; I said there was no place.

POET
>   If not in a place, where are the People weeping?

LIBERAL
>   They creep weeping in the face, not place.

POET

>   Is it something with which we may cope—
>   The weeping, the creeping, the peepee-ing, the peeping? (93)

At this point, one is inclined to answer, "no," as the "eclogue" degenerates into a sort of Marx Brothers routine (or scene from Beckett). The Liberal means something as mundane and practical as seawater (that it is no place to be), while he thinks the poet is speaking of hope or of "the poetical face of Europe." The shepherd-Poet at this points drops his classical mask and sounds a lot like a modern man on the street. When the Poet attempts to regain composure and to express compassion for "the People" who are weeping "in a place," the deracinated (and deraced), comically literal Liberal responds, with no apparent feeling, that they are "weeping in the face, not place." The Poet descends into a babbling wordplay that brings his level down to that of a nursery rhyme, as if to say, We may not cope with Europe's fate on its own terms—certainly not on the Liberal's terms, and certainly not by mixing codes. An eclogue is, in fact, no place for the Liberal, the politician from the metropole; he cannot speak poetry, and when he tries to speak in a poem, the poem "crashes." The two languages cannibalize each other, so that we get neither good poetry nor good theory.

In this, Tate's separation of spheres, there can be no mixture or stasis: his is a zero-sum economy in which creativity is always flowing in one direction or the other. In another of the *Reactionary Essays,* "The Profession of Letters in the South" (1935), Tate writes that the fault of antebellum southern culture was that "[i]t was hag-ridden with politics." Since, on Tate's account, the South was an aristocracy, and "[a]ll aristocracies are obsessed politically," this result was inevitable under the circumstances: "The best intellectual energy goes into politics and goes of necessity; aristocracy is class-rule; and the class must fight for interest and power." Accordingly, "the South had less excess of vitality for the disinterested arts of literature than it might have had ordinarily" (*Reactionary* 153). In this trope, creative energy, like electricity, can be concentrated, diverted, or divided; it can go into either politics or the arts, but not both. Politics is feminized, devouring, and monstrous, like a succubus. It saps the (presumably male) aristocrat-poet's vital bodily fluids; the South here has the same problem as 1930s Europe, "[h]er face pinched and her breast slack," rather than being a fecund object of male contemplation and control. And the reason is that politics is the realm of "special interests"—of "passion" that can be "inflamed" by "furious contentions" (153), propaganda and oratory—rather than the universal, unclassed, "disinterested" perspective of art. Passion, that traditionally feminine and notoriously disruptive force, diverts "the best intellectual energy" of full members of the political community of the South, who are (it literally goes without saying for Tate) male, white, and propertied.[5] Nonetheless, at one time, both politics and poetry, according to Tate, were arts with a common source. The separation from that source has turned them, in this fallen world, into polar opposites. Now we must have separation of spheres, with poetry in the private sphere.

What, then, is a poet to do? Tate continues, in his preface, to explain that the relation of politics to poetry "will concern the poet only in his faculty of critic, not in his job as craftsman. The poet's special question is: How shall the work be done?" (x). The poet, in other words, is not concerned with the political content of, motivation for, or effect of the poem on the readership. Poetry for him is a value-neutral craft-object that concerns neither politics, economics, nor philosophy. "A poet whose main passion is to get his doctrine . . . into his poems," Tate continues, "is trying to justify a medium in which he lacks confidence. There is a division of purpose." (xi). Poetry is a medium, not a message. The two "purposes" are de facto divided, and when they are mixed, one suffers from a divided mind, a schizophrenia.

We see in this side of Tate a version of idealist morality rather than communitarian ethics. Thus Tate writes, in "Aeneas at New York" (1932), "Appreciation of victory contains no views."[6] The military action itself is the thing, not the cause for which it is conducted. Aeneas at New York is Aeneas at Latium. Both are figures of the poet who is a craftsman regardless of the particular situations in which he finds himself or the "sides" that happen to be fighting it out around him. This transhistorical contentlessness comes to look rather like the abstraction Tate (like Pound) elsewhere deplores. That is, art, on this account, is about what Charles Taylor calls "procedural norms" rather than substantive "moral sources"; Taylor sees such norms as characteristic of liberalism, and he opposes them because they imply mere technique without moral content.

It is precisely on such grounds that Tate could defend the 1949 bestowal of the Library of Congress's Bollingen Prize to Ezra Pound for the poems the latter wrote while imprisoned on charges of treason against the very government granting the award. This decision predictably generated a general hue and cry both from poetic populists and from members of Congress on both sides of the aisle. Tate, who as Poetry Consultant to the library both secured the award for the library and suggested the *Pisan Cantos* as the recipient, wrote to Librarian of Congress Luther Evans, "If a democratic society is going to justify itself, it has got to maintain distinctions and standards and allow for decisions which are above politics. Pressure groups and popular hysteria have nothing to do with intellectual standards" (quoted in Ninkovich 2). Politics, pressure, and popularity line up in this quote as hysterical (i.e., "hag-ridden," feminized, and unruly), antidemocratic, and anti-intellectual. A democratic society is here justified and distinguished by liberty—by "allow[ing] for decisions which are above politics" and outside of the realm of state intervention (even in an award granted by an arm of the state). But this freedom for distinctions and standards is also a freedom *from* public authority: this is the old liberalism, which stresses liberty, not the new, egalitarian version. In other words, a democratic society is not justified by popular sovereignty or social responsibility but by negative liberty and abstract norms—that is, for Tate, democracy here means that older, libertarian liberalism.

Tate expresses many of these sentiments in his poems as well as his essays. For instance, in "Causerie" (1927), he uses poetry to complain of the decline of the social conditions necessary for literature:

> And whores become delinquents; delinquents, patients;
> Patients, wards of society. Whores, by that rule,
> Are precious.
> 					Was it for this that Lucius
> Became the ass of Thessaly? For this did Kyd
> Unlock the lion of passion on the stage?
> To litter a race of politic pimps? (*Poems* 82)

In this vision, all manner of boundaries break down: sexuality and generation become associated with politics, which in turn is associated with pandering to illicit desire, which in turn collapses crime into social engineering, and this into medicine, medicine into state protection, and protection by the state into a perversion of value. The problem here seems to be not only that a masculinist subject is threatened by the preciousness of a whore, but also, and by the same token, that the validity of art is undermined by the activities of politic pimps. The passion of the stage has been diverted into the passion of politics, which inflames. The result is not culture but bureaucracy; the emerging welfare state is a threat to art.

For Tate, as well as many of his contemporaries, a private subject and sphere came to seem increasingly beleaguered, fragile, and in need of protection from a public realm that had spilled over its original boundaries. The New Deal and the welfare state seemed just as threatening for Tate as did European totalitarianism; centralized planning of any sort came to seem inimical to individual creativity and to a living culture that could foster poetry. Accordingly, in "The Profession of Letters in the South" (1935), the writer asserts that "the Southern man of letters" sees "the old system" as "better than the system that destroyed it, better, too, than any system with which the modern planners, Marxian or other color, wish to replace the present order" (*Reactionary* 158). "Planning" here becomes the enemy, whether Marxian, New Deal, or Fordist. Just as the early New Critics fuse "sentimental" (efficacious, transitive) poetry with Marxist poetry, so all of these utilitarian socioeconomic "systems" blur in Tate's view. Social liberals and leftists seem just as bad in this vision—all represent a world "out there" that threatens the tranquillity and integrity of a personal social vision. Moreover, for Tate in the 1930s, "the public" includes not only the state and "politics," but the market as well: "There is no reason why the Southern writer should not address a large public, but if he does he will learn sooner or later that—but for happy accidents—the market, with what the market implies, dictates his style" (164). This is by now a fairly familiar plaint on the part of high modernist writers, bourgeoisie assuming a stance against a bourgeois audience. What is noteworthy is that here (as in Pound's prose of the same period) the pressure on the artist to conform to the dictates of the market is seen as contiguous with political correctness. Both the controversialism of the *New Masses* and the middlebrow populist flattening of tastes present in *The Saturday Review* become equally insidious: popular tastes seem predictable, demotic, "planned." What the public wants is equated with what Mr. Ford or Mr. Roosevelt wants, and both are destructive to liberty.

By contrast, Tate praises Emily Dickinson (in an eponymous essay of 1932) because "she never had the slightest interest in the public" (*Reactionary* 23). Dickinson wants not popular acclamation ("flattery and fame"), and "she never needed money." These two qualities go together in Tate's thinking about authorship as in his thinking about culture generally: "correctness" in the public eye (and the lucre that goes with it) is the same in demagogic politics as in debased literary consumption. If the southern writer is tempted to throw his hat into the ring, such a temptation never afflicted Dickinson: "She never felt the temptation to round off a poem for public exhibition. Higginson's kindly offer to make her verse 'correct' was an invitation to throw her work into the public ring—the ring of Lowell and Longfellow." Dickinson, however, is "one of the rarest literary integrities of all time" (23); she offers no "message to society; she speaks wholly to the individual experience" (24).

The disinterested integrity of the individual is equally threatened by popularity, marketability, and social engagement; the alternative seems, from Tate's point of view, Dickinsonian seclusion—or rather, being "rare." Thus Tate seems to take seriously Arnold's advice, in *Culture and Anarchy,* "to stand more aloof from the area of politics at present, and rather to try to promote . . . an inward working" (26). The alternatives are the poems of Mike Gold on the one hand, written to contribute to the collectivist ends of a political party, or Walt Mason on the other, written for the masses in order that a newspaper syndicate may make money.

The artist mustn't take pervasive public affairs or fads into account for fear of ruining art; but the artist can't produce art because of the intrusion and presumption of the public. "Publicness"—considered as public authority, public sphere, and public taste taken together—has created, in Tate's imagination, an atmosphere in which art cannot thrive: "The prevailing economic passion of the age once more tempts, even commands, the Southern writer to go into politics. Our neo-communism is the new form in which the writer from all sections is to be dominated by capitalism, or 'economic society.' It is the new political mania" (*Reactionary* 166). Good writing is destroyed, but what's remarkable is the thing that destroys it: domination by a generalized "mania" that is at once communist and capitalist, economic, political, and social. In other words, everything that is not the private sphere, and a goodly sector of that which formerly was (including the market), begin not only to encroach upon the private, creative subject, but tempt, then command, then dominate the writer. For Tate, writing against this state of affairs in the 1930s, there is no longer a distinction between public authority (the state) and the public sphere (political debate); both seem equally threatening. And this is not surprising, given the pervasiveness of political debate in the literary world of the 1930s, and given that social liberals were themselves busy blurring the lines, extending state authority into the market, even as the power of the market seemed to expand. "And there is no escape from it," Tate concludes, echoing Wallace Stevens's lament over the plight of the artist in the politically polarized 1930s: "There can be no thought of escape" (*Opus Posthumous* 226).

This anxiety reflects a gradual redefinition of privacy within modern societies; here Tate's version of classical liberalism betrays its twentieth-century cast. As Nancy Rosenblum puts it, private life in classical liberal philosophy "means life in civil society, not some presocial state of nature or antisocial condition of isolation and detachment" (61). As time goes on, however, the meanings of public and private shift: "Public becomes an inclusive category that refers not only to officials but also to cooperation in the workplace, combinations based on the cash nexus, neighborliness, voluntary associations, and so on. Private refers to interior life, to purely personal spaces, activities, and intimate relationships" (63). From the late nineteenth century on, "Autonomy is the rationale for privacy but it no longer simply means moral agency. It appears as a self-creative enterprise that embraces personality" (71).[7] Classical liberalism sees both freedom and privacy as "a matter of non-intervention, of not being prevented from doing what you want to do." But in their modern incarnations, freedom and privacy come to be seen as "not being required to do what you do not want to do. . . . It does not concern activity or choice but preservation of personality itself, especially emotional integrity" (72). By the same token, that which is "public" de facto becomes larger and more threatening.

Indeed, "there is no escape from it." The apolitical, antiutilitarian self can be created only by the political user of ends; the poet can practice poetry only by becoming a critic, which Tate does, increasingly, throughout the late 1920s and the 1930s. Tate allows this in the conclusion to his essay "Remarks on the Southern Religion," his contribution to *I'll Take My Stand,* saying: "The Southerner is faced with the paradox: He must use an instrument, which is political, and so unrealistic and pretentious that he cannot believe in it, to re-establish a private, self-contained, and essentially spiritual life." "The Southerner" is hemmed in by communism/capitalism, but also by his own hermeneutic circle, and "[s]ince he cannot bore from within, he has left the sole alternative of boring from without" (Twelve Southerners 175).

In these passages, Tate seems painfully aware of the problem that increasingly confronted high modernists. On the one hand, he condemns those poets who speak "a message to society"; on the other, Tate's poetry is, as we have already seen, rife with such messages. For example, in "To the Lacedemonians" (1932/1936), "An old soldier" asks:

> where have they, the citizens, all
> Come from? They were not born in my father's
> House, nor in their fathers': on a street corner
> By motion sired, not born; by rest dismayed. (*Poems* 15)

In these lines and in the body of this long poem, Tate presents an eloquent indictment of disenchanted modernity and a poignant elegy for his own version of an older agrarian order. The subject of paternity and of the domicile (the paterfamilias et fil) is replaced by the restless, modern public denizen of the street corners (the potential member of a "hysterical" mob). Or, as in the World War II "Our Young Pro-Consuls of the Air," Tate directly attacks Archibald MacLeish and Van Wyck Brooks for their abandonment of the apolitical stance and newfound belief in poetry as public speech:

> Brave Brooks and lithe MacLeish
> Had sworn to thresh
> Our flagging spirit
> With literature made Prime!
> . . . .
> Spirits grown Eliotic,
> Now patriotic
> Are: we follow
> *The Irresponsibles!* (98–99)

But while these poets chose to publish or broadcast the sort of public poetry that emphasized the newer liberal value of responsibility over the older form of individualism, Tate chose to go public by publishing a satire of that very poetry.

Not surprisingly, then, the idea of publishing poetry about the threat to poetry from the public appeared to be an embarrassment to some readers of the day. Before MacLeish's "conversion," a letter to the editor of the *New Republic* (one which appears alongside Tate's "Aeneas at New York") asks of "Invocation to the Social Muse": "Why, if Mr. MacLeish prefers the comfortably detached and comparatively safe position of the 'estranged' poet, does he expose himself to the suspicion of being in style along with the rest of us?—'being in style' meaning, of course, being a partisan in politics. . . . Disliking political poetry, Mr. MacLeish wrote a political poem against it" (Platt). With minor variations, this question could profitably be asked in the later twentieth century of the Two Blooms, or any of the other politically correct cultural conservatives who attack other scholars on the charge of political correctness—that is, correct according to a politics contrary to their own. The 1930s Agrarian/New Critics and high modernists, by contrast, owned up to their passionate engagement with the politics of their day, an engagement whose paradoxes they were fully aware of and (reluctantly) compelled to accept.

It is not unusual that a poet would write some pieces in what is, after all, the well-established subgenre of political poetry contra political poetry (e.g., Stevens's "Owl's Clover"). The remarkable feature is the *prevalence* of social, cultural, economic, and political commentary in the poems of a poet ostensibly wary of political poetry. Even Tate's more "private" poems frequently hinge on an assessment of cultural decline within monopoly capitalism and social liberalism, and he includes his most blatantly political works in his collected poems in 1948.

In fact, Tate wants to have his Blake and Eton too—to have both artistic liberty and union to a larger culture, mythos, and history. This is, it seems to me, a tension that ran throughout the poetics of the U.S. high modernists for reasons that are not unique to, but are especially acute in, the United States. On the one hand, Tate can long for a golden age in which "a poem was a piece of free and disinterested enjoyment" ("T. S. Eliot" [1931] 105), in which Dr. Johnson "hates Milton for a regicide" but can produce a judgment of *Paradise Lost* that "is the most disinterested in English criticism" (106). On the other hand, he wistfully asserts that "[u]nder feudalism the artist was a member of an organic society" (*Reactionary* 147). Indeed, "The 'message' of modern art at present" for Tate "is that social man is living, without religion, morality, or art, without the high form that reduces all three to an organic whole, in a mere system of money references through which neither artist nor the plutocrat can perform as an entire person" (160). Art here merges with normative values (religion and morality)—a tendency not uncommon in high modernism, and one that is hardly libertarian.

This tension between desire for individual liberty and longing for subsumption in a communal union derives from a recurrent fear within classical liberalism that the freedom of the individual from the sovereign invites disunity. Individual liberty, as Tocqueville and other classical liberals perceived it, opened the possibility of anarchy, mob rule, or tyranny of the majority. Thus the framers of U.S. liberal democracy attempt to undergird the abstract and formalist nature of the social contract with a presupposed preexisting social and cultural unity, as in the Declaration of Independence's appeal to the English people based on "ties of common kindred," or Alexander Hamilton's appeal for a federal system embracing "one united people" with "the same ancestors, speaking the same language, professing the same religion" (7). Tate harks back to this vision of political liberty as secured by the unity of society via an organic notion of the People and their (its) culture.[8]

For Tate, however, the problem *is* America. In "American Poetry since 1920," he comments that "the stylistic excellence of contemporary American poetry is equalled only by the variety in the chaos that it holds up to the view. In this chaos there are several different Americas, none of which contains all the values of the whole and which, with respect to the whole, represents disorder" (82). Here, stylistic excellence, the ideal of neutral technique, unleashes a chaos of variety or eclecticism. Either "the whole" or "disorder" exist as alternatives for poetry in this scenario: difference, the multiplication of Americas, is the problem for Tate as it was for Jay and Hamilton, and for precisely the same reasons. While the

Federalists solved the problem by positing an organically unified America ratified by a single social contract, Tate solves the problem by an antifederalist "return to the provinces" that "will put the all-destroying abstraction, America, safely to rest" (88). Within these "small, self-contained centres of life," unity and stability can be reconstituted out of an America that has come to represent a disorder of values, factions, and interests.[9]

Moreover, classical liberalism solves the unity/plurality problem by a return to civility. Freed of obedience in all things to the sovereign, as J. G. A. Pocock records, members of civil society not only engaged in economic activity, they also began to develop "manners," a culture for free agents: "These new freedoms became known by a variety of names, among which 'manners,' 'politeness' and 'sociability' are perhaps the most prominent. Each denotes the individual's capacity to comport himself —now and then herself—in a society where increasing circulation and exchange were rapidly multiplying the occasions which individuals had for encountering and interacting with one another" (90). In other words, manners and the notion of polite society offer means of suturing and neutralizing an increasingly diverse, libertarian, market-driven society through culture.

For Tate, such manners are very important and are what distinguish his version of traditional society—and "manners include poetry, which also pertains to the conduct of men in society" (*Collected Essays* 544). Hence protecting poetry from the public means not only shielding the individual poet or reader from the public but also rendering the public realm a less threatening place. This project involves inculcating social order as Tate understands it; he thus associates observing social formalities with formalism in poetry. Tate would write later that "[f]ormal versification is the primary structure of poetic order, the assurance to the reader and to the poet himself that the poet is in control of the disorder both outside him and within his own mind" (quoted in Breslin 28). Wolin claims that, in classical liberalism, the basic concept that was pitted against the political was "society" (290). Society came to be seen "simultaneously as an entity distinct from political arrangements and as the shorthand symbol of all worthwhile human endeavor" (291). "Social," in this sense, is clearly quite different than the common meaning in twentieth-century thought (as in "sociology"). Instead, the individual has freedom, but freedom to be a member of society. Accordingly, the seemingly antisocial (and modern) Dickinson emerges as both an independent artistic "integrity" and as a carrier of social tradition: she "demands of the reader a point of view—not an opinion of the New Deal or the League of Nations"—that is, *not* participation in the public sphere —"but an ingrained philosophy that is fundamental, a kind of settled attitude that is almost extinct in this eclectic age" (3). Thus a "settled," "fundamental," "ingrained" attitude of the New England mind puts Dickinson beyond the reach of (even out of relation to) "planners." The individual expresses his or her individuality in relation to a (mannered) social order: the (unfortunate) separation of the two in the modern world, and the attempt to bridge that separation, here becomes a source of great art.

So for Tate, freedom is to be used to convert "the public" into "society," the great (free) poet is a natural aristocrat of that society, and real politics is a politics of the same—that is, no politics at all. Hence, for Tate, freedom and conformity, the public and society, begin to merge. For him, "the ideal task of the critical quarterly is not to give the public what it wants, or what it thinks it wants, but what—through the medium of its most intelligent members—it ought to have." Moreover, "[a]t a time when action has become singularly devoid of intelligence, there could not be a 'cause' more disinterested" ("The Function of the Critical Quarterly" [1936], *Collected Essays* 72). This cause that isn't a cause, this disinterested coercing of the public into accepting the editor's own "sense of the moral and intellectual order upon which society ought to rest" (71) paradoxically encourages the reader "in self-knowledge" (66).

In this topos, the free subject freely submits to the good of the whole, submits to tutelage in freedom by being guided by the most intelligent representatives (individuals of integrity) who are themselves guided by a disinterested understanding. This complex of ideas is also present in Kant's Third Critique, in the *Federalist Papers*, in Arnold's "Function of Criticism at the Present Time," and in Mill's *On Liberty* (not to mention postwar American foreign policy). For Mill, individualism has been prevented from descending into chaos or mediocrity in government or culture only when "the sovereign Many have let themselves be guided (which in their best times they always have done) by the counsels and influence of a more highly gifted and instructed One or Few" (63). Liberty exists to allow "exceptional individuals" to express their individuality and to keep everyone else from misusing theirs. Thus in Tate's antitotalitarian phase in the 1950s, he would write, "Will it not be borne in upon us in the next few years that Hitler and Stalin *are* the Common Man, and that one of the tasks of democracy is to allow as many men as possible to make themselves uncommon?" (quoted in Jancovich 181 n. 22). Here, once again, the point of equality in liberalism is to remove restrictions on the *natural* development of hierarchy, over against a Tocquevillean egalitarianism within despotism. Or, as Herbert Marcuse puts it, "Liberalism proceeds from the essential inequality of men, which is considered the presupposition of the harmony of the whole" (271).[10]

In this, the Agrarian poet and the utilitarian prophet of early-nineteenth-century liberalism agree. Substantive equality, the sort sought by U.S. liberals of the 1910s to 1930s, would mean either chaos or despotism for classically minded liberals. Thus the atomistic public must be converted into The (organically unified) People for Tate. Poetry provides one "medium" for doing this, and the artist, as teacher-hierophant, the figure to do it. Hence Tate, despite his love of autonomy, becomes an example of what Wolin, anticipating Foucault, calls "the liberal addiction towards social conformity" in which social codes are internalized by the pressure of "non-legal, privately enforced norms" (343), which "could be understood as a species of control distinct from political power or legal authority" (344–45).[11]

One can see this dynamic at work quite clearly in the later Tate poem "The Swimmers" (1953). Here the sheriff in "Montgomery County, Kentucky, July 1911," having been unable to prevent the lynching of a black man, deposits his corpse on the courthouse square, as if to indict the entire town. The speaker, then a boy in the town, comments at the end of the poem:

> My breath crackled the dead air like a shotgun
>   As, sheriff and the stranger disappearing,
>   The faceless head lay still. I could not run
>
> Or walk, but stood. Alone in the public clearing
>   This private thing was owned by all the town,
>   Though never claimed by us within my hearing. (Pratt 111)

It is not whim that the poem is in the terza rima of Dante (rather than, say, the abortive Augustan couplets of the "Eclogue of the Liberal and the Poet"): the courthouse, site of rational legal norms, becomes, instead, the end point in a tale of infernal medieval bloodletting. Here society imposes its own discipline apart from public authority, and its members silently "own" or internalize that practice: it is a "private thing," not the res publica. The figure in public is at once lifeless, alone, and faceless, or depersonalized. The public "clearing" is not free and clear of the private and what has happened in the woods; the abstract public subject is, as physical body, subject to the discipline of the raced "private" or social norms, but the reverse is not necessarily the case. At the same time, individuation and individual responsibility, rather than being confirmed in the separation of spheres, vanish altogether: though the town owns "it," the individual members of the town do not. Political freedom is given with one hand by the law only to be removed by the invisible hand of society—a dynamic which, as the poem graphically yet implicitly reminds the reader, was only too well known by southern African Americans in the early twentieth century. The social contract, Tate reminds us, is here not only fraternal but racial as well.

Given this tension between politics and society, it is understandable that Thomas Jefferson emerges for Tate in a dual aspect. On the one hand, Jefferson discusses "the possibility of morals" and "calls his judgment 'taste'—reliance on custom, breeding, ingrained moral decision" (Twelve Southerners 170). Here, aesthetics, custom, and manners form a harmonious "ingrained" whole. Yet, on the other hand, Jefferson is also the representative of "the scientific mind" that believes that "[t]he ends of man are sufficiently contained in his political destiny" and achieved "by the operation of mechanical laws" (173). The two halves, the private man of letters and slave owner on the one hand and the rationalist public figure, that proponent of rights and liberty, on the other, are too implicated in one another to provide for a comfortable separation of roles for Tate and for antimodern modernism. And this was a central contradiction for Tate's (and Pound's) hero Jefferson, who argued (at first) for abolition on political principle yet concluded that the Negro could never be part of the new American Republic because of too-deep cultural and, literally, organic differences.

This contradiction in Jefferson points to the central problem for Tate's vision of antebellum southern American "aristocracy": Tate must *reason* himself back to a pre-Enlightenment set of values. Those values are invented, but they must be spontaneous—organic—to count at all. And if an organic society must be recreated, in what sense can it be said to be organic? Ultimately, in fact, there is no way out of this tension between liberty and union, between being Enlightenment subjects "fighting for our liberty . . . when our rights were threatened" and at the same time a feudal "band of brothers, native to the soil." Accordingly, Tate finds himself describing tradition as "a body of ideas that can bear upon the course of the spirit and yet remain fixed as a rational instrument" (*Reactionary* 4) and "the intelligence trying to think into the moving world a rational order of value" (*Collected Essays* 63). Rationalism becomes the instrument for the imagined reestablishment of traditional values in these statements, but it is instrumental rationalism that also allows for the atomism and anomie in modern liberal-democratic societies that makes Tate long for traditional values in the first place.

So Pound, too, would claim that "[t]he thing is mechanical in action.

In proportion as [the author's] work is exact . . . so is it durable and so is it 'useful' " ("How to Read" [1929], *Literary Essays* 22). Here literary art, as technique, *resists* politics: it is not right or wrong but exact, durable, and (if you must) useful—a tool. Pound writes, in 1927, "The artist is concerned with producing something that will be enjoyable even after a successful revolution. So far as we know even the most violent bolchevik has never abolished electric light globes merely because they were invented under another regime, and by a man intent rather on his own job than on particular propaganda" (379). The author in this vision is a professional, an inventor, not a politician or a prophet transforming civilization.

But the project of the *Cantos* is to use poetry as neutral technique to write a poem that both embodies and composes coherent, central cultural values—"vital statistics and fragments of history which ought to be the common possession of every man in the street" (*Guide to Kulchur* 55), a common possession that at once proves and enacts, is and ought to be, a common civilization. If "a civilization was founded on Homer," then it is the loss of that civilization that spurs much of Pound's work. Thus the *Cantos,* as well as books like *Guide to Kulchur* and *ABC of Reading,* resemble early versions of E. D. Hirsch's list of "What Every Literate American Knows."[12] Thus Pound too becomes increasingly caught up in public debate because he has to defend a definite normative vision that he wishes society to embody.

For both Tate and Pound, this means not pandering to public tastes and anxieties but demanding that the heterogeneous public come round to a consensus propounded by the intelligent few. The project of Tate, Pound, and, to a certain extent, Eliot can be seen as an attempt to recast society by returning it to that common center of energy, that *foyer virtuel,* from which both politics and poetry once sprang—namely, community. Hence Tate, in "Remarks on the Southern Religion," holds "that my private fable was once more public and general, and that our public have fallen away from it on to evil days" (Twelve Southerners 156).

And they won't come back. By Tate's own admission as by Pound's, it doesn't cohere: the fact that the "fable" is private and must be reconstructed in opposition to public taste marks it as a quixotic quest. The poet, *il miglio fabbro,* sees the constructed, even rationalist, nature of his project: the materials of the *Cantos* ought to be what every American knows, but they aren't, and aren't likely to be. Hirsch, purveyor of bestsellers and board games to the public, does not admit this normative motivation—he claims to be merely describing what a "Literate American" already knows (and don't *you* want to be a literate American)? However, in the work of the high modernists, "the long journey from private judgment to social conformity appears as the desperate effort of liberals to fashion a substitute for the sense of community that had been lost" (Wolin 350)—although a quite different and older notion of community than their progressive liberal contemporaries had in mind. The effort to reconstitute the free yet fallen public as an organic community through literature constitutes these writers' defining project, one that the best of them realized to be "paradoxical," if not impossible. Nonetheless, this bind was bequeathed to and influenced the social form of poetry, particularly in the postwar U.S. academy—in no small part via the promotional and political activities of Allen Tate.

This may be, but what of other strains in the modernist canon—for instance, that practiced by Wallace Stevens? Tate and Stevens expressed admiration for one another's work in an extensive correspondence during the 1940s. Tate invited Stevens to deliver the lecture that became "The Noble Rider and the Sound of Words," of which the former wrote, "[T]here is no other single, brief statement about poetry by a contemporary with which I feel so much in agreement."[13] Indeed, Tate would be instrumental in publishing the essays contained in *The Necessary Angel.* Stevens for his part said of Allen Tate's appointment as poetry consultant to the Library of Congress that "a better choice could not possibly have been made."[14] And it is significant that former Fugitive poet John Crowe Ransom, in "Poets without Laurels," would choose Wallace Stevens and Allen Tate as his two examples of modern poets who "aim at poetic autonomy; that is, speaking roughly, at purity" (508).

Readers know Stevens for (as Ransom says) his "calculated complexity" (perhaps above all else), and his poetry had a reputation in the 1920s and 1930s, as in the 1980s and 1990s, for being hermetic, aestheticist, apolitical. Certainly, the reflexivity and abstraction of many of Stevens's poems do not lead easily and obviously into public debate or any exposition of values—nor did the poet express a desire that the poems should do so. Yet the separation of poetry from a putative public sphere, and the very existence and role of the public, proved far more ambiguous for Stevens as both poet and critic than Ransom's comments might suggest.

CHAPTER THREE

The Modernist as Liberal:

Wallace Stevens and the Poetics of Private Insurance

In December of 1936 Wallace Stevens delivered his first lecture.[1] The talk, entitled "The Irrational Element in Poetry," introduced the poet's reading of the first section of his long poem "Owl's Clover," "The Old Woman and the Statue," which, Stevens explained, took as its subject "the effect of the depression on the interest in art" (*Opus* 225).[2] Here Stevens explicitly examines the relation between current events and the art of poetry: "The pressure of the contemporaneous from the time of the beginning of the World War to the present time has been constant and extreme. No one can have lived apart in a happy oblivion. . . . We are preoccupied with events, even when we do not observe them closely. We have a sense of upheaval. We feel threatened. We look from an uncertain present toward a more uncertain future. One feels the desire to collect oneself against all this in poetry as well as in politics" (229). In this passage, as in many poems and letters from the 1930s, Stevens seems compelled to consider poetry in light of contemporary politics. The Stevens of this period appears not as a retiring aesthete writing hermetic verses, but as one of many writers caught up in the social and aesthetic controversies of the day. At the height of these controversies, the poet, who loathed reading in public, chose to read publicly his most "public" poems, prefaced by a rationalization of his choice of a "social" subject.[3]

Stevens critics have occupied themselves with the question of the poet's relation to politics because the question also preoccupied Stevens. Nonetheless, critics in the 1980s portrayed Stevens as an *isolato* who tried to "evade" historical reality (Perloff 1985), a solipsist who squelched or "appropriated" any voice except his own (Bruns 1985), or a dissatisfied, alienated consumer (Lentricchia 1988). This Stevens tries to block out or keep a lid on what's going on around him, but alienation, historical reality, or the Other comes back (unconsciously) to haunt him. However, this isolated Stevens does not come across as the same man who wrote that, between the wars, "No one can have lived apart in a happy oblivion."

Other studies attempted to deal in greater detail with the relationship between Stevens's poetry and the larger culture of which it is a part. Some of these critics seem to want to save Stevens for politics.[4] For instance, Harvey Teres, who depicts a Stevens who is a sort of social democrat of the mind, says that the poet attempts to make a place within politics for "the unencumbered imagination" and "autonomous poetry" (154). James Longenbach reads the poet's attempts to avoid referentiality, historical specificity, or political positions as a conscious stance for imaginative freedom; he goes so far as to say of the offhanded and noncommittal political comments in the poet's correspondence that "the creed is so elusive that it is not easily appropriated by the forces of tyranny" (33). Still later, Stevens even emerges as a Popular Front author (Filreis 1994) or a New Dealer (Szalay 1998). But why should inconclusiveness per se represent either resistance to dogma or acceptance of statism rather than (as *New Masses* critic Stanley Burnshaw claimed Stevens recognized) confusion?[5]

That literary critics and historians can find so many different Stevenses in his poems and pronouncements is, it seems to me, a function of the abstractness of Stevens's work. The lack of specificity and referentiality in Stevens's poems invite a search for historical correspondences or analogies while preventing any definitive statement about the specific historical milieu in which they are written. And that, I would argue, is precisely the point. Stevens was neither an *engagé*, nor a civic-minded champion of freedom, nor an aesthete who believed one could ignore politics in the 1930s. The unease Stevens expresses in "The Irrational Element in Poetry" arises not so much from a specific form of political thinking or organization but from a much more abstract and indefinite sense of "events," "the pressure of the contemporaneous," "a sense of upheaval," of threat, of uncertainty. It is precisely the fear of and inevitability of uncertainty that disables any consistent political stand on Stevens's part. "One" wishes merely to "collect oneself against all this," whether in poetry or in politics.

Stevens's response to developments in the 1930s gives us insight into his poetics if we view it not as the expression of a deeply held political conviction, but in light of the poet's notions of the nature and function of poetry and of the imagination. The place of poetry, for Stevens, has less to do with the right to free speech than with the much older rights to privacy and to property and with the separation of spheres that undergirds those rights. The influence of liberal habits of thought upon the poet may or may not have taken conscious shape. Nonetheless, an examination of Stevens's work in these terms can reveal much about modernist views of the relation of literature to political discourse and about the liberal subject in the twentieth century. As we shall see, this tension between poet and the public (in all senses of the word) both gives rise to and defines modernist constructions of poetry as a genre.

In the literary world of the United States of the 1930s, as more and more writers and intellectuals became radicalized, radical writers competed with conservatives and social liberals for hegemony of a truncated literary public sphere. This competition grew in intensity from the late 1920s until its decline in the 1940s and virtual cessation in the 1950s—a decade which also marked the widespread academic acceptance of New Criticism and of the literary category "modernism." In the 1930s, as Allen Tate and Archibald MacLeish waged war on proletarian aesthetics in the pages of the *New Republic* and, in the process, introduced the tenets of New Critical formalism to a general audience, Stevens also began to "collect himself" against the "pressure" of "events" in his published contributions to the political-aesthetic debates.

The debate between these opposed blocs emerged, of course, within the context of a much broader social and political conflict. If Wallace Stevens, home-office vice president at Hartford Accident and Indemnity, found himself rather less vulnerable to the Depression than most people, he nonetheless felt insecure. In addition to feeling threatened by news of war in Spain, he may have had a much more immediate cause for concern. In 1935, the debate over Social Security became ubiquitous in the popular press. As James Longenbach points out, this debate possessed a personal relevance for Wallace Stevens, because, "[a]s Stevens immediately recognized, the Social Security system was modeled on the principles of private insurance. . . . And to many members of the insurance community, the Social Security Act appeared to be the government's first step toward nationalizing the insurance business: they feared for the future of their livelihood" (193). And, as Longenbach cogently argues, the security of that livelihood had afforded Stevens the peace of mind necessary to resume his writing career after a decade's hiatus. The pressure of events was, in fact, hitting closer to home.

Many of Stevens's colleagues saw in Social Security the leading edge of a social-welfare—or even totalitarian—system's replacing the older liberal system of markets. In 1937 Stevens responded to these developments by publishing an article entitled "Insurance and Social Change" in his company's magazine, the *Hartford Agent*.[6] There the author distinguishes Social Security, which had begun, two years earlier, in order to protect people against economic catastrophe, from a hypothetical insurance that would completely cover all conceivable risks: "To be certain of a regular income, as in the case of social security, is not the same thing as to be able to repair any damage, or to meet any emergency. Obviously, in a world in which insurance had become perfect, the case of social security would be a minor case. In short, universal insurance or insurance for all is not the same thing as ubiquitous insurance or insurance for everything" (233–34). Social Security, in other words, will not edge out private insurance altogether. However, the vision of perfect insurance holds a certain fascination for Stevens; the poet goes on to construct a fantasy world in which everyone is guaranteed an income and, by dropping "a personal or peculiar penny" in a box at the corner, one insures oneself, one's family, and one's property against everything. "The circle just stated: income, insurance, the thing that happens and income again," Stevens continues, "would widen and soon become income, insurance, the thing that fails to happen and income again. In other words, not only would all our losses be made good, but all our wishes would come true" (234). That is, while actual insurance responds to risk, perfect insurance would eliminate risk.

While this scenario sounds utopian—no insurance will make all our wishes come true—nonetheless, Stevens implies, some people take the fiction for fact: "If Mr. Wells has preferred the machine to insurance as his field, he has only left insurance to others. How far have others gone?" the author asks. He then launches into a description of nationalized insurance in Italy, Germany, Britain, and the Soviet Union.[7] Stevens concludes by saying that, "[e]ven if the point is considered from the view of the nationalization of the business, it is not to be supposed that any government can maintain an entire population indefinitely at a loss" (236). Nonetheless, he points out that Italy has issued national life insurance since 1912, and he does not preclude the possibility that a government could run an insurance organization at a surplus, or at least solvently. And while the European nations he mentions may have failed to perfect insurance, the poet seems to imagine that such systems take as their *telos* a utopian insurance or a utopia underwritten by insurance. Indeed, Stevens paints this fantasy of perfect insurance in particularly vivid strokes. Although perfect insurance cannot exist because risk cannot be eliminated, such insurance works quite well on an imaginative plane. As the poet says, "[W]e may well be entering an insurance era" (234).[8]

This possibility would be very bad news for Stevens the poet-theorist as well as for Stevens the insurer. In a perfect world nothing happens, including poetry. "If each of us could put his hand on money whenever money was necessary: to repair any damage, to meet any emergency, we should all be willing to stop so far as money goes," the executive declares (233). Moreover, "[t]he objective of all of us is to live in a world in which nothing unpleasant can happen. Our prime instinct is to go on indefinitely like the wax flowers on the mantelpiece. Insurance is the most easily understood geometry for calculating how to bring the thing about" (234). These wax flowers recall lines from "Owl's Clover," written the previous year, in which the speaker entreats "celestial paramours" to:

> Bring down from nowhere nothing's wax-like blooms,
> Calling them what you will but loosely-named
> In a mortal lullaby, like porcelain. (79)

The wax flowers here symbolize a utopia, a nowhere, a nothing that serves as a cipher for any name one gives it. While the wax blooms may be malleable, they are also as inert as those on the mantelpiece. Their transformation by people does not erase this suggestion: the "mortal lullaby" evokes a painless descent into death, a suggestion reinforced by the likeness to porcelain, which in Stevens's poems tends to become associated with cold, inert, inhuman perfection.

For Stevens, "utopian" schemes like nationalized insurance would mean not only an ignorance of things as they are, but also, paradoxically, an attempt to escape the ceaseless imaginative striving occasioned by the pressure of those things. The argument that social insurance would cause people to shirk or cease striving had long since become common. Berkeley professor Albert H. Mowbray put it thus in 1930: "The most common objection in the United States to proposals for the introduction of social-insurance systems is that they are paternalistic, contrary to the spirit of our people, and that paternalism stifles individual initiative, the cause of our growth and progress" (Tuan 340).

For Stevens, likewise, national insurance would stifle the will to strive and so stifle the spirit. At one point, the poet remarks, rather cryptically: "In a late number of the Accident Company's Confidential Bulletin, it was said that . . . '[c]emeteries have been found by a number of offices to be a very definite market for the Hartford's All Risk Securities Policy.' This observation would apply to the Hartford's policies generally under Communism, and, to some extent, under Fascism" (236). At first this quote from the house organ looks merely like an in-house joke, but in fact cemeteries are vulnerable to accidental damage by fire, flood, tornado, or earthquake. Stevens's point, however, is that All Risk policies do not cover loss due to deterioration or depreciation; and cemeteries, or at any rate their residents, are beyond the need for that kind of coverage. Deterioration represents a certainty, not a risk; it cannot be insured against, but one can rest assured of it in the perfect security of the grave. Yet under totalitarian systems of insurance, insurance is cradle-to-grave and beyond—a "mortal lullaby" indeed—and even the dead are "covered."

While this phenomenal expansion of the Hartford's business in "the vast monopoly of communism" (236) might be, from one point of view, attractive to the executive, it appears, from another, horrifying. Under communism, everything, including insurance, is static, and therefore dead, as in the opening lines of "Mr. Burnshaw and the Statue," the second section of "Owl's Clover," where

> The thing is dead . . . Everything is dead
> Except the future. Always everything
> That is is dead except what ought to be. (78)

Communism "and, to some extent," Fascism kill the living, vibrant present to pave the way for a future that is so perfect as to be static, and so static as to be dead, a future in which the dead are themselves insured by the living. There exists, in fact, nothing but insurance in this fictional world. In Stevens's imagination, national insurance should in theory eventually eliminate the very need for that imagination and so eliminate the conditions necessary for the imagination's functioning.

Throughout "Owl's Clover," utopian impulses lead to stasis. In "Mr. Burnshaw and the Statue," the speaker addresses a group of "Mesdames," saying:

> one might believe that Shelley lies
> Less in the stars than in their earthly wake,
> Since the radiant disclosures that you make
> Are of an eternal vista, manqué and gold
> And brown, an Italy of the mind, a place
> Of fear before the disorder of the strange,
> A time in which the poets' politics
> Will rule in a poets' world. Yet that will be
> A world impossible for poets, who
> Complain and prophesy, in their complaints,
> And are never of the world in which they live. (80)

The "radiant disclosures," the Shelleyan prophecies of heaven-on-earth, are both hyperborean and tawdry. While the real Mr. Burnshaw was a communist sympathizer, the Italy of the mind, in 1936, "to some extent" evoked other political orders as well. This world, "an eternal vista, manqué and gold," resonates with Stevens's picture of a static world of perfect insurance. But while a political vision might offer a buffer against fear of change, the vision is still "a place of fear" and denial, one that rules over true poets. Poets cannot live in utopia because they complain and prophesy; in utopia nothing remains to complain about and, since history has ended, there is nothing to prophesy. Moreover, since poets "are never of the world in which they live," if that world demands a direct engagement with itself on its own terms, then poets would become impossible indeed. In other words, in Stevens's perception, the political theory, not the politicized aesthetic, threatens true art. Radical art comes off as second-rate because its theory seeks to lay the ground of art's obsolescence: if poets become the acknowledged legislators of a "poets' world," then poetry ceases to be Poetry. Later in "Owl's Clover," ugly Socialist art takes the form of

> "Concerto for Airplane and Pianoforte,"
> The newest Soviet réclame. Profound
> Abortion, fit for the enchanting of basilisks. (93)

The wax flowers and the abortive Soviet réclame both serve as examples of dead art, art devoid of the spirit of the imagination.

Stevens goes on, in "Mr. Burnshaw and the Statue," to offer an alternative vision of life lived in uncertainty:

> But change composes, too, and chaos comes
> To momentary calm, spectacular flocks
> Of crimson and hoods of Venezuelan green
> And the sound of z in the grass all day, though these
> Are chaos and of archaic change. (82)

The poem ends by toppling the lifeless statue of public art and replacing it with a Keatsean urn in a time

> when, at last, you are yourselves,
> . . . .
> No longer of air but of the breathing earth,
> Impassioned seducers and seduced. (83)

The poem, then, subsumes the political vision by including and dismissing it at the same time; the poem goes on to offer what Stevens elsewhere calls "the poetic view of life" (199), in which change is as ancient and beautiful as crimson birds in Venezuelan forests, in which life is whirling in a dance, but where some, at least, can sit on the porch "all day" and listen to crickets making "the sound of z in the grass." In this world "change," not ideology, composes; yet this change proceeds chaotically, not predictably, and it leads only to "momentary calm." Stevens would write in a commentary on the poem that "the future of the mass is not an end of the future, but that change is incessant. . . . Life is chaos, notwithstanding its times of serenity"; moreover, "progression from one thing to another is archaic, as archaic as being born and dying" (*Letters* 367). Anything organic and alive must change in this way.

If nationalized insurance and everything it represents to Stevens is a dead effigy, then private insurance grows organically because it depends upon individual imagination. As Stevens writes in the essay "Surety and Fidelity Claims" (1938), "a business alive and expanding in other respects must be alive and expanding equally in respect to claims. The truth is that the most conspicuous element from the point of view of human interest in the handling of claims is the claim man himself" (239). By the same token, Stevens made the connection between the imagination required to untangle a complex claim on a private insurance policy and that required for the composition of his poetry: "Poetry and surety claims aren't as unlikely a combination as they may seem," he remarked in an interview. "There is nothing perfunctory about them, for each case is different" (Nichols 3). It is the claims man, another type of "the poet, meaning by the poet any man of imagination" (*Opus* 233), who keeps the business a living rather than a dead thing, who brings order out of indeterminacy.[9]

The agent, the representative of the private insurer who actually "writes" insurance, is an equally important figure for Stevens. Hence it is notable that "in Italy postal officials are among those that sell life insurance" (235). Likewise, the Soviet system "would put insurance agents on a footing with letter carriers or government employees generally," so that "under both Fascist and Communist systems, the finely-tailored agent, wearing a boutonniere, gives way to the letter carrier" (236). Indeed, the postal savings program had already usurped one function of American private enterprise. If individual agency and judgment, represented by agents and claims men, give way to a manqué ideal of perfect insurance, under which even the dead are insured, then the noble figure of imagination and beauty, the man with the blue guitar and the pink carnation, must give way to the bureaucrat. If the "violence from without" is insured against and even death, "the mother of beauty," made prosaic, then the role of the insurance man vanishes, and the "man of letters" takes the debased form of a Bartleby, the employee of the dead-letter office, the figure who can refuse but who cannot create.[10]

Stevens's reaction to both social insurance and public poetry may have as much to do with the culture of his youth as with the culture of the 1930s. Many advocates of social insurance had been sounding a resoundingly utopian chord since the turn of the century, a chord consistent with the celebration of progress evident in both oratory and poetry. For instance, Rufus Potts, the Progressivist director of insurance for the state of Illinois, was moved in 1916 to exclaim:

When I consider all the possibilities potential in a general system of insurance, which will make secure and permanent the welfare of all, ignorant and educated, rich and poor alike, the vision of a new and happier world rises before me, a world flooded with the sunshine of universal happiness, where the people of all the nations of the earth live in undisturbed contentment, and where peace reigns secure because the time has come foreseen by the great poet:

"When the war-drum throbb'd no longer,
   and the battle-flags were furl'd,
In the Parliament of man, the Federation of the world . . .
And the kindly earth shall slumber,
   lapt in universal law." (Tuan 335–36)

Not only will universal peace prevail, Potts adds, almost as an afterthought, "but there will also exist security of economic welfare and freedom from poverty and misery by reason of universal insurance" (336). This world takes the form of a utilitarian version of that envisioned by the imperial and progressivist poet of "Locksley Hall," not that of the wiser, circumscribed post–World War I modernist. Potts's vision, like Stevens's, makes Social Security (or indeed, national health insurance) seem "a minor case," and its advocates pikers. Now, Stevens implies, we see this utopianism reborn and transformed, with disturbing results, in the 1930s. If we were able to follow the path of universal insurance, we would wind up in a world where Tennyson and Shelley are the great poets.[11]

Stevens presents the fantasy of "perfect insurance" to diminish the perceived threat to the insurance industry from state-sponsored insurance schemes. But it is a fantasy tinged with anxiety that, as the New Deal attempted to make life more secure for more people, and as the trend toward nationalization increased abroad, the importance of insurance executives and of modernist poets (and not that of politicians) might diminish. If state insurance becomes available to people who cannot afford private insurance, if it covers ever more risks and is as easy to obtain as a book of stamps, then, while it may not create a utopia, it will reduce the pressure of reality, both physical and economic. As the early social insurance advocate I. M. Rubinow admitted, the purpose of all insurance is "an evident gain in the freedom from anxiety concerning the possibility of the larger loss" than that incurred from the payment of premiums (Tuan 367). And national insurance, by making coverage more certain and more widespread, decreases anxiety still further. Instead of one individual's turning to other, qualified individuals for protection, under social insurance a policy (in both senses) and a polity insure everyone systematically. The "pressure of the contemporaneous" becomes less daunting and hence, to some extent, "the disorder of the strange" meliorates without the need for the poet's prophecies or for the snappy agent's actuarial tables.

"Owl's Clover" suggests that any separation between politics and poetry is never complete or secure. Rather, for Stevens, they compete with one another as imaginative discourses; as alternative mediations of reality, they vie for people's attention and allegiance. Accordingly, the debate *about* poetics proves decisive for Stevens. The poet's theory establishes the rationale for his poetry. Stevens, like Bryant and Emerson before him, enabled this process by abstracting an essence, "Poetry," that expresses itself in specific works of writing. That is, the poems foreground the theory they embody, and the poetic theory tells us how to use the poems: "The theory of poetry is the life of poetry" (202), and "[p]oetry is the subject of the poem" (*Collected Poems* 176).

In Stevens, as in other modernist poets, the textual-formalist separation of the categories "Poetry" and "Politics," a separation that stemmed from a reaction against the "efficacious" or hortatory verse of the Edwardian period, became, in the 1930s, a standard reaction against a leftist poetics as well. And leftist poetry is not "Poetry"—it is "Politics." In a letter, Stevens writes, "You will remember that Mr. Burnshaw applied the point of view of the practical Communist to IDEAS OF ORDER; in MR. BURNSHAW AND THE STATUE I have tried to reverse the process: that is to say, apply the point of view of a poet to Communism" (*Letters* 289). A Communist, even one who writes in verse, is just a Communist; a poet, regardless of his politics, is preeminently a poet.

Returning to "The Irrational Element in Poetry," one finds an echo of this symmetrical exchange, this artistic effort to reverse the process of political critique: "We look from an uncertain present toward a more uncertain future. One feels the desire to collect oneself against all this in poetry as well as in politics. If politics is nearer to each of us because of the pressure of the contemporaneous, poetry, in its way, is no less so and for the same reason" (*Opus* 229). Here change does not compose but must be composed, through either politics or *poeisis*. Both are attempts to "collect oneself against" uncertainty. Stevens, despite (or perhaps because of) his personal degree of economic and social security, felt an extraordinary pressure simply from reading the newspaper (which he did, cover to cover, every morning).[12] In poetry, accordingly, "the subject is not the contemporaneous, because that is only the nominal subject, but the poetry of the contemporaneous. Resistance to the pressure of ominous and destructive circumstance consists of its conversion, so far as possible, into a different, an explicable, an amenable circumstance" (230).

Here the Stevensian poetics resists not the forces of tyranny but any ominous or untoward "circumstance." In the *Adagia,* the poet goes so far as to say that "[p]oetry is a purging of the world's poverty and change and evil and death. It is a present perfecting, a satisfaction in the irremediable poverty of life" (193). Poetry and politics, then, perform similar functions, "for the same reason." Indeed, years later, in the address "Imagination as Value" (1948), Stevens would claim that "the scale of poetry" had been surpassed by that of international politics, particularly communism, considered as "a phenomenon of the imagination" (*Necessary* 142–43). But politics, a kind of poetry manqué, deals directly with the contemporaneous in order to bring a utopian world into actuality. Poetry, by contrast, converts the contemporaneous into the poetry of the contemporaneous, and by so doing imaginatively transforms things as they are into something more explicable and amenable. Poetry is a *present* perfecting, partial and deferred, of a poverty that has no remedy, only palliatives. Poetry—real Poetry—does not make our wishes come true, but it does make our losses good.

No utopia or sublime can shut down change; change, accident, must be dealt with. This view of events informs the jacket statement from *Ideas of Order* (1936), where Stevens writes that "[w]e think of changes occurring today as economic changes, involving political and social changes. Such changes raise questions of political and social order" (222). But Stevens wishes to transmute such questions in his poetry: "[T]his book, although it reflects them is primarily concerned with ideas of order of a different nature," such as "the dependence of the individual, confronting the elimination of established ideas, on the general sense of order; the idea of order created by individual concepts, as of the poet" (222). Likewise, on the jacket of *The Man with the Blue Guitar and Other Poems* (1937), the poet insists that, "In one group, *Owl's Clover,* while the poems reflect what was then going on in the world, that reflection is merely for the purpose of seizing and stating what makes life intelligible and desirable in the midst of great change and great confusion" (233). Stevens wishes, "in short, to isolate poetry," an example of "things imagined," from "things as they are" (233). Both statements instruct us to read the poems in terms of a private and universal, rather than a public and historical, experience. Stevens's repeated use of "individual" underlines his view of the function of poetry. The blue guitar is "a reference to the individuality of the poet" (233); the poems express the reflections of a private individual grappling with his life. While public events may press upon that life, they do not form the sphere of the poet's immediate concern. Nonetheless, unsettling occurrences create the need for poems; the poems "seize and state" that which makes life worth living despite the unavoidable assaults of change. By encompassing political changes within what seem to him more fundamental concerns, Stevens affirms the interiority, primacy, and privacy of the reflecting poetic subject.

As "great change and confusion" caused by public events threaten the privacy, individuality, and safety of the reader, that reader, if he or she uses Stevens's poems according to instructions, can begin to do the opposite—to extend (imaginatively) the private sphere to encompass the public.[13]

Those poems, as Stevens says, treat "the general sense of order . . . created by individual concepts, as of the poet." It is this very generality that makes these ideas of order "of a different nature" than "economic changes, involving political and social changes" (e.g., the nationalization of insurance). And the generality of these ideas protects the individuality of the reader; by abstracting general concepts from historical particulars, the speaker of the poem (and presumably the reader, as well) gains a perspective from which Depression, war, and totalitarianism become less personal, more distant, and therefore more amenable.

Many of the poems from the 1930s and 1940s play out the competition between "politics" and "poetry." For instance, angry mobs figure prominently in *Ideas of Order,* and they are usually threatening to figures of artists or to the speaker. In the poem "Farewell to Florida," the first in the book, the speaker complains, "My North is leafless and lies in a wintry slime / Both of men and clouds, a slime of men in crowds" (*Collected Poems* 118). This "wintry slime" made of "men in crowds" threatens to subsume the individuality of the speaker, to liquefy or evaporate him. In

"Sad Strains of a Gay Waltz," "mountain-minded Hoon" finds that "There is order in neither sea nor sun," but rather, "There are these sudden mobs of men, // These sudden clouds of faces and arms" (122). The integrity of the subject once again dissolves in the "cloud" of a crowd or mob, a mob that seems at once to dismember the body and to vaporize it.

The title of the poem "Mozart, 1935" should alert the reader: Stevens is not the sort of poet who dates his poems. It opens with a command: "Poet, be seated at the piano. / Play the present . . ." (131). An unnamed "they" "throw stones upon the roof / While you practice arpeggios," but the speaker entreats the poet-as-pianist:

>   be thou
> The voice of angry fear,
> The voice of this besieging pain. (132)

The poet must neither hide under the bed sheets nor rush into the streets, but convert the fear and pain outside into "[t]he unclouded concerto." The poem ends with:

> The snow is falling
> And the streets are full of cries.
> Be seated, thou.

Here, too, we have said farewell to the mythical Florida of the 1910s and early 1920s: we see less of the colorful and fanciful icing of the imagination here than in *Harmonium*. Now, in the depths of the Depression, as Stevens begins writing after a ten-year hiatus, it is winter and the snow is falling, and the poet inside must make the cloudy cries in the public thoroughfare into the poetry of the contemporaneous, into an aesthetic order emanating from and reaffirming a "thou" who is a poet.

But many of the poems in *Ideas of Order,* as in *Harmonium,* convey not so much a sense of risk to or pressure on the speaker as a nostalgia for the loss of a world in which things cohered aesthetically and metaphysically. The voice in these poems is that of a saddened and contemplative observer, not the voice of Wallace Stevens in the thick of it—not the voice we find in his prose of the 1930s and 1940s. It is almost as though Stevens's poetry—interior, reflective, often quasi-metaphysical or -psychoanalytic—has already lost out to a competing version of political or aesthetical correctness. Or not quite. Take, for example, these lines from "Academic Discourse at Havana":

> Politic man ordained
> Imagination as the fateful sin.
> Grandmother and her basketful of pears
> Must be the crux for our compendia.
> That's world enough, and more, if one includes
> Her daughters to the peached and ivory wench
> For whom the towers are built. The burgher's breast,
> And not the delicate ether star-impaled,
> Must be the place for prodigy, unless
> Prodigious things are tricks. (143–44)

At first it seems that politics has brought about the imagination's demise, by decree or ordinance. In typical fashion, the name Stevens names sublimates all particulars into an ideal abstraction: "Politic man." This formulation points to the similarity between Stevens's poetics and classical liberal formulations of subjectivity: both are punctual, abstract, and universal. In "politic man," Stevens attempts to parody this conception even as he too abstracts the specific, historical instances to what Kant describes as "this archetype of taste" (76). Any given ideology or opinion can fit within the category "politic man." But for Stevens, this archetype has already attained hieratic or mythical status: like a god, it ordains fate and determines what constitutes sin. The passage quoted above follows a verse paragraph that ends with an "urgent, competent, serener myth" that "[p]assed like a circus" (143). Thus politic man replaces this older, better myth, one "[c]onceiving from its perfect plenitude." The new, tawdry myth has won out over the imagination only to enjoin it. The "crux" of ordinary life, the old woman, the family member with her produce, replaces the Cross as the object of reverence; the old woman, who in "Owl's Clover" represents for Stevens "a symbol of those who suffered during the depression" (*Opus* 226), becomes "the central" of a new system of principles.

But the quotidian begins to slip at this point—grandma is world enough only if one includes "Her daughters to the peached and ivory wench / For whom the towers are built." This "wench" comes off as a sort of travesty of Helen of Troy, and the daughters, bathetic versions of her (citizens, perhaps, for whom towers are built by industrialists or by the WPA); the new world and the classical merge, but neither can quite make it. Moreover, while the burgher and what he harbors in his breast may be the stuff of politic life, he invites unflattering comparison to "a delicate ether star-impaled," that in its denial presents itself as possibility. In other words, the imaginative fight between "politic man" and "serener myth" reasserts itself despite the apparent dominance of the former. One can still conceive of "prodigy," even if such a conception is false consciousness or a "trick." The subject of the poem thus once again returns to poetry, and poetry once again defines itself by its difference from and subsumption of politics.

This is not to say that Stevens lacks awareness of the problems with abstraction—at least in a political sense. In "A Duck for Dinner," the penultimate section of "Owl's Clover," Stevens considers what the park would look like "[i]f these were theoretical people" walking in it. He then comes up with an incisive critique of classical liberal subjectivity:

> The civil fiction, the calico idea,
> The Johnsonian composition, abstract man,
> All are evasions like a repeated phrase,
> Which, by its repetition, comes to bear
> A meaning without a meaning. These people have
> A meaning within the meaning they convey,
> Walking the paths, watching the gilding sun,
> To be swept across them when they are revealed,
> For a moment, once each century or two. (Opus 95)

The eighteenth-century liberal ideal is a fiction that is not only unnecessary but empty as well. The classical model includes only theoretical, abstract, fully rational, conscious, and equal individuals—in other words, it has nothing to do with the world. Though meaningless, the model of Johnson (or Franklin) seems to take on a meaning by repetition and pervasiveness. But it is a meaning without substance, a meaning that explains nothing. The real people, on the other hand, embody layer upon layer of meaning; this meaning resides both inside and outside, both "within" and "swept across them when they are revealed." Presumably "A Duck for Dinner" attempts to be that (bi)centennial revelation: only the fleeting insight of the great poem can reveal the depths of human nature. The legal fiction of a contract (social or otherwise) produced for mass consumption only scratches the surface.

Yet Stevens's own poems in the 1930s (including "Owl's Clover") deal with "man" in abstract terms. As Stevens suggests, this habit of abstraction lies at the heart of classical liberalism as well; and, as we have seen, the poet understood his own poetic abstraction as individualistic. Stevens and his critics have pointed out that his poems are not "an affair of people," or, at any rate, not an affair of people who speak.[14] I would suggest that Stevens's poems contain persons rather than people. "These people in the park," the "mesdames," "man number one," "the poet"—the figures in the poems of this period become as abstract and indefinite as a "person" at law: the outline is there and could apply anywhere to anyone in a similar category or context. Only the names have been changed (or left blank). "Persons" at law are, in fact, theoretical people, and Stevens's poems are full of them. Likewise, places or things: one image or word becomes an example or symbol of a general "idea," in Kant's sense of the word. In other words, as Stevens says of insured risks: "There is no difference between the worm in the apple and the tack in the can of sardines, and not the slightest difference between the piano out of tune and a person disabled" (234). From the point of view of the insurance business, each instance can be abstracted into an actuarial table and a uniform premium can be affixed. "The beggar in Rome / Is the beggar in Bogota," as the poet writes in "Owl's Clover" (90). Or, as he says in "The Pleasures of Merely Circulating" (1934):

> Mrs. Anderson's Swedish baby
> Might well have been German or Spanish,
> Yet that things go round and again go round
> Has a rather classical sound. (*Collected Poems* 150)

Swedes, Germans, Spaniards: we are all equivalent and abstract individuals in both liberal theory and in Stevens's poetics. Moreover, that things are interchangeable and go round and round has rather the sound of classical political economy: money can circulate due to its alienable and abstract character. If "[m]oney is a kind of poetry" (*Opus* 191), then Stevens's poetics would reverse the formula as well.

That this poetics comes from an insurance attorney specializing in claims against surety bonds should not surprise us. The practice of "underwriting" began when, in the original Lloyds's coffeehouse, insurers wrote their names under the specific maritime risk that they chose to assume; investors in Lloyds's are known to this day as "names." These names underwrite the entire system, but they are place holders, much like the proper names Stevens uses to represent "figures" in his poems (e.g., "Lenin," "Cotton Mather," "Mr. Burnshaw"). The signature, the sign, becomes both the content of and the surety for the system. That the names attach to this or that individual or this or that document is rather less important than that there be names; the presence of persons assumes more importance than the absence of people.

Wallace Stevens's specialty, the surety bond, underwrites a contract; when such a bond is written properly, if one party defaults, the losses of the other party are made good. The claims man (or the judge) insures that the bond will be interpreted properly.[15] Likewise, the indeterminacy of an abstract poetics requires the poet to take the role of self-interpreter in order to insure that the poems are not misinterpreted or used improperly. Stevens devoted his career to such interpretation, to insuring that persons would fulfill the terms of contracts. In dealing with these "abstract men," Stevens may have felt as though he were becoming one. As he says in "Surety and Fidelity Claims," "A man in the home office tends to conduct his business on the basis of the papers that come before him. After twenty-five years or more of that sort of thing, he finds it difficult sometimes to distinguish himself from the papers he handles and comes almost to believe that he and his papers constitute a single creature, consisting principally of hands and eyes: lots of hands and lots of eyes" (239).

The monstrous paper man in the insurance office in Hartford seems a sorry alternative to the letter carrier in the post office in New York or Rome, but this is the dilemma Stevens faced. If the dangerous historical particulars lead to a bureaucratic totalitarian dystopia, then the alternative, for Stevens, becomes a poetry of generality that can accommodate the world to the needs of the individual who interprets it. But that abstract alternative threatens to collapse back into an equally totalizing, ideal and dystopian rut. The man in the home office becomes paper, the agent becomes nothing more than his suit and his flower, and both emerge as figures of a disembodied punctual individuality.

In sum, then, a liberal political economy must be maintained for Stevens's poetic economy to work. Political action and discourse, such as the demand for national insurance, could (but should not be allowed to) replace either the poet or the rigors of the free market. Otherwise, "we should all be willing to stop"—or to become letter carriers. And while we might receive better salaries, benefits, and job security as letter carriers, life would be less challenging and aesthetically less appealing.

Stevens's theory depends upon a sphere of civil society free of the demands of public life but able to refer to the public sphere and imaginatively subsume it. If nationalization seeks to make private enterprise public, then Stevens does the opposite; he would privatize not just government functions but the rest of life as well. As Nancy Rosenblum points out, classical liberalism conceived of the private as a space apart from the state, and the private individual as an actor in public affairs. But by the twentieth century, the state had expanded, and formerly "private" realms had begun to seem threatening to the private self (for example, through the market's mutation into monopoly capitalism). This twentieth-century emphasis on the private self, Nancy Rosenblum points out, usually responds to radical instability: "It is a response to the fragility and unsafety of public life. It springs from the conviction that to act in the world is to expose oneself to suffering and dependence. For antipolitical souls, alternative political or social ideals are unimaginable" (84). It is precisely this sense of threat, of chaotic change or insecurity, that leads the insurer-poet to argue not for an explicit political or social ideal but for the legitimacy of his privatizing poetic.[16]

But that very argument demonstrates the impossibility of the classical liberal subject in the twentieth century. As in the case of Allen Tate, for Stevens the ongoing contest between an overtly politicized, radical poetry and a poetic that would absorb the category "public poetry" altogether occasions a public poem against public poetry, namely, "Owl's Clover." In order to establish poetry as an activity of the private self, the poet-critic must acknowledge, paradoxically, poetry's participation in public debate about poetic theory. The poet-essayist, Stevens as well as Tate, cannot leave well enough alone. Rather than simply ignore young Stanley Burnshaw's numbering Stevens among "[a]cutely conscious members of a class menaced by clashes between capital and labor" (42), the poet instead turns Burnshaw into a personage in "Owl's Clover." In spite of Stevens's insistence on the inherent privacy of true poetry, his poems enter what remains of the literary public sphere; as such, the poet enters or is drawn into a pervasive public debate. As the poet states, "[e]veryone takes sides in social change if it is profound enough" (198).

In the 1930s, this observation spelled trouble for the poet-businessman; political conditions were making it impossible for Stevens to maintain a privatized, privatizing poetic sphere—that is, the general cultural-political conditions necessary for that poetics had evaporated. Stevens confesses in "The Irrational Element in Poetry" (1936), "If I dropped into a gallery I found that I had no interest in what I saw. The air was charged with anxieties and tensions. To look at pictures there was the same thing as to play the piano in Madrid this afternoon" (226). The entire gallery (not to mention the literary world) is framed by the charged "air," the atmosphere of tension induced by world events. To look at pictures during the Spanish Civil War seems like fiddling while Rome burns. Art, in other words, regardless of its content or its theory, is always subject to interpellation and articulation by political society; in a politically charged and polarized moment, pretensions to the contrary seem quixotic. Rather than the private subject's subsuming the public, the political here seems to crowd out the private. But the answer doesn't lie in supporting the Abraham Lincoln Brigade or refugee relief. Rather, the modernist poet redoubles his imaginative efforts to establish a privatizing poetics that can reduce the anxiety occasioned by current history by absorbing it in abstraction.

While the voice in Stevens's poems often seems detached or even self-effacing, Stevens reluctantly joined the public debate at almost the same time he resumed publishing poems after a decade's silence. In the poems and essays that emerge from this period, we see a sort of compromise-formation between what the author represents as a world-historical reality principle on the one hand and a desire for autonomy—a desire to "hug the purely local"—on the other. This tension expresses an important moment within modernism and in liberal subjectivity.

CHAPTER FOUR

Publicity, Sabotage, and Arturo Giovannitti's "Poetry of Syndicalism"

As U.S. modernists attempted to secure artistic autonomy in the private sphere, they found themselves repeatedly drawn into public debate in order to justify that choice and to shape their poems' reception. They did so not only in response to the literary Marxism of the 1930s, but also in response to the literary culture of the 1910s and 1920s. At that time, it seemed natural for magazine critics to discuss poets' ideals and biographies, and the popular conception of poetry was of a fundamentally publicly oriented art.

By the same token, Arturo Giovannitti (1884–1959), immigrant poet, orator, political theorist, and labor organizer, is an important (albeit unlikely) figure for understanding the new and unstable meanings poetry took on in the United States prior to the political and poetical polarization of the early 1930s. It is not surprising that a poet like Giovannitti, though frequently anthologized in the 1920s, would suffer critical neglect after the codification of the modernist canon. During the early 1910s, Giovannitti was a poet published in both wide-circulation literary magazines and propaganda for the syndicalist union Industrial Workers of the World (IWW, or "Wobblies"). Giovannitti, in defiance of Kant's famous antinomies of poet and orator,[1] was both; he simultaneously assumed the role of an orator borrowing from (his own) poetry and a poet writing in an oratorical style.

Post–New Critical canons of taste suggest one reading of Giovannitti—namely, that he was a bad poet, too swayed by the Edwardian twilight and too oratorical in style. In his contemporary context, however, his poems' meaning was overdetermined by his public image. In 1912 to 1914, Giovannitti was "bad" in a different sense: his poems complicated the distinction between poetry and rhetoric, the material and the ideal—more so than either proletarian poets or self-described reactionary critics would twenty years later. I would suggest that while at the time Giovannitti's work was first published it was received warmly, twenty or even ten years later, by contrast, such liminality between art and news seemed suspect by new political-cultural standards. In this sense, Giovannitti is an interesting test case of the changes in the social form of genre over time.

Giovannitti, not unlike Wallace Stevens, idealizes the political and turns "private" poetry into public utterance. For Stevens, poetry serves (among other things) as a means for the private subject to sublimate the public world in general, and politics in particular, into a poetic essence. However, Giovannitti does the opposite. Giovannitti's poems form a connection between the private self and public self via the fiction of poems as private utterances that are, in fact, heard in the sphere of public debate. For example, Giovannitti's famous prose poem "The Walker" would turn poetic uplift into an indictment of the textile kings of New England and in the process turn meditative poetry into public speech.

In Giovannitti's case, it is publicity, in the narrow sense of notoriety as well as the larger sense of "making public," that collapses distinctions between the poetic sphere of the private subject and the public sphere of economic and political issues. His poems lack the attention to historical detail found in social poetry of the 1930s; as we shall see, they tend to deal in the types and idealizations characteristic of much Edwardian (and Victorian) verse. However, by bracketing the poems within the social-economic movement, literary critics and propagandists alike shaped the meaning of the poems and publicized the syndicalist movement at the same time. Since many of Giovannitti's poems were written or published during or just after his imprisonment during the 1912 Lawrence, Massachusetts, textile strike, the movement became hard to ignore.

It is just this historical milieu that produced Giovannitti's liminality between ideality and ideology and that turned the "poetry of revolt" writ large into (as the *Atlantic Monthly* put it) the "poetry of syndicalism" specifically. Although by many accounts the bourgeois public sphere was largely a thing of the past by the twentieth century, its publicist impulse gained strength in the years preceding World War I, in the investigative New Journalism, in the Progressivist ideal of open government, and in the defenses of a moral-practical-social poetics of the 1900s and early 1910s. And if the U.S. press of Giovannitti's day was reluctant to give a hearing to syndicalist ideas, they were willing to engage what they saw as syndicalist *poetry*. It was precisely these literary-critical and reportorial responses that translated Giovannitti's utterances in both verse and prose into a mode of discourse that is personal expression and oratory at once. In the early twentieth century, the conversation about poetry frequently became a conversation about the shifting field of U.S. politics. Accordingly, poems could become political critique, and critiques of Giovannitti's poems could (and did) end in a discussion of or debate with his philosophy. This liminality would prove important to literary culture in one way, to union organizers in another.

At first glance, it would seem that the literary world received the poems of the young Italian immigrant favorably. For instance, *Current Opinion* published his work alongside that of Sara Teasdale, saying of the poet's volume *Arrows in the Gale* (1914) that "a number of these poems are unsurpassed in power by anything ever published in America" ("Voices" 54)—high praise at the time for a non-"Nordic" writer. "The Walker," Louis Untermeyer asserted in 1919, "is one of the most remarkable things our literature can boast" (*New Era* 191). Likewise, Charles Ashleigh, writing in Margaret Anderson's *Little Review,* tells the reader to concentrate on the "spirit" of *Arrows in the Gale,* not its technique, because "[a]ll through it flares that spirit of impatient revolt, that spurning of most of the scaffolding of our decrepit civilization which is usually held up for admiration to the budding youth of this country" (22). In short, Arturo Giovannitti's work held appeal for a wide variety of poetry readers, those excited by the literary and cultural revolts of the 1910s, as well as those adhering to more traditional conceptions of poetry.

This was possible because most of the poems included in *Arrows in the Gale* don't go into specifics. They certainly contain the *spirit* of revolt, as the reviewers note, but the nature of that revolt—its ideological and historical specificity, if any—is nowhere to be found. Giovannitti's poems tend to conflate historical epochs; they speak of "human labor," of the rich and the poor, the old versus the new. The prison poem "The Walker," for instance, doesn't mention the United States or Massachusetts at all; the turnkey, the "white-haired man dressed in blue," is "greater than Mohammed and Arbues and Torquemada and Mesmer, and all the other masters of men's thoughts" (27). Even the "inflammatory" "Sermon on the Common" addresses "ye, Plebs, Populace, People, Rabble, Mob, Proletariat," implying that these terms, if not synonymous, are at least equivalent (75). Indeed, while no poem mentions the Salem jail where Giovannitti and his colleagues were jailed, one does mention the Bastille.

Many of the poems take the reader to biblical times and settings, or take on an archaic diction and subject. This is the case particularly when the poems assume their most polemical edge, as in "Utopia," where the speaker declares:

> A day shall come when gold shall not enthrall thee,
>   When theft and murder cease to be thy rule;

> So I, who call thee now a friend, shall call thee,
> Forsooth, a true and upright man, "Thou fool!" (57)

Likewise, in the "Samnite Cradle Song," a mother tells her infant:

> For the despair of my life, my lost hope,
> And for this song of the dawn that I sing
> Die like a man by the ax or the rope,
> Spit on their God and stab our good king. (87)

While these figures are rebellious, they are not proletarians per se; one is tempted to sigh, "The poor ye have always with ye." In fact, "The Walker" speaks of the roads leading downward and the stairs leading upward that all people tread:

> And they all climb the same roads and the same stairs others go down;
> for never, since man began to think how to overcome and overpass
> man, have other roads and other stairs been found. (24)

This view of man's inhumanity to man is not much less abstract (or pessimistic) than Wallace Stevens's treatment—there is no dialectic here.[2]

One of the prose poems in *Arrows*, "The Cage," appeared both in the *Atlantic Monthly* and in a limited edition print on vellum published by the Hillacre Bookhouse in Riverside, Connecticut. Like the other poems, "The Cage" doesn't mention a judge, let alone his name or the particulars of the case or the venue; rather, "Old and hoary was the man who sat upon the faldstool, upon the fireless and godless altar. / Old were the tomes that mouldered behind him on the dusty shelves." While the *Atlantic*'s introduction to the poem does discuss Giovannitti's career and thereby shapes readers' impression of the text, the point of the poem itself is the abstract decrepitude of the room and the old men as compared to the youthful figures in the cage, figures who are connected to the living world outside the room. "The Cage" is a quasi-surrealistic allegory, and "The Walker" suggests a spiritual aspect to imprisonment that could as easily apply to anyone (indeed, *Current Opinion* compares it to "The Ballad of Reading Gaol"). In general, the poetry is universal and adjectival; it almost always avoids any direct reference to contemporary (or even socialist) politics. In these respects, Giovannitti's poems do not differ formally from other Victorian or Edwardian poetry in English.[3]

However, Giovannitti's work appeared and received notice in places other than his slender 1914 volume or literary periodicals. Though one wouldn't necessarily know it from his poems, in 1906 Giovannitti became a socialist and subsequently editor of the Italian socialist paper *Il Proletario* in New York.[4] In 1912, his friend Joe Ettor, an organizer for the IWW, invited Giovannitti to help organize a strike of foreign-born textile workers in Lawrence, Massachusetts. Giovannitti went to Lawrence and became active in the strike, particularly in organizing relief for the children of striking workers, in boosting morale, as an interpreter, and in exposing attempts by the Woolen Trust to discredit the Wobblies.

But the authorities cut short the activities of Ettor and Giovannitti. Seventeen days after the beginning of the strike, someone shot and killed a striker, Anna LoPizzo. The police seized Ettor and Giovannitti on a charge of accessory to murder; the district attorney alleged that their inflammatory speeches had incited the unknown assailant. The same day, on the same picket, militiamen bayoneted a Syrian boy, killing him. This fact, along with the paucity of evidence against the two Italians, the history of framed-up charges against IWWs, and racist remarks by the mayor of Lawrence about "hunkies," led many to believe that the charges held no weight and that the real perpetrator acted on orders from the Woolen Trust.

Nonetheless, Ettor and Giovannitti spent the next year in prison. The two were moved to Salem (an irony that did not escape the defendants or some reporters); here Giovannitti wrote most of the poems included in *Arrows*. Big Bill Haywood, Carlo Tresca, Elizabeth Gurley Flynn, and various other Wobbly luminaries took over the fight in Lawrence; the IWW wasted no time in organizing the defense of Ettor and Giovannitti —or in using their case to further the ends of the union. Justus Ebert, writing about Giovannitti in an IWW newspaper prior to the trial, included a poem by the prisoner called "The Prisoner's Bench" (also in *Ar-*

rows), which Ebert introduces by saying: "The following Whitmanesque lines are at once suggestive of Giovannitti's undaunted spirit in the present crisis, and his reciprocated devotion to his companion in the class war on the textile kings of New England" (4). Farther down the column reads the stern remonstrance, "What injures Joe Ettor injures you. Remember that." Still lower is an ad for the *I.W.W. Song Book,* "To Fan the Flames of Discontent." In the end, the jury acquitted the defendants. A pamphlet published after the trial entitled *Ettor and Giovannitti before the Jury at Salem, Massachusetts* included both men's speeches to the jury and ends with Giovannitti's poem "The Walker."

Despite the presence of Giovannitti's poems in these propaganda pieces, the weekly and monthly magazines attributed considerable poetic value to his work. We may conclude from this, and from the universal nature of the poems themselves, that readers found the ability to look at the poet's work objectively, to consider its literary merit apart from the poet's biography, and to set aside his political ideology in order to understand his art. We may reach this conclusion, but nothing could be further from the truth. Even when critics claimed to ignore Giovannitti's politics and public persona, they seemed unable to do so.

The *Atlantic,* in "The Poetry of Syndicalism," argues with the poem "The Cage" as though it were a manifesto: "It was the law which freed Giovannitti. This law, read by 'dead men' out of 'dead books,' had in it the spark of the eternal life of justice. The logic of facts is against the poet's repudiation of the past" (854). The article is not literary critique so much as a reading of a political-cultural movement. Alfred Kreymborg writes that, although "The Walker" may be a masterpiece of a poem, it is also "the most impassioned American tract against the prison system" (475). Like all of Giovannitti's critics, Kreymborg ineluctably places this poem in its biographical/political context: for him, it is at once poem and tract, and Giovannitti is simultaneously artist and agitator.

Likewise, Louis Untermeyer, in his review of the poet's work, admits that "[t]his is not the place for an analysis of Giovannitti's political views or his economic theories. But they must be considered, no matter how sketchily, since they form not only the background but the impetus of his poetry" (*New Era* 183). Untermeyer seems to say that literary criticism is not the place for a discussion of political and economic opinions, but criticism must address those issues in the case of Giovannitti. And what are they? "The old clash between employer and employed, the tragic enmity between labor and capital, the terrible hypocrisy of 'law and order' in many of our mining camps, the absurd fiction of free speech maintained by a 'kept' press—these are matters which concern the man so deeply that they have forced the poet to speak" (183–84). Very specific issues of public import concern the private "man" so deeply that they force the poet to go public with his feelings (even though the poems don't mention those specific issues). In this way, the poetry for Untermeyer bridges the separation of spheres.

Nor did critics farther to the left shy away from moving from literary to political criticism and linking the spirit of poetry to the spirit of politics. For instance, in the preface to *Arrows in the Gale,* socialist Helen Keller writes, "He has tried to render his ideas of the world he lives in. As a poet he is to be judged by his success in rendering these ideas in verse, and not by his relations to Syndicalism or Socialism or any other movement in which he happens to be active. The laws of poetic beauty and power, not one's beliefs about the economic world, determine the excellence of his work" (9). Giovannitti merely "renders"; he is (to paraphrase Allen Tate or Ezra Pound) a craftsman, and it doesn't matter what his politics are. But then Keller tells us that the poetry is "inspired by this consecration to a glorious cause. It is 'only living aloud his work, a singing with his hand'" (11). Moreover, "[h]e is a poet, a better poet than has come out of the privileged classes of America in our day. He is also a practical strike-leader and organizer. . . . Giovannitti's real crime was helping the strikers." "His work" becomes a slippery phrase in this passage. At first it seems that Giovannitti's work is his mastery of poetry, then it appears his poetry only expresses his work of union organizing. Thus "poetic beauty and power" dovetails with "helping the strikers"— the preface makes the articulation between the two. Giovannitti is the practical poet in an era of practical poetry; his practical action in both verse and life is "social" in nature.[5]

Indeed, the poet himself, in the "Proem" of *Arrows in the Gale,* writes: "These are but songs—they're not a creed / They are not meant to lift or save," but rather, "They are the blows of my own sledge / Against the walls of my own jail" (18). Here the poet seems to reject a reading of his poems as "political" in any direct sense—as well as the popular received notion of poetry as expressing belief, lifting the spirit, or saving the soul. He also makes what seems a strong declaration of individual autonomy as an artist; the poems, in the rhetoric of the "Proem," are not expected to do anything for anyone other than the artist. Why, then, do the commentators find in these writings "The Poetry of Syndicalism"? Why are these ostensibly private poems read as public utterance?

According to historian-theorists such as Jürgen Habermas and Reinhart Koselleck, the "public sphere" originated in debates about culture and art and then gradually spread to include discussions of public authority and public affairs. Both art and criticism moved from disinterested moral-aesthetic judgment to interested political action by another name. Accordingly, "[b]y engaging in literary, aesthetic and historical criticism, Voltaire indirectly criticized Church and State" but soon realized the direct influence of that critique (Koselleck 113). Publicity, accordingly, was a necessity for and a vehicle of public opinion, which in turn formed the basis for the legitimacy and power of the public sphere and the criticism originating therein. Thus publicness—openness, making public—became the medium and sine qua non of legitimate debate in the public sphere and formed the link between the moral understandings facilitated by literature and by political critique.

Giovannitti's poetry invoked this process in a volatile period, when liberalism was divided between social liberals (such as those writing in *Current Opinion* and *Survey*) and classical liberals (such as the spokesmen for the laissez-faire mill owners) and under attack (by syndicalists, conservatives, and others). Critics understood Giovannitti's poems in terms of the artistic expression of the private person: as the *Bookman* put it,

Giovannitti's poems express an "attitude of extreme individualism" (Bradley 208). But it becomes important that public events "concern the man so deeply that they have forced the poet to speak," as Untermeyer puts it. Giovannitti's reviewers assume that the poetry is meant to critique church and state, but, according to his defenders, this critique issues from the spontaneous concern of a free person with the heart of a poet.

This is why it is important that his poems do not directly engage the politics of the day. For Kant, the interested economic identity of private agents could be reconciled, via the rational-critical debate defined by publicness, to the role of "spiritually free human beings" (Habermas 112). Hence it is crucial that publicity *about* Giovannitti turn the poems into public speech. Critics simply could not understand them apart from the historical circumstances in which Giovannitti wrote them, any more than a reader of *Ettor and Giovannitti before the Jury* could do so, but the content of Giovannitti's poems is not directly responsible for this understanding. While Giovannitti's "sledge" in his "Proem" may be metaphorical, "the walls of my own jail" are not. "The Cage" takes on a particular meaning if you know Giovannitti wrote it in the Salem jail while awaiting trial for a capital offense related to an IWW strike. In 1913, or even 1923, Giovannitti and his union were news, and so were the poems. They are, to paraphrase Marianne Moore's "Poetry," imaginary toads in a real garden.

Indeed, Giovannitti wrote his most famous poems in the midst of a political *culture,* during a "strike that sang," one in which art and propaganda, poetry and politics, merged. During the Lawrence strike, one striker's banner pointed up this fusion of aesthetics and economic democracy: "We Want Bread—and Roses, Too!" Syndicalism, both in the United States and France, had been gaining in visibility and notoriety since the turn of the century, and the Lawrence strike (for all practical purposes a general strike in that mill town) made "syndicalism" a household word. The poet's socialism, sympathy toward syndicalism, and defense of sabotage were well known (his translation of and introduction to Emile Pouget's *Sabotage* appeared in 1913). And Giovannitti occupied center stage in the first major appearance of the IWW before nationwide public opinion.

By the same token, writing from prison carries its own challenges, especially when you are on trial for allegedly speaking words that incited someone to murder. In 1917, just before the United States' entry into World War I, Giovannitti would write that "I find that poems are the best safe-conduct for revolutionary utterances . . . Besides you can always hang somebody at the end of an ode, while in an arricle [*sic*] you cannot go further than libeling them."[6] Likewise, publicity cut both ways for the IWW when its organizers on the West Coast were being clubbed by police and vilified in the press for speaking publicly on behalf of their cause. Accordingly, Giovannitti, in many poems, masters the art of naming-by-not-naming; it is the critics who fill in the specifics. In its original form in the *Atlantic*, "The Cage" bears the inscription "Salem Jail, Sunday, October 20, 1912," and several other prison poems have similar notes; "The Republic," ostensibly dealing with the rise and fall of the French Revolution, bears the dates "July 4–July 14." Giovannitti seems to be taunting when he isn't flaunting; these seemingly historical or symbolic poems took on a specific contemporary meaning for their original audience, and no one knew that better than he. If a first-time reader of the poems who encountered them in *Arrows in the Gale*, where they are shorn of these dates, rather than in their original publication context had any doubt about the occasion of the poems, Keller's preface to the book makes it abundantly clear.[7]

In fact, the very universality of Giovannitti's poems is part of their political point. Giovannitti uses universality not only to save himself, but also to travesty the classical liberal idiom that produced it, the "old" laissez-faire liberalism of the Woolen Trust—as opposed to the "new" progressivist liberalism of some of the magazines that published (and sympathized with) him.[8] Rather than "taking logics of the 'universal subject' so dear to poetry critics and carrying them to their shockingly democratic extreme," as Hester Furey suggests (37), "The Walker" shows the undemocratic core of that subject and reveals the type of oppressive equality and sham consensus it enforces. "I hear footsteps over my head all night," the poem begins. The speaker asks, "Who walks? I know not. It is the phantom of the jail, the sleepless brain, a man, the man, the

Walker" (*Arrows* 21). This is the subject of the jail who is subject to the jail, a nightmare liberal self: "a man" becomes representative as "the man," but this man is nothing more than a phantom or a disembodied brain, an abstract being, defined in relation to the prison, who merely walks. Yet the jail-keeper is not abstract or disembodied, but "a coarse hand with red hair on its fingers." The jailer may be nothing but a hand, but the hand metonymically suggests a particular class and ethnicity, not a universal self; by the same token, in the historical context of the poem, the carceral subject is not so much a "perpetrator" as a "hunkie."[9]

Moreover, the jail itself comes to be an analog for the liberal state and its reduction of all to an abstract equality:

> Wonderful is the supreme wisdom of the jail that makes all think the same thought. Marvelous is the providence of the law that equalizes all, even in mind and sentiment. Fallen is the last barrier of privilege, the aristocracy of the intellect. The democracy of reason has leveled all the two hundred minds to the common surface of the same thought. (26)

That thought, as it turns out, is of "a little key of shiny brass" that opens the jailhouse door. The jail mirrors the drive to social conformity within liberal equality—democracy here is perfected by consensus, but it is a consensus built not on freedom but coercion. Equality consists in the desire of everyone to get out. "Equal justice under law" means leveling all to a small brass thought that exists only on "the common surface." Reason, in the purposive rational control expressed by the prison, eliminates privilege by eliminating freedom. In so doing, however, it has (in good Tocquevillean fashion) eliminated all but the most narrow thoughts. Consequently, says the speaker, "I, who have never killed, think like the murderer." In fact, "I think, reason, wish, hope, doubt, wait like the hired assassin, the embezzler, the forger, the counterfeiter, the incestuous, the raper [*sic*], the drunkard, the prostitute, the pimp, I, I who used to think of love and life and flowers and song and beauty and the ideal." In other words, the speaker is a Poet, not a felon—but it doesn't matter.

But despite the declaration of a self that is here a carceral subject, the speaker is not actually thinking like the criminal but is writing poetry instead. Poetry, in the popular, premodernist, progressivist version, becomes both a vantage from which to critique the system and a way of rising above it, of attaining spiritual freedom ("beauty and the ideal"), if not equality.[10] That poem and others affirm the existence and value of spiritual freedom, despite an actually existing carceral society. Hence Giovannitti, in his public image, can be both man and poet, both autonomous artist and union organizer—can be a socialist critic of liberalism and be accepted as a liberal subject, too.

While it is Giovannitti's organizing that colors his poetry, his status as (lyric) Poet by the same token lends cultural or even spiritual credibility to his organizing. It is the generic status of poetry as "free" that made it useful as propaganda in the 1910s and, by the same token, the writer's devotion to a noble "cause" that vouches for his status as poet. For instance, *Current Opinion* says that Giovannitti is "not the usual type of labor agitator. The usual type is not a very complex one. . . . But in Giovannitti there is something else. He has the soul of a great poet, the fervor of a prophet, and, added to these, the courage and power of initiative that mark the man of action and the organizer of great crusades" ("Social Significance" 24). A picture of Giovannitti wearing his trademark cravat accompanies the article: the poet did little to dispel his romantic image. As Eric Amfitheatrof recounts, "Giovannitti was a dashing and flamboyant figure. Dark, with patrician good looks, just under six feet tall, he wore a velvet jacket, a Byronic collar and large, scarflike cravats . . . His [spoken] language was rich and fabulous" (184). Amfitheatrof suggests that Giovannitti's poems and status as poet helped generate sympathy for the defendants among Americans. In the publicity surrounding the trial, the organizer-poet is no scrappy Joe Hill; rather, he retains an exalted, hieratic status as poet. James P. Heaton, writing about the trial days after the verdict, affirmed that the poet-orator, "slender, pale, trembling, courteous always rather than assertive, showed himself truly the poet who lives, as well as writes with ink on paper" (304). It is precisely his status as pale,

Arturo Giovannitti, c. 1912.
Brown Brothers, Sterling,
Pennsylvania

trembling poet that suggests that he is not a murderer: as Mary Brown Sumner wrote, "Surely we are not so rich in lyric poets that we can afford to send this one to the chair or keep him longer in prison" (166). He has "something else" in his soul as a poet. As Furey writes, his "poetry signified something inseparable from his character" (38).

This is one reason, I think, that the poems make no more reference to specifics than they do: in 1913, this feature makes Giovannitti's poems valuable as both literature and (by the same token) propaganda. Giovannitti is not a social realist before his time; despite his protomodernist use of "rough speech" and stated rejection of spiritual uplift, he is, in a sense, writing social poetry within a late romantic tradition that would be recognizable to his audience—uncomfortably so, given the content of the poems and the identity of the author. Giovannitti's commitment to equality does not level so much as attempt to merge the exploited industrial worker and the autonomous soul of the poet in their common role as rebels.

In this respect, Giovannitti's naming-by-not-naming acts in much the same way as sabotage. Giovannitti, in his introduction to Pouget's *Sabotage*, avers that the practice has always been around. It becomes dangerous only when it becomes a propagated idea: "[T]here is no danger in any act in itself when it is determined by natural instinctive impulse and is quite unconscious and unpremeditated—it only becomes dangerous when it becomes the translated practical expression of an idea even though, or rather because, this idea has originated from the act itself" (Pouget 15). The poems (and everything they represent), while appearing as spontaneous expressions, became a publicized idea available for use. This is important for Giovannitti, since "if by public opinion we mean the people at large, these are and always will be favorable to the cause of any class of workers . . . because they are workers themselves" (31). Only when the worker "hears his woes . . . re-enacted on the stage does he become conscious of it, and therefore dangerous to the digestion of his masters" (19). The saboteur, like the "respectable" poet-syndicalist, is "a spy in disguise in the camp of the enemy" (33) whose acts become ideological through publicity.

Consequently, for some critics, Giovannitti's writing awakens the working classes to a *personal* conception of *society*—the same sort of conception Keller and Untermeyer both claim the texts of the poems embody. Kenneth Macgowan writes in "Giovannitti: Poet of the Wop," "Whatever its future, the I.W.W. has accomplished one tremendously big thing—a thing that sweeps away all twaddle over red flags and violence and sabotage. And that is the individual awakening of 'illiterates' and 'scum' to an original, personal conception of society and the realization of the dignity and the rights of their part in it. They have learned more than class-consciousness; they have learned consciousness of self. The I.W.W. is making the 'wop' into a thinker" (611). The jail, in Macgowan's ethnocentric reading, becomes the common plight of the Italian workers, Giovannitti included; it is at once a material jail as well as a metaphorical jail of ignorance and unconsciousness. Giovannitti's poetry elevates the movement to the status of "culture" and makes it visible to a middle-class WASP audience as more acceptable than it would be via speeches or pamphlets by southern or eastern European immigrants; the poetry spiritualizes the material struggle. But more than that, despite the collectivist cast of the poet's philosophy, the poetry becomes the vehicle by which individual selfhood is formed—an audience not acculturated to poetry is, in Macgowan's imagination, individuated by exposure to it. Thus, on this reading, Giovannitti's poems exist at once as stimulating private reflection and, at the same time, as public speech (it makes the "illiterates" think about society).

This generic liminality of Giovannitti's writing becomes apparent when we compare the poet's speech from the dock at his trial with his poems. Heaton attributed to Giovannitti the status of Poet not because of his poems, but because of the eloquence of his speech to the jury. That is, it is Giovannitti's skill in moving people that proves him a poet.[11] Accordingly, Giovannitti makes a point of assuring the jury of the spontaneous and free nature of his remarks. He asks, "[D]o you believe for one single moment that we ever preached violence, that a man like me as I stand with my naked heart before you and you know that there is no lie in me at this moment, there is no deception in me at this moment [*sic*]. You know that I know not what I say, because it is only the onrush of what flows from my lips today that I say" (*Address* 9). Giovannitti thereby attempts to establish himself as the man Kant describes as one "who is possessed of an imagination that is fertile and effective in presenting his ideas, and whose heart, withal, turns with lively sympathy to what is truly good—he is . . . the orator without art." Kant contrasts such oratory with that "which borrows from poetry only so much as is necessary to win over men's minds to the side of the speaker before they have weighed the matter, and to rob their verdict of its freedom" (192) and so to move men "like machines to a judgment" (193 n. 1).[12] Giovannitti, however, assures the jury of his good intentions and his sympathy for "the better and nobler humanity where there shall be no more slaves" (3) and makes a case for the socialist version of this vision. In his version, it is not oratory but the wage system that makes a person "the slave of the machine" (7). Giovannitti says his words are free, unlike "those words that have been put into my mouth by those two detectives" (1–2).

Giovannitti uses the same rhetorical strategies, many of the same tropes, and much of the same cadence and tone in both prose poems and speeches. Like "The Walker," Giovannitti's speech stages him as a poetic soul reduced to the condition of miscreants and murderers. The defendant faces the same fate "that has destroyed the life of the wife murderer and the patricide and the parricide [*sic*]" (12), and he sits in the "same cage where the drunkard, where the prostitute, where the hired assassin has been" (3). Like the speaker of "The Walker," who thinks "of love and life and flowers and song and beauty and the ideal" (*Arrows* 26), Giovannitti says to the jury, "I have a woman that loves me and that I love . . . I have an ideal that is dearer to me than can be expressed or understood. And life has so many allurements and it is so nice and bright and so wonderful that I feel the passion of living in my heart and I do want to live" (10–11). But, as Giovannitti keeps reminding the jury, their verdict is freely given, they may decide in favor of either side of the question, may send the men to the chair, or their judgment may "be such that this gate will be opened and we shall pass out of it and go back into the sunlit world" (11). Just so, in "The Walker," "the apostle and the murderer, the poet and the procurer, think of the same gate, the same key and the same exit on the different sunlit highways of life" (*Arrows* 27).

On the other side, "[t]he District Attorney and the other gentlemen here who are used to measure all human emotions with the yardstick may not understand the tumult that is going on in my soul in this moment" (*Address* 1). Unlike the poet's tempestuous soul, the D.A. comes across like "The Walker," the subject of the prison:

> He has measured his space, he has measured it accurately, scrupulously, minutely . . . so many feet, so many inches, so many fractions of an inch for each of the four paces. (*Arrows* 21)

In the context of the speech, the D.A. also represents a version of the old man on the judge's bench among "the tomes that moldered behind him on the dusty shelves" in "The Cage" (88). Only the men in "the green iron cage" experience "all the fierce and divine passions that battle and rage in the heart of man" (89). The formal, parsing, abstract, universal sham equality of the older liberal legal system stands in stark contrast to language of the heart, of that which is "new and young and alive."

If Giovannitti thinks in terms of historical archetypes or sees a sort of eternal recurrence in his poems, his "Address" does the same thing. The principle of the IWW and socialists is the same for which "Lloyd Garrison in this very Commonwealth . . . [was] dragged through the streets with a rope around his neck" (*Address* 2), and it is opposed to the principle of wage slavery, which emerges as a version of the chattel slavery that "Abraham Lincoln, by an illegal act" put an end to (6). Moreover, says the speaker:

We are fanatics. But yet so was a fanatic Socrates, who instead of acknowledging the philosophy of the aristocrats of Athens, preferred to drink the poison. And so was a fanatic the Saviour Jesus Christ, who instead of acknowledging . . . that Tiberius was emperor of Rome . . . preferred the cross between two thieves. And so were all the philosophers and all the dreamers and all the scholars of the Middle Ages who preferred to be burned alive by one of these very same churches which you reproach me now of having said no one of our membership should belong to. (3–4)

Similarly, the Giovannitti poem "The Stranger at the Gate," one of what we might call his "historical" poems, has a setting in ancient Palestine. A traveler, leaving a certain city, asks the sentinel why the authorities crucified a certain man the day before. Was it because he pitied the poor and lowly, because he mingled with the rabble and flattered it, or because he preached a new religion? At each query, the keeper of the gate responds that no, the people of the city do the same. He ends by saying:

"Aye, I will tell thee, stranger, though thy curiosity is great for a walker of Caesar's roads. It was not because of any of these things, but because of all these things, because he said and did them all at once and because he talked too much and was beginning to be heard and because . . . But whither art thou going, stranger?"

"Where the highroad leads, keeper of the gate." (*Arrows* 34)

Given the trial of Ettor and Giovannitti for talking too much, and given the latter's explicit comparison, in his speech, of the defendants to Christ, the poet implies that U.S. radicals are suffering the same fate for the same reason—and indeed, that they, and not the Christians who persecute them on religious grounds, are on the same side as Christ. Giovannitti deploys this religious rhetoric in his address to the jury: "[W]e are the apostles of a new evangel, of a new gospel," he proclaims. Their radical version of a social gospel is a "message of love" being preached by "Comrades of our same faith" in "other parts of the world,—every known tongue, in every civilized language, in every dialect" (8).

This polyglot preaching was precisely what Giovannitti had been doing at the time of his arrest, but whether or not the message was one of love is perhaps debatable. In Lawrence, Giovannitti found an outlet for his oratorical skills, and, as it happened, his poetry as well—sometimes in the same breath. Elizabeth Gurley Flynn, also a strike organizer, recalls tactics Ettor and Giovannitti employed: "Giovannitti . . . was a poet and a magnificent orator. . . . [Ettor] selected interpreters to bring order out of this veritable tower of Babel. . . . They held meetings of all the strikers together on the Lawrence Common (New England's term for park or square), so that workers could realize their oneness and strength. It was here one day that Giovannitti delivered his beautiful 'Sermon on the Common'" (117–18). Like much Wobbly poetry, the "Sermon on the Common" travesties a respected religious text, in this case, the Sermon on the Mount:

> Blessed are the strong in freedom's spirit: for theirs is
>   the kingdom of the earth.
> Blessed are they that mourn their martyred dead: for they shall
>   avenge them upon their murderers and be comforted.
> Blessed are the rebels: for they shall reconquer the earth. (73)

The "Sermon" in effect literalizes the inversion of gospel humility as well as the analogy between the poet and the Savior: through this poetic "conceit," Giovannitti makes himself a sort of socialist Christ literally addressing the new evangel to a new gathering of the nations. Giovannitti delivered poems as oratorical utterances in other political mass gatherings as well.[13]

This is not surprising, given the historical context. For readers of the 1910s (as in the mid- and late nineteenth century) poetry was efficacious. Poetry worked on a personal level and a social level at the same time. It was the vehicle for a soul to speak to another soul, and, by the same token, it could work spiritual change in the reader/recipient. This personal change, many believed, issued forth in social change. The proposition that poetry would have political effects or that the poet was also an organizer seemed somewhat less suspect in the 1910s than Allen Tate and company would attempt to make it in the 1930s; in the 1910s, published poetry was understood to have a public, social function (even when it acted on the individual).

This is a far cry from the mid-twentieth-century academy's separation of spheres between poetry and public speech; that distinction becomes reified, in the form we know it today, as a result of New Critical canons of taste. That is why everyone forgot Giovannitti and the historical moment he represents. But we must also remember that the New Critics did not invent out of whole cloth the dichotomy between rhetoric and poetry. The former became associated with Kant's *ars oratorica* (manipulative rhetoric), while only the latter, according to Kant, can guarantee a disinterested "free play of the imagination" (184). Indeed, several of Giovannitti's contemporary critics implicitly acknowledge this premise. But it is precisely the fluid boundary between literary and political discourse in the 1910s that challenges Kant's distinction between poetry and rhetoric/oratory and that allows for the poems' inclusion in propaganda and the critics' understanding of them as at once propagandistic and literary. That is, Kant's categories, whether invoked implicitly or explicitly, are never determinate when considered historically: they are categories of judgment —a faculty—not the objective social standards that early Agrarian/New Critics made of them. That is, it is Kant's very idealism that necessitates a critique of judgment in the first place.

But for many of Giovannitti's contemporaries, his poetry existed in both public and private spheres at once, as personal artistic expression and political manifesto. Louis Untermeyer, in his 1919 consideration of Giovannitti's poetry in *The New Era in American Poetry*, says that "The Walker" is, pace its author, "a poetic epitome of a creed, a movement that is both political and religious" (191). "If it is propaganda at all," the critic continues, "it is propaganda in the highest and most widespread sense of the word; it takes on the quality not so much of the Commune as of communion." In other words, the poems of Giovannitti (the former Presbyterian seminarian who turned atheist) may be "interested" politically but contain that numinous spirit of poetry that collapses party and division. The critic goes on to say of the poet that "all he has written, whether in the form of pamphlets or poems, has been done in 'an effort to express a multitude of men lost in an immensity of silence'" (*New Era* 185). In this statement, typical of artistic judgments sympathetic to the "new liberalism" of the 1900s and 1910s, pamphlet and poem provide different forms for the same expression, one that is at once political and poetical.

In the 1923 *American Poetry since 1900*, however, after the publication of "The Waste Land" and increased visibility of modernist poetics, Untermeyer revises his remarks by saying, "The poetry of Giovannitti rouses [*sic*] the problem of the relations of art and propaganda. Is Art, as many have claimed, cramped and distorted by the message? Or is the message weakened by Art?" "The propagandist in Giovannitti," concludes Untermeyer, "sometimes plays traitor to Giovannitti, the poet, but in his longer poems the balance is nicely adjusted" (276). Five years earlier, poetry and propaganda seemed indistinguishable, and the difference, for Untermeyer, irrelevant with regard to Giovannitti. In 1923, the proponents of art sans propaganda and propaganda sans art are two forces that cannot be ignored or merged but only balanced: "The answer . . . lies somewhere between the two replies demanded by the interrogations of the two factions" (276).[14] In the 1920s, a central ground between "the two factions" was easier to find than it would be by the 1930s. But there were more than two options with regard to poetry and politics in 1912 — or even, as we shall see, in 1921.

CHAPTER FIVE

Poetry as Crossing: The Newspaper Verse of Anise (Anna Louise Strong)

In the 1910s, elements of avant-garde and popular writing styles not only existed side by side but sometimes merged within the same works. Indeed, one of the reasons this decade is such an exciting moment in retrospect is that it is not always possible to draw sharp distinctions between poetry, journalism, religious writing, propaganda, graphic art, and humorous writing—because several of these modes may describe any given work. In this respect, the 1910s have much to teach us, not only about what poetry might have become, but also about later decades (such as the 1990s) in which the lines between poetry and other genres and media (acting, popular music, video, computer art) once again became especially blurry or unstable; indeed, this undecidability could suggest possibilities for sites and techniques for poetry in the future.

Particularly illustrative in these respects is the early work of poet, journalist, and revolutionary Anna Louise Strong (1885–1970).[1] Her biographers, Tracy Strong Jr. and Helene Keyssar, write that Anna Louise Strong's poems display an "assertive, unmannered style" (70); "[u]nabashedly derivative," they "drew with equal ease from religious sources, well-known literary works and contemporary events" (72). By way of contrast, Cary Nelson believes that Strong's poems "represent a key moment in the development of modernism and in its extension to a working-class audience" (86–87). Both Nelson's argument and Strong and Keyssar's are accurate: Anna Louise Strong's writing does mark a key moment in the development of modern poetry, and it is also largely derivative. This strange combination was not as unusual in the 1910s and 1920s as it would seem for later generations.

Strong's writing suggests an expansive, hybrid notion of poetry—not the romantico-modernist notion of Poetry as pure aesthetic (not to mention ethical and cultural) Value but an impure assortment of different sorts of values.[2] Strong's medium allowed her access to effects foreclosed by the generic boundaries of either "theory" or "poetry." Her poems, as both journalistic and literary productions, combine effects of propaganda and of art-writing, critique and idealization, commitment and uncertainty. Strong's feature "Ragged Verse," which appeared daily under the pen name "Anise" in the *Seattle Union-Record* newspaper from 1918 to 1921, combined several traditions in U.S. letters—social protest, newspaper verse, satire, and avant-garde technique.

These generic crossings are especially important in that they allowed Strong an entrée into public debate and a means of participation in the labor movement that few women possessed at that time. Strong combined aspects of two historically feminized genres, poetry and features journalism, to create a new medium and an oppositional voice for herself as a woman writer operating in a traditionally masculinized public sphere.

By the same token, Strong's verses reconceptualize the relation of poetry to the public by using the former to imagine multiple, overlapping, and competing public spheres. The ending and aftermath of World War I was also a moment of political transition and instability, in which pub-

The Newspaper Verse of Anise

Anna Louise Strong, c. 1913.
Manuscripts, Special Collections,
University Archives Division,
University of Washington Libraries,
Seattle, negative no. UW 340

licness included "an unstable mixture of different types of publicity" and was "a site of discursive contestation for and among multiple, diverse, and unequal constituencies."[3] Strong's verses smudge the sharp classical distinction between unitary public and private spheres, between private, individual reflection and collective public rhetoric. I have argued that canonical modernist poetics represents a classical liberal reaction against the newer social liberalism of the twentieth century, as well as illiberal political-cultural tendencies. Accordingly, modernist poetics, while very interested in a public role for poetry, tends to disavow that role and to reclaim a sharply demarcated private sphere. Strong, by contrast, propels private concerns into public and claims poetry for an oppositional, "proletarian" counterpublic sphere.

The significance of this intervention becomes apparent by looking at the changes in Strong's poetry in the decade before the "Ragged Verse" was composed. Anna Louise Strong self-published her first two poetry books in the decade of the 1900s. In February 1907, when Strong was a Ph.D. student at the University of Chicago, *Current Literature* bestowed rather faint praise on her second volume of poems, *The Song of the City*. The book is part of the long tradition of social protest verse written in conventional form and published in literary milieus. For instance, the reviewer quotes "Tenement Back Yards":

> Close by the elevated the worst of the back-yards lie,
> Barren, desolate spaces under an ashen sky,
> Bottles and boxes and papers and pieces of glass and tin,
> And rotted boards of fencing that shut the scrap-heap in.

Into this unappealing landscape, a stanza later, comes, as the reviewer puts it, "the poetic sense of life":

> For over the dust and ashes roll surges of conquering life,
> Life and the glory of living, the joy and the pain and the strife,
> Love and the faith of loving, and wan hope's fitful gleams;
> Ay, even the lost are haunted by the pallid beauty of dreams.
>   (Strong, "Tenement" 199–200)

The rather naturalistic sense of Chicago's South Side is redeemed for Poetry and the ideality it represents for contemporary readers, as the poem moves (in dactylic pentameter) from a catalog of the material ugliness of ghetto life to abstract nouns and "the pallid beauty of dreams." While the 1907 poems imply a denunciation of the forces that produce ghetto life and substandard working conditions, they do not make that point explicit; rather, their silver lining recoups misfortune through a very old poetics of sympathy. In this movement, the poem conforms to the project of Hull House (where Strong lived during this period), in that it makes the tenement area a topic of fit contemplation in liberal, bourgeois magazine poetry.

Strong's work appears again on the national scene in 1917, when *Current Opinion* reprinted the free-verse poem "The Woman Speaks." The editors aptly remark of the poem, which had initially appeared in the New

York *Evening Mail*, "here is an unusual poem to be found in a daily paper." Domestic love, the speaker fears,

> fetters a man,
> With iron driven through his heart and the heart of his dearest,
> So that he no longer springs gladly to battle
> Against intrenched wrong.

How can love "Cease to be for us an enemy," she asks, and

> How shall I give what I have to give,
> Whether to many lovers or one only,
> Joy without dishonor,
> And the comfort of woman without bondage?

Love itself is "an enslavement" that can consume a man with and bind him within the domestic. Subsequent events suggest that this poem coincides with a decision by Strong to avoid such enslavement herself by pursuing a life of public service rather than a traditional domestic role as either wife or poet.[4]

Concomitantly, the poem also marks a formal textual change for Strong's writing. Although it is not unlike her earlier work, and would be recognizable to most readers as Poetry by, for instance, its elaborate metaphors and personification of love, at the same time, its unconventional sentiments, confessional quality, free verse, and more direct, conversational tone mark the influence of the New Poetry.[5] A formally similar poem from the same year, "In Court," sets up a contrast not unlike that in Giovannitti's "The Cage":

> The age-long contrast,
> Here in the quiet, stuffy court-room,
>
> . . . .
>
> The placid judge rocking back and forth in his leather chair,
> High above conflict,
> Sustaining and over-ruling, watching the clock for the times of recess
>
> . . . .

> The witness,
> A bronzed, sturdy logger just in from the woods,
> Breathing the unhurried, solid calm of the old forests,
> Earth-born, earth-nourished, taught in the ways of earth,
> Untaught in the nervous thinking of civilization . . .[6]

In both poems, Strong has gone beyond genteel form and diction as well as social gospel politics.

Indeed, the late 1910s marked a time of rapid transformation for Strong, not only stylistically, but personally as well. Her newfound socialism and consequent reassessment of the causes of poverty led her, in 1916, to abandon her post as an organizer with the National Child Labor Committee in Chicago, when she also joined her widowed father in Seattle. In the process, she had abandoned a third career (having been an academic and then a religious journalist), most of her religious devotion, and the Social Gospel. When Strong arrived in Seattle, she moved into a city full of political ferment and possibility. She was elected to the school board; over time, she became familiar with radical unionists, pacifists, anarchists, and others whose friendship with her was largely unknown to respectable Seattle. When she appeared as a defense witness at the 1917 sedition trial of her friend Louise Olivereau, who was accused of circulating an anticonscription tract, it became known that Strong had been writing pseudonymously for the socialist newssheet, the *Seattle Daily Call*. All of these facts led local conservatives to brand her a "Bolshevik" and to lead a successful recall campaign against her in March 1918.

Strong's writing in 1917 and 1918 evinces the disparate influences that would later go into making her verses during 1918 to 1921. The antirecall campaign reprinted her poem "City Comradeship" (1907) as part of a handbill. The poem ends:

> Face on face in the city, and where shall our fortunes fall?
> Face on face in the city,—my heart goes out to you all.
> See, we labor together, is not the bond divine?
> Lo, the strength of the city is built of your lives and mine.

The Newspaper Verse of Anise

The reverse side reprints "My Country's Share," with the note: "Dedicated to President Wilson, as an effort to express the ideal he has uttered for my country."[7] In the meantime, unbeknownst to the voters, Strong was writing politically radical free verse as well as satirical rhyming ballads for the *Seattle Daily Call*—albeit not with her name attached.

Shortly after the recall, the *Daily Call*'s printing presses were wrecked by "a gang of 'patriots'" (Strong and Keyssar 69), and in April 1918, Strong went to work for the *Seattle Union Record,* which became the nation's first labor daily at the same time. At this point, Strong moved her poetry out of both the parlor and the bourgeois public sphere[8] and used it, instead, to imagine a proletarian public sphere where the two were to be less distinct—as, too, was the generic and social status of her writing. At the *Union Record,* Strong wrote daily poems that were collected, later in that same year, in the volume *Ragged Verse*. The title distinguishes her new work from the polished poetry that she had attempted previously (and that was fashionable at the time) and associates her poems instead with the ragged workers who were their intended audience. Indeed, the "Ragged Verse" was as much an aesthetic as a political statement; Strong anticipates what leftist Chilean poet Nicanor Parra later would call "antipoesia" —a writing that borrows traits historically associated with Poetry while rejecting that title and everything it represents.

"The Woman Speaks" had appeared in August 1917. As soon thereafter as July 1918, in the poem "What's Money, Anyway?" money had displaced love as the hindrance to action in the world:

Is it the prize method
 $ $ $
For TYING MEN
 $ $ $
With a SETTLED HOME,
 $ $ $
And a SETTLED JOB,
 $ $ $
And a SETTLED WAY
 $ $ $
Of LIVING?
. . . . . .
But when folks say
 $ $ $
They need money to be
 $ $ $

INDEPENDENT
$ $ $
That's just FUNNY.
$ $ $
I guess they need money
$ $ $
To be TAME
. $ $ $

And TIED.
$ $ $
And to bring up FAMILIES,
$ $ $
And other things
$ $ $
The WORLD wants.
(*Ragged Verse* 25)[9]

These are reflections on a man who exemplifies the Wobbly hobo—moving from job to job, talking to men in jails, to congressmen "who should have been there," and to artists "who might be there some day." Such poems indicate that her new style and venue allowed for considerably more latitude and unpredictability, and a more explicitly political edge, than her writing evinced until then.

This shift in voice and concerns—from Anna Louise to Anise—also signals a changing relation between the speaking subject(s) of the poems and a changed understanding of the public spaces they engage. When the editors of *Current Opinion* introduced Strong's "The Woman Speaks," they remarked, "The writer . . . has the one requisite of success as a poet—the ability to put her own (we cannot doubt that it is her own) deepest experience into metrical expression" (123). Poetry here is sincere and personal: "[W]e cannot doubt that it is her own . . . deepest experience." By contrast, "Anise" rejects the familiar turn-of-the-century notion of poetry as the sincere and sententious expression of a multilayered yet self-possessed subject. Rather, Anise is at once a nom de plume, a nom de guerre, and a character in the poems. As a politicized woman writer, Strong faced the continuing exclusion of women from the discourse of universality, from the freedom needed to participate in disinterested debate in the bourgeois public sphere, and from the "free" production of art. Unlike male poets of the same period, the development of a public personality for a woman, one that would shape the reception of her poems, was decidedly dangerous (as, for instance, Amy Lowell's experience testified).

The Newspaper Verse of Anise

The Anise persona is more a nose-thumbing gesture than actual "cover" for a woman recently pilloried for her political views, whom the Seattle establishment had attempted to shame into silence by subjection to a gendered public scrutiny. Anise is a contraction of Anna Louise; Strong does not discuss her choice of pen name, but it may have struck her ears as somewhat foreign sounding. In the midst of Red scares and spy scares, this may have been the desired effect and, given Strong's parodic sense of humor, may have been a dig at the paranoia of nativist, nationalist city fathers. The Anise persona is a sort of female flaneur, roaming the city as both subversive voyeur and reporter. Many poems record overheard private conversations, either actual or staged. In one piece, for instance, two "Employers of labor" having lunch lament that prohibition hasn't made workers more reliable—in fact, now they spend their money more slowly. That a businessman could imagine his "private" comments parodied by a woman in print the next day gives these poems the context that can make satire dangerous. Likewise, other poems lampoon the power elite of the city, as in the 1918 "Why Have Lawyers, Anyway":

The SEATTLE LAWYERS
   ? ? ?
Are talking of
   ? ? ?
Discouraging DISLOYALTY
   ? ? ?
By REFUSING to
   ? ? ?
DEFEND anyone
   ? ? ?
CHARGED WITH SEDITION
. . . .
(It is one of these IDEAS
   ? ? ?

So GRAND
   ? ? ?
And yet so SIMPLE
   ? ? ?
That it takes a LAWYER to
   ? ? ?
THINK OF IT).
   ? ? ?
Why not discourage
   ? ? ?
ALL CRIME
   ? ? ?
By refusing to defend anyone
   ? ? ?

Charged with ANY CRIME
    ? ? ?
At all?
    ? ? ?
And then
    ? ? ?
All those EXTRA LAWYERS
    ? ? ?
Can go to the
    ? ? ?
FRONT LINE TRENCHES
    ? ? ?
Where their country
    ? ? ?
REALLY NEEDS THEM.
    (*Ragged Verse* 7)

Like many other Anise verses, this one "talks back" to the official wartime discourse by taking it to its illogical (yet funny) conclusion. The scrappy, wisecracking "Anise," though a very thin mask, is nonetheless an effective character.

Strong attempts, in both her poetry and persona, to imagine and contribute to the creation of a counterpublic in which "the woman speaks." For instance, during the February 1919 general strike in Seattle, the *Union Record* published "They Can't Understand," later reproduced as a handbill:

It is your SMILE
    * * *
That is UPSETTING
    * * *
Their reliance
    * * *
On ARTILLERY, brother!
  . . . . . .
It is the milk stations
    * * *
That are getting better daily,
    * * *
And the three hundred
    * * *
WAR Veterans of Labor
    * * *
Handling the crowds
    * * *
WITHOUT GUNS,
    * * *
for these things speak
    * * *
Of a NEW POWER
    * * *
And a NEW WORLD
    * * *
That they do not feel
    * * *
At HOME in.
    (History Committee 2)

Anise takes the liberty of directly addressing union brothers here in order to interpret their collective experience—one that isn't shared by the capitalists and their papers. Since the *Union Record* had as many as 100,000 subscribers at this time, the potential audience for the verses was quite large. In addition, several other poems were reprinted as handbills and broadsides. Indeed, there is reason to believe that the *Union Record*'s audience read Anise's verses avidly and appreciated them immensely. Earl Shimmons, Tacoma bureau chief of the paper and a bitter enemy of Strong, wrote that "when Anise' ragged verse failed to appear on the editorial page there was an avalanche of letters from the discontented, demanding to know whether the Union Record had 'sold out.'"[10] Numerous letters to the paper praised her verse as "[b]eloved by thousands—yes and ten, of women, children, and honest workingmen."[11]

As Strong wrote these verses, her stated view of artists and art generally began to change. By February of 1919, she would write, "[A] fiery, brilliant youth, poet and revolutionist, and yet a revolutionist whose poetry has nothing to do with revolution—such is Max Eastman. . . . Even Eastman's latest book, 'Colors of Life,' contains so little trace of revolution, and so much passionate adoration of beauty and love that it is hard to connect the writer with the daring and witty orator of Saturday and Sunday in the Labor Temple" (18 Feb. 1919). Eastman's separation of spheres between poet and orator, between fiery public revolutionist and youth who passionately adores beauty as a private individual, seemed contradictory to the more radicalized Strong. She ends the article with poems by Eastman that celebrate, respectively, the coming of April and Isadora Duncan's dance. These "bourgeois" lyrics might have seemed a bit embarrassing to present in a union daily; Strong accordingly introduces them with a bit of tongue-in-cheek coaxing to readers of her own poems (one appears next to the article): "Editor's note: Adjust your mind for a complete change. We will try to make it as gradual as possible, by starting with a poem to Lenin."

But this editor's note could also serve as a preface to Strong's own work. She had abandoned the wrought poetry of the sort she (or Eastman) had admired in her twenties, shifted the sites in which her poems appeared and the audience that would read them, and squandered whatever cultural capital she had accrued.[12] That is, the shift in the *textual* form of her writing, from mannered free verse to a more "experimental" style, coincides with her experiments in the *social* form of poetry—its potential uses and locations as a medium of communication and cultural-political interaction.

However, the shift in form was not from social poetry of the Edwardian twilight to a high modernist poetics of disinterested, objectified technique. Rather, Anise develops something like an antimodernist modernism—if we limit modernism (as poetry critics typically do) to the sort of performatively reactionary aesthetic ideology espoused by Pound, Eliot, or Allen Tate. Rather, the Anise poems utilize *techniques* identified then and now with "modernism": abrupt transitions that mimic sometimes fluid or meandering thought processes; typographical collages or mobiles; wordplay or reflexive language; short lines, compact diction, and "Imagistic" plainness; line-breaks across syntactical units; and the attempt to both embody and critique modernity. But in the process, she employs these techniques in a leftist union newspaper, using them for political ends in a way that complicates the still-dominant high modernist narrative. Strong was aware of such contexts for avant-garde writing; in 1921, as she headed eastward toward Poland and Russia, she wrote that "[Lincoln] Steffens was in Berlin and introduced me to the head of the Theater Guild, New York, who was interested in what I told him about certain cubist plays in Moscow."[13]

Strong's verses don't look particularly formally innovative in retrospect. But blue-collar readers in the western city of Seattle (the verses' actual audience) might not have seen it that way in 1918. This audience, used to seeing newspaper poetry of the sort Strong had written ten years previously, might have found the look of the Anise poems a bit hard to get used to. This does not make Anise into H.D., but why would it? The two wrote poems for very different audiences.

But why would she want to adopt these formal features in the context of a union newspaper? I would suggest that, at a moment when new textual and social forms for poetry emerged and when old ones were still popular, Strong found in the practices of avant-garde poets a largely underdetermined space that allowed for a hybridization of different forms of writing. This crossing of modes allowed the voice(s) of "Anise" a greater freedom and room for play than Anna Louise Strong enjoyed as either a traditional poet or an editorialist. For this reason, whatever the verses' interest as literature today, they are of decided interest for literary history.

The physical appearance of Anise's poems indicates this influence. Anise uses capitalization, as Cary Nelson says, "sometimes to honor terms she values, sometimes to mock concepts we take for granted that she wants to deride, and sometimes for simple emphasis" (86); but I think we might also say that she uses this technique, along with very short lines separated by dingbats, as a way to defamiliarize terms, ideas, situations. The capitalized words have the effect of headlines (sometimes the word "headlines" is capitalized) or of poster captions or signs. Or, as in "A Sad Story" (figure 1), the caps form a little poem imbricated within the more discursive text:

EDITOR DO NOT SEND ANY MORE TOO BUSY WORK WAR GARDEN MEETINGS TIME PAPERS MINUTES STREET-CARS SEAT GOING COMING STANDING YOUR PAPER READ IT LABOR AGES WORKING EXTRA FOOD ISN'T TIME ENERGY EDUCATED SPOILED INCONVENIENCES SHORT HOURS BODIES THINKING APPARATUS TIME DOING PLAN

Like some dadaist or futurist poems in the same form (or Bob Brown's "readies"), this poem-within-a-poem embodies acceleration, mechanization, and the arbitrary effect produced by decontextualization. In this poem, capitalized words also "telegraph" the gist of the poem; it contains a critique of the "basis . . . of any democracy" that grows oxymorons like "WAR GARDENS," reduces people to bodies, or turns them into a "THINKING APPARATUS." In other poems, capitalized words pro-

POETRY AND THE PUBLIC

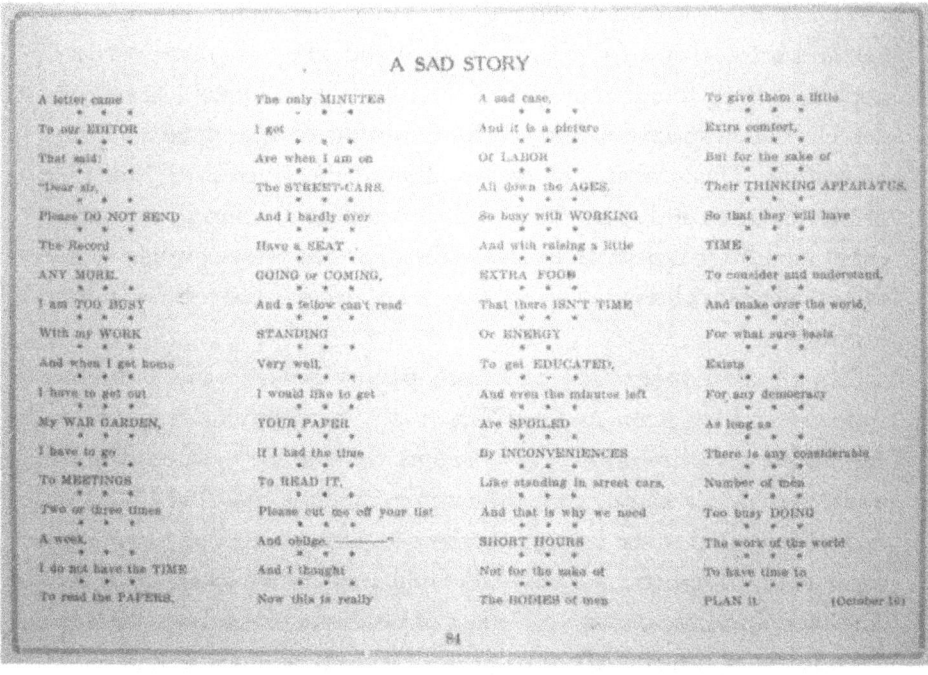

Figure 1. "A Sad Story," as it appears in *Ragged Verse by Anise* (1918)

duce meanings that work against those produced by the syntactic chain of the entire text or that throw terms into harsh relief. The lineation and layout have the effect of preventing the verse from being read in the same way as editorial prose—by breaking up the text spatially, building a little verbal suspense or undercutting expectations, and allowing for time to take in each unit of meaning or syntactical bite.

These techniques, along with the then "modern" fashion of compact, unadorned language, may have appealed to an already shortened attention span. Many of the poems borrow tricks from popular print culture. Dollar signs, question marks, exclamation points, or asterisks grab readers' attention, slow them down, break up an already brief utterance into moments reminiscent of cartoon frames or frames of a film.[14] In "Little Lessons in Advertising," Anise avers that the chief of police is publicizing the IWW through his attempts to suppress it. "It doesn't take / BRAINS,"

The Newspaper Verse of Anise

But just a few
    ! ! !
POLICEMEN
    ! ! !
And a JAIL,
    ! ! !
Stir in a few
    ! ! !
WOBBLIES,
    ! ! !
And add
    ! ! !
Some newspaper HEADLINES

    ! ! !
And a dime-novel tale
    ! ! !
About SPIKES in logs
  . . . . .
    ! ! !
Presto! 'Tis done!
    ! ! !
Two wobblies grow
    ! ! !
Where ONE grew before.
    (*Ragged Verse* 5)

The dingbats, caps, and diction mimic the very sort of advertising layout and copy that was employed in the paper itself—even as it is clear that the poems themselves are advertising ideas (figures 2 and 3).

But especially when read aloud, the poems make everyday speech seem a bit strange, as when Ferdinand of Bulgaria says of the Kaiser,

He is GOING TO WIN,
    * * *
And WE want to be
    * * *
On the WINNING SIDE. (79)

One may well wonder at this point who "we" are and what a "winning side" means in such a war. When the Bulgars free

All the PACIFISTS
    * * *
Who had been put in
    * * *

FOR LIFE
    * * *
By Ferdinand,

Figure 2. An advertisement in the *Seattle Union-Record*, 15 November 1919. Note use of capitals and question marks.

the "pacifists'" crime becomes "life," or they go to jail on behalf of life, as well as receiving life sentences. The poems often produce the auditory effect of a news broadcast read by Laurie Anderson,[15] and indeed the poems parodied the messages the wire services conveyed in a similar form.

Moreover, these editorial poems allow for a degree of ambivalence, ambiguity, pessimism, and mischievousness that the standard editorial does not. In "Poverty and Progress," Anise relates that five years of bad crops, mortgages, and foreclosures turned Oklahoma farmers into so-

The Newspaper Verse of Anise

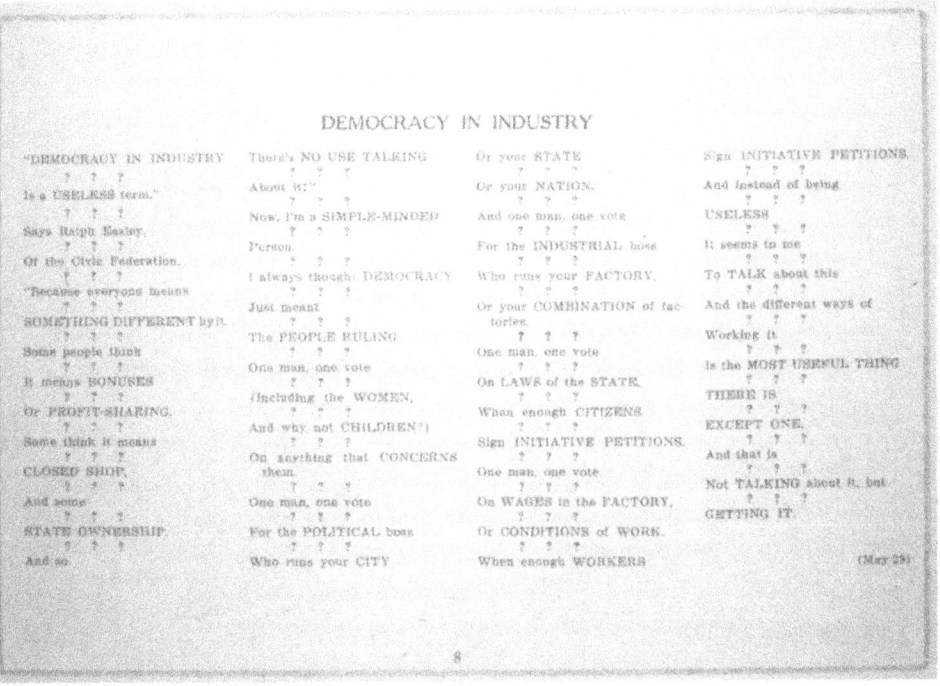

Figure 3. "Democracy in Industry," originally published in the *Seattle Union-Record*, 29 May 1918. Note use of capitals and question marks, as in advertisement (figure 2).

cialist tenant farmers. "Then last year / Was a year of / BUMPER CROPS," she goes on to say, so that now all the "RED-HOT RADICALS" have money to found a socialist paper. She concludes by saying:

"God moves in a
    $ $ $
Mysterious way
    $ $ $
His wonders to perform."
    $ $ $
But I can't help wondering

    $ $ $
Whether they won't soon stop
    $ $ $
PROGRESSING
    $ $ $
Now that they have MONEY!
    (*Ragged Verse* 20)

Rather than presenting agitprop, this poem muses, rather cynically, on the power of capital to dissipate anticapitalist sentiment. "Now Begins

Work" echoes this pessimism. The speaker reads of socialist revolts in Austria, of the imminent demise of the Kaiser, the Red Flag flying in Vienna and over labor temples in Australia,

And I wanted to start
* * *
CHEERING,
* * *

And say: "It is here
* * *
AT LAST,"

until she remembers the story of "the aged Russian exile" who goes home to die "In a contented Russia, / In the heart of his family," only to be told by the soldiers that

"NOW BEGINS WORK!"
* * *
Now begins MORE fighting,
* * *
And MORE dying.
* * *
You old ones cannot understand
* * *
That the job

* * *
Is NOT FINISHED.
* * *
Are there not
* * *
ENEMIES WITHOUT,
* * *
And TRAITORS WITHIN?"
(*Ragged Verse* 100)

While the *Union Record* generally takes a favorable attitude toward the Bolsheviki, these poems give Strong a place to express conflicting emotions, impulses, and perceptions exacerbated by the uncertainty fostered by stories and rumors from Europe.

I would not, however, suggest that typography or ambivalence make Anise a modernist—at least not by any current conventional definition. Rather, she produces a hybrid poetics that merges elements of modernism (writ large) with other traditions. For example, the voice of the "Anise" persona is as much an attempt to attain and maintain a broad audience as it is an attempt to embody a particular politics or aesthetics. The same could be said of the then-popular newspaper poems of Walt Mason or T. A. Daly. In fact, the poems of Anise may have as much in common with humorous newspaper verse or protest poems of the progressive era as with newer poetic movements. And radical women unionists were not the only ones to publish such verse; Philip Foner quotes a poem called "Keep the Girls off the Cars," published in *Motorman and Conductor* in August 1918, when the federal government moved to continue the wartime employment of women as conductors and brakepersons (?) on streetcars:

We wonder where we are drifting, where is the freedom of the stripes and stars
If for the sake of greed and profit we put women conductors on the cars.
Woman is God's most tender flower, made to blossom and to bear
To keep our homes, raise our children, and our joys and sorrows share. (204)

For rhetorical effect, the poem merges several common aspects of popular poetry: the patriotic ode, the idealization of domesticated womanhood (associated since at least the early nineteenth century with the genre of poetry), and the denunciation of perceived social injustice (in this case the fear that women workers would drive down wages for men). Fortunately, not all political poetry from the 1910s is quite so solemn—or cynical, as the case may be. From 1914 to 1917, Alice Duer Miller wrote a column, "Are Women People?" for the *New York Tribune*. The poem "Selfish Creatures," like many by Anise, takes the form of a conversation between a first-person speaker and a worker:

> I stopped to ask a scrub-woman
>   "Why labor like a man?
> You cannot feed your children? Well,
>   There must be some one can."
> She said: "I merely work because
>   I need a feather fan." (Dresner 34)

Miller's verses form part of a widespread use of newspaper verse, often as part of columns, to lampoon dominant ideas or to establish new modes of debate. This was a poetry that thumbed its nose at Poetry and at those with pretensions to patrician culture. Such humorous poetry

POETRY AND THE PUBLIC

flourished throughout the "modernist period" much as it had in the 1890s and, as much as modernism, it influenced Anise.

For example, in "The Spy Never Sleeps," "Dr. William Otis / At the university" attempts to generate paranoia and suspicion of German Americans. Anise looks about the lecture hall trying to pick out the spies and then begins to get suspicious of her neighbors:

But then I remembered
! ! !
How the sign says
! ! !
In the street car,
! ! !
"The SPY NEVER SLEEPS,"
! ! !
And I know
! ! !
The Man NEXT DOOR
! ! !
SLEEPS
! ! !
Because I can HEAR HIM
! ! !
Sometimes.
! ! !
So I felt SAFER
! ! !
About him.
! ! !
But how does THE SPY
! ! !
Manage to be so lively
! ! !
Without ever resting
! ! !
Like us others?
! ! !
I'm sure no good American
! ! !
Could do it.
! ! !
It must be some more
! ! !
Of the thing they call
! ! !
GERMAN EFFICIENCY.
(*Ragged Verse* 29)

In this instance, exclamation points mimic the panic generating and generated by neighborhood spying; caps mock the pomposity of prowar sloganeering; and through the joke the critique is easy to get. The reader is thereby invited to view official public space and speech critically and askance—and enjoy it.

While many newspaper poets specialized in such mockery or buffoonery, others (who often appeared in the same papers) express what David Perkins calls an "unashamed frankness of sentiment" (90). For instance, the conservative commercial daily *Seattle Post-Intelligencer* published such verse; these poems typically appear in small print at the bottom of the editorial or magazine/features pages. In the case of the editorial page, the verses have nothing to do with the prose that surrounds them; the verse, in effect, offers a little oasis in the midst of economic conflict, wars, and rumors of war. Sometimes they comfort, sometimes entertain, sometimes edify; they offer the reader a private space slightly apart from, and slightly more elevated than, the world of business or the cares of running a household. "Poetry," so positioned, served as a synecdoche for "Culture," that is, high culture. As Perkins notes, in a nation questioning its identity under the pressures of "frontier violence, a flood of arriving immigrants, rapid growth of large cities . . . the huge frauds and cunning of the robber barons, and the garish luxury of the gilded rich" (94), poetry might compensate or even "be a corrective, a formative influence on readers and, through them, on society as a whole" (95).[16]

Those very problems form the material of Strong's poetry. At the same time, however, she sometimes addressed them in a serious, utopian, or inspirational mode, even while retaining the typography, diction, and politics that characterize the ragged verses. But poems in this case no longer offer a framed experience *in* but not *of* the paper; here the separation of spheres between private contemplation and public affairs dissolves. In one, for instance, the poet finds herself above the city, witnessing a Wordsworthian symbol:

The cloud lifted a moment,
    * * *
White and majestic and ghostly
    * * *
THE MOUNTAIN
    * * *
Offered itself to our gaze
    * * *

And we sent up a shout
    * * *
Forgetting the chill and the damp
    * * *
Because we had seen
    * * *
THE VISION.
    (*Ragged Verse* 36)

This scene resembles one limned by Mrs. H. A. Waite in the *Post-Intelligencer* in her poem "The Mountain That Was God: Mount Rainier at Sunset":

> Pearly white, O glorious mountain,
>   With thy dome against the blue,
> Thou hast stood for countless ages
>   Unsurpassed in form and hue. (29 Aug. 1911)

However, Strong's mountain becomes a symbol of the vision of a new earth; it stands by impassively as the industrialist Schwab returns from a banquet with his retinue of autos "HURRYING / Through THE FOG." If the symbol, the tone, and the sentiment are familiar, the Anise poem weds them to a utopian social energy. Even when Anise's poems make no direct reference to events in the news, they nonetheless do so indirectly by appeal to teleology or to collective values.

In this process, Strong did to poetry what she did to prose: she adapted both traditional and innovative textual forms to the interests of a local proletarian counterpublic sphere in which women were to be seen and heard. As a journalist and organizer, Strong had considerable experience gearing analysis, theory, and history to what she conceived to be the needs of a broad readership interested in union and working-class issues. For instance, the *Union Record* staff came into possession of a Rand School pamphlet version of Lenin's 1918 address to the Congress of Soviets. Strong describes the use she made of it:

> [W]e promptly reprinted it for popular circulation among workers. We discarded Tractenberg's scholarly foreword with its puzzling explanations about Mensheviks and Social Revolutionaries and other people who didn't seem to matter, and inserted a foreword of our own which I innocently and blithely wrote, explaining in vivid, simple terms that this document was a "description of the problems faced by a working-class government on coming to power," and therefore should be read by all workers who expected to take power. I also added "headlines" above each paragraph, summarizing their contents in short phrases so that workers, accustomed to reading

newspaper headlines, might quickly grasp what each section described. (*I Change Worlds* 68)

Strong here excises any material that doesn't seem to matter to the immediate local situation. Speed and ease in reading become cardinal virtues. The method was a success, as twenty thousand copies sold out in the Northwest, and other organizations reprinted the document whole and sold another twenty thousand copies; "for some time," Strong says, "these little pamphlets were seen by hundreds on Seattle's street cars and ferries, read by men of the shipyards on their way to work" (68). That is, by reformatting the work, addressing it to a different audience for a different purpose, and using new distribution channels, Strong changed the presentation context of Lenin's speech, altered its social form, and turned it into a new medium.

 Strong produces a similarly unexpected transformation in poetry. The ragged verses make news stories into something more strange, funny, or outrageous than they are as a dry, conventional relation of that which is new in public affairs. Strong reconfigures poetry "for popular circulation among workers"; if the verses turn difficult topics into something innocent and blithe, they also propagate theory and make it palpable and compelling. Finally, the brevity of the poems and of the lines, the emphases in the text, and the simplicity of the language make for ease of apprehension. This final point can be accounted for with a 1 April 1919 article entitled "What the Women Want." It offered working women's self-representations of their experiences of reading—or lack thereof: "We interviewed 25 girls picked at random in shop and office. Many said they had no time to read anything; when they did read they wanted something amusing. Most of their spare time, they said, was spent in taking care of their clothes or other work at home." Not only do these observations confirm those in "A Sad Story," they also help to explain the reflexive language, punctuation, and playfulness of the texts. These flourishes are not simply part of a new literary concern with the materiality of language, but rather add to the pleasure of the text, its entertainment value—and this value counted for a lot in a feature in the *Union Record*.

This desire to draw readers, especially women readers, may also explain why, when editor Harry Ault recognized Strong's talents and offered her any job she wanted with the paper, she chose the features editorship. "Features" or "magazine" pages in their early days typically included humor, poems, "human interest" stories, and advice columns; in some papers, these features were included in the "women's," "society," or "home" page. This journalistic innovation did not become widespread, however, until popularized by Joseph Pulitzer in his *New York World* (Marzolf 205–6); in this respect, the features page came into being at the same time and from the same source as the muckraking New Journalism, and both represented part of a wider trend to reconfigure "news" to attract a wider and more diverse audience—in this case, one that included women readers.

However, historian Marion Marzolf reports that such sections did not pass without criticism from the intelligentsia: "'Don't talk to me about the Advancement of Women as long as any newspaper has a woman's Page,' snorted one of [Pulitzer's] female friends. 'The Spectator' . . . agreed that the women's pages were 'a hopeless case.' He found them an insult to intelligent women, filled as they were with recipes for removing sunburn and freckles, menus for a household of six at 50 cents a day, fashion 'dots and doings,' sunshine poetry and advice to young mothers" (207). Yet in the late nineteenth and early twentieth centuries, women journalists typically found themselves doing just such stories (205). The features section formed a sort of domestic space within the story of public affairs told by the paper as a whole; in the features page, women's publishing was somehow less public, and women reporters were sequestered from the world of politics and restricted to speaking to other women.

Strong's version of the feature story, however, violates this textual separation of spheres (and genres) by moving into the editorial section at the same time that it maintains the capaciousness and flexibility of the features format. Indeed, Strong wrote editor Harry Ault that her "plan would be flexible, and would give me considerable freedom in planning and executing," even to the extent of taking over some local news stories.[17] Features writing allowed her access to a body of material that the front page would not have supplied: "Most revolutionary news thus came in my province, for little of it arrived by cable. It came by chance lecturers, by men escaped across borders; it was dug out of letters, translated from pamphlets or culled from illegal bulletins which drifted to us [from] across the world" (*I Change Worlds* 67). The most important news, Strong suggests, may not come over the wires and may not fit into copybook form. The speakers she reports on and interviews "dealt in picturesque anecdote and practical success," the same material treated by many of the verses.

Accordingly, instead of writing sunshine poetry, Anise uses her features-page poems as license to expand what counts as news and to allow herself more latitude in how she may treat that news. The poems elevate marginalia, unsubstantiated report, eyewitness account, illicit propaganda, hearsay, rumor, anecdote, personal feelings, and experience to the status of journalism. Yet such material is, unlike rational disinterested debate in the classical public sphere, admissible in writing that is a "feature" and a poem rather than a news story or official editorial. So for Anise, "stories" from her and her readers' everyday lives form as important a current of current events as does news of wars and strikes; from the point of view of unionists, the elevator operator or shop woman who won't unionize are the most important newsmakers, because they make or break strikes.

Many poems recount the speaker's reaction to a conversation she has had or has overheard, or to an experience from her day. She then relates this experience to that of women generally, the Seattle community at large, or to the worldwide community of working-class people. In "Left Behind," Anise reports on two conversations. In one, "a woman of fifty" asks Anise if she knows

["]Where WOMAN'S PLACE is?"	* * *
* * *	"Woman's place
"Why yes," I laughed,	* * *

is IN CONGRESS!" "The KITCHEN," she said,
* * * * * *
She was DEEPLY PAINED. "The KITCHEN!"
* * * (*Ragged Verse* 59)

Anise argues that the other woman has to work in a shop because no man will support her, and that even women who do work in the home need representation "To get pure food / And good water." Anise has to assure the reader:

Now this Even if you can't
* * * * * *
Is a TRUE story, BELIEVE IT.
* * *

Here the poet/person-on-the-street thematizes the news that isn't news. That people "HUG / THEIR OWN CHAINS" is not news, in that it is not novel nor are the people involved "public figures." But the fact that it is true but unbelievable makes it news. Anise concludes that it all goes to show that

The SURVIVAL * * *
* * * Of folks like that)
Of the FITTEST * * *
* * * TAKES TIME!
(Which will get rid

This "analysis" is also a call to join a movement rather than be "left behind" as an individual.

In this manner, Strong, in a moment of generic and political instability, simultaneously drew upon two historically "feminized" genres in order to allow for more flexibility, even as she subverted and revised the conventions of both. In some poems, she inverts the concerns of typical features pages. "A Wasted Waist" reads like a parody of advice columns on home economics. The poem begins, "I bought a waist . . .":

The Newspaper Verse of Anise

It was white
    $ $ $
With a GREEN COLLAR
    $ $ $
And GREEN CUFFS
    $ $ $

And GREEN POCKETS.
    $ $ $
I paid all of
    $ $ $
FIVE DOLLARS for it
    (*Ragged Verse* 19)

The dollar signs (and GREEN) alert the reader that this is not going to be a description of fall styles or advice to the homemaker, despite the description of how to wash a waist:

I wore it three times
    $ $ $
And then I WASHED IT—
    $ $ $
Oh, SO CAREFULLY!
    $ $ $
First I soaked it in
    $ $ $
SALT WATER
    $ $ $
To set the COLOR

    $ $ $
and then I put it through
    $ $ $
HOT SUDS
    $ $ $
Very quickly,
    $ $ $
And then—
    $ $ $
IT RAN,

and shrank, and became good for nothing but rags. Rather than ending with advice, the poem ends with a reflection on the difference between use and exchange values:

The MAN who MADE it
    $ $ $
KNEW
    $ $ $
That the stuff would run
. . . . . .
I guess this waist was
    $ $ $

NEVER MADE
    $ $ $
For ME to WEAR,
    $ $ $
But only
    $ $ $
for HIM to SELL.

POETRY AND THE PUBLIC

That it was a "MAN" who made the shirtwaist suggests that the problem here is not simply a manufacturer's gypping a consumer, but the male-controlled market contaminating and circumscribing the domestic life it idealizes.

Another poem, "Ostracized!" directly attacks the features page as an institution:

We feel for you, ladies!
* * *
The other day
* * *
When you held your great meeting
* * *
On behalf
* * *
Of the WORKING WOMEN
* * *
Of our State,
* * *
When you exposed the deeds
* * *
Of Governor Hart
* * *
Concerning
* * *
The Minimum Wage,
* * *
And made your plea
* * *
Against him,—
* * *
And then,
* * *
When Mr. Goss
* * *
Of the Post-Intelligencer
* * *
Came up on the stage
* * *
And warned: "If you take part
* * *
In this meeting,
* * *
Your names will be DROPPED
* * *
From our SOCIETY PAGE!"
. . . . . .
And yet, somehow . . .
. . . . . .
We believe that any woman
* * *
Who comes forth to fight
* * *
For her sister-women,
* * *
Is probably brave enough
* * *
To stare down
* * *
EVEN
* * *
A Society Editor . . .

(16 Oct. 1920)

Such poems do seem to have reached women readers. For instance, Mrs. Clara H. Waller writes: "Dear 'Anise'—for such you are to me—I'm one of your '*humble*' followers. I have gloried in your ragged verse . . We will await your return most eagerly, knowing full well we will *then* get the *real* —ideal—*news*—so needed—from a wide, deep and *woman's* point of *view.*" Another writer recalls that "I was sitting in the car with Paul in Woodland Park and drew his attention to this 'literary find.' I have read, and mailed most of your verse. It would, no doubt, do you good, to read the favorable comment from my friends. over many miles. your verses have appealed to." [18] Anise's poems present news that is at once real and ideal, and (not coincidentally) from a woman's point of view.

Anise's self-consciously unbeautiful poems also deal directly with the exclusion of women from the bourgeois public sphere. One poem comments on the way the Walla Walla Commercial Club threw Mrs. Ina P. Williams, former legislator and candidate for Congress, out of their hall. She's

the champion	INFORMATION CONVEYOR
* * *	* * *
CHAIN-LIGHTENING	Of the State
* * *	

says Anise, and the poem gives a taste of the sort of information she conveys—about patronage, vote-trading, machine politics—and of "the chuckling INDECENCIES / Those men threw at her" in order to discredit her public morals bills (*Ragged Verse* 14). The poem thus becomes an exposé of the complicity of the businessmen (in a private gathering) with "public indecency." While women's pages typically reported on "unusual women in public affairs" (Marzolf 206), to record the way a respectable woman was insulted and ejected from a respectable organization's meeting constituted a breach in decorum.

Such pieces form a marked contrast with the serialized novel *My Husband and I,* by Jane Phelps, which the paper ran beneath Anise's poems. The protagonist, Mildred, constantly fears saying anything that will anger her husband; she tries to anticipate his whims and fend off threats to the marriage. Even so, her husband, Clifford, treats her with contempt: "Unless I told Clifford that I knew Mabel Horton had been in Chicago with him, and asked him to explain things seemingly unexplainable to me, I was sure he would never mention the fact of her visit to me. And even after the years we had spent together, I feared to question Clifford, feared to rouse his anger" (20 Apr. 1919). Anise's use of poems (sometimes in a series) to intervene in a public world of letters becomes all the more striking in juxtaposition with this suffocating serialized novel of domestic containment. "Anise," though a mask, is also an agent; the character Mildred is a sort of antifeminist exemplar, beyond the help even of the women's pages. That the *Union Record* ran *My Husband and I* speaks to the endurance of traditional gender roles within the labor movement, as well as the remarkable extent to which Anise travestied those roles.

Moreover, by linking the struggle of women and girls with that of workers, political prisoners, and consumers in a forum and a form accessible to many of those overlapping groups, Anise envisions "the public"—in all the senses of that word—as multiple, and as the negation of the classical public sphere. By the same token, however, the Anna Louise Strong of 1935, as a Stalinist looking back at her youth, would fault the poems, not for their literary defects, but for their political naïveté: "There are verses sharply aware of the inconsistencies and cruelties of capitalism, satirizing the campaigns of local patriots, the absurdities of spy scares. . . . Other verses have a fine glow of optimism dealing with futures, "new worlds," "new freedom," the marching progress of the world's workers. But I search in vain for any positive plan or theory concerning the organization of this march. . . . We passionately believed that a Great Change was coming, but when or how we did not know" (*I Change Worlds* 73–74). Strong here implicitly and negatively associates her poetry with indeterminacy, with roads that lead "no one knows where" —as she had said in one of her editorials about the Seattle General Strike of 1919 (the first to call itself by that name in North America). This indeterminacy makes the "revolution" of the 1910s look, to 1935, "poetic" in a turn-of-the-century sense—ideal, spiritual, emotional, aesthetic—rather than material and political in character. To the Strong of the polarized 1930s, as to Ezra Pound in the same decade, political correctness—that is, adherence to a particular literary/cultural ideology—counted for more than the more unfettered or unpredictable poetries and politics that allowed both writers to develop in the late 1910s and early 1920s. Indeed, the Anna Louise Strong of the 1930s replicates the tendency of the New Critics and those they continue to influence: she reads one historical moment anachronistically through another. The surprises and vigor of social and literary movements of the 1910s were as distasteful to Communist Party members of the 1930s as they would be to Red baiters (in both university and Congress) of the 1950s and later.

If, however, one understands the Anise episode as an experiment in the preliminary development of a public space antithetical to *either* the totalizing space of the classical public sphere or totalitarian statism, it looks more understandable and even promising. "Historical fissures," write Oskar Negt and Alexander Kluge, "—crises, war, capitulation, revolution, counterrevolution—denote concrete constellations of social forces within which a proletarian public sphere develops. Since the latter has no existence as a ruling public sphere, it has to be reconstructed from such rifts, marginal cases, isolated initiatives" (xliii). Indeed, the Seattle of World War I and its aftermath was one such moment; it was also a moment of considerable flux and instability in poetics. Langdon Hammer writes that today's reader of little magazines of the 1910s and 1920s encounters "a modernism bearing little resemblance to the literary period represented in textbooks: it is unstable, various, and unsorted . . . it all feels precarious—liable at any moment to close up shop and disappear, as little magazines very frequently did" (x). The interest of the Anise poems, it seems to me, is precisely that they express and exploit both of these historical instabilities to produce something that is not merely novel, but that is written into and in order to shape their historical moment. And if 1918 to 1921 was an especially propitious time for such an enterprise, so too were the 1990s.

CHAPTER SIX

Poetry and Its Publics in the 1990s

In the academy, poetry seldom appears as part of American literature, a field traditionally defined by prose fiction. F. O. Matthiessen discovered a renaissance for American literature that did not include poetry — other than that of Walt Whitman, that representative man and representer of "America." Neither the complex sensibilities of Dickinson nor the conventional sentiments of popular nineteenth-century poets quite made it.[1]

Fifty years later, despite increased suspicion toward "theories of American literature," the identification of American fiction *as* American literature persisted. For instance, in the 1992 MLA compilation *Redrawing the Boundaries: The Transformation of English and American Literary Studies* edited by Stephen Greenblatt and Giles Gunn, neither Cecelia Tichi's nor Philip Fisher's essays on American literary criticism treat poetry criticism. Rather, these historicist essays primarily cover criticism of fiction and popular culture. Fisher's own anthology *The New American Studies* (1991) includes poets, again, only in the person of Whitman; the same is true (with the addition of two Emerson poems) of John Carlos Rowe's *At Emerson's Tomb: The Politics of Classic American Literature*. Meanwhile, "poetry studies"—even studies of American poetry—remained distinct from "American literature." Nonetheless, in the 1990s, some criticism of modern poetry, despite its domination by a narrowly defined modernist canon, inched closer to "cultural studies."

Why, then, at a moment when historical scholarship became the norm in criticism of American literature, did "American literature" continue to neglect poetry? And why did it take poetry criticism so long to catch up (even to the limited extent that it has)? Textualist high-modernist poetics maintained its influence in English departments throughout the 1990s—and not only among poetry critics. As Alan Golding pointed out, "much New Americanist work implicitly perpetuates the historical essentializing of poetry as the least 'social,' most 'transcendent' of genres, treating it by default as a private aesthetic space untouched by the material and historical determinants shaping literary production in other genres" ("Dissensus" 6). In fact, as I shall argue, a new generation of Americanists became unwitting allies of the New Critical program for literature and, by the same token, called into question the bases of their own enterprise.

As we have seen, the transcendence of poetry goes back a long way. Poetry began this century as detextualized spirit and became an objectified, even reified, text. However, in both incarnations, "Poetry" remained an alternative to the slings and arrows of contingent historical fortune. Archibald MacLeish in the 1920s praised Amy Lowell's Imagist objectivity because her work was "secure in that kernel of poetry which . . . escapes for its handful of generations the familiarities of time" (521). Previously, the essence of poetry had insured its power to lift one above the daily grind; in the 1920s, the "kernel of poetry" offered a vicarious escape from "the familiarities of time." The modernist conception of poetry was more hermetic than the genteel, but every bit as sacralized.[2] Seventy years later, Americanists of all methodological and political stripes allowed this conception to remain unchallenged, and, as a result, poetry, that most "literary" form of literature, was on the outs. At the close of the twentieth century, poetry still appeared to American scholars as what *Scribner's Magazine* characterized in 1925 as "literature in its rarest, its quintessential form" (Black 538). Today, in the United States, you'll find the "Poetry" section on one side of the bookstore, the "Literature" section (meaning novels—the real thing) on the other, and this split obtains in the U.S. academy as well.

Of course poets have attempted to sell their work as an alternative to the novel since the novel was born. Poetry also seemed "out" in 1821, when Shelley wrote, "There is this difference between a story and a poem, that a story is a catalogue of detached facts, which have no other connection than time, place, circumstance, cause and effect; the other is the creation of actions according to the unchangeable forms of human nature, as existing in the mind of the creator, which is itself the image of all other minds" (1075). As Catherine Gallagher points out, in this passage, "[s]tory . . . must rely on particulars of time and place for what little organization it has, [and so] never quite achieves *form,* which would subdue such ephemera" (233). Poetry, however, becomes *pure* form and moves "toward the Platonic notion of form as a transcendent Idea" whose "essence is simply the representation of timelessness" (234). Likewise, for early-twentieth-century U.S. readers, poetry offered a refuge from an increasingly modernizing and materialist society and, by the same token, an alternative to the naturalist and later the "proletarian" novel. In 1912, Hermann Hagedorn's antimodernity resonated with Shelley's opposition of "detached facts" to "unchangeable forms": "It is a platitude that in the realistic novel you cannot see the woods for the trees—that is, you lose sight of the eternal laws in an orgy of detail. The result of this has been that the man of today has been a part of the grinding machinery of this vast Success Factory, the life of twentieth-century America, not only in his working-hours, but in his hours of recreation, seeking new worlds, he has been flung back upon his own [*sic*]" (775). In the following decades, the lingering (though unacknowledged) influence of romanticism would enable New Critics to regard the intrinsic properties of the text in isolation—a proper poem would body forth "the unchangeable forms of human nature" as "existing in the mind of the creator, which is itself the image of all other minds"—the unacknowledged representative of all, not just a specific nationality or age. Poetry, for high modernists and New Critics, meant a discursive, meditative and intellectual discourse of which John Donne was the exemplary craftsman.[3] The narrative poetry of Robert Frost or John Maesfield may have been popular, but the poets "have actually received critical sentence because their tales 'might have been done in prose'" (Hill 10)—that is, if they are popular, it is because they are really novelists and not poets. Poetry defined a domain of pure aesthetic value apart from "mere historical value."

Likewise, Roger Gilbert's study *Walks in the World* (1992) frankly bases its thesis upon the generic integrity and superiority of poetry. Because the writing of journals provides a record of daily life, Gilbert writes, they "come closest to the latent poetry of experience" (5). But this is bad: "[I]t is precisely for this reason that the journal comes to embody a major threat to the project of American poetry. For if poetry and journalism merge entirely, poetry must give up its heightened aesthetic aura and its claims to canonical status." "[T]he project of American poetry" consists in the exercise of maintaining the category "poetry" as something apart from the rest of letters. Poetry's "canonical" or "privileged status" constitutes "Poetry."

Gilbert significantly designates the keeping of journals as "journalism." Arbiters of taste in the 1910s condemned journalism as a kind of anti-literature, even as poetry rose to the status of hyper-literature. Journalism, "getting the story," emerged as the counterpoint to poetry's universality; the reporter, unlike the poet, produced "a catalogue of detached facts." As the novel in the late nineteenth century turned toward realism, critics reinscribed the lines between poetry and journalism even more sharply. Robert Underwood Johnson added his plaint in 1916: "Another obstacle to poetry is the demand for novelty, the restless inability to base one's content upon the great, simple and noble things common to human nature, as expressed in literature. . . . It is the bane of the magazines and discriminates literature from journalism" (178). This formulation accords with Shelley's views, as well as with Pound's dictum that "[l]iterature is news that STAYS news"—rather than, one infers, the sort that ends up on the bottom of the bird cage (*ABC* 29). One reader faulted the new little magazine *Poetry* because "[t]he paper of the magazine has been poor, the type that of the newspapers, the cover and form inadequate to the dignity of the cause" (Rice 371). This dichotomy survived in criticism unto the end of the century, even as literary studies had taken journals and journalism into the fold.

When "poetry" takes on such a strong structural referent, apart from the historical uses of the word, it also takes on a (de)legitimating function. "Poetry" turns into an evaluative epithet, as in, "Well, it's good for what it is, but is it *poetry?*"—which is as much as to ask, "Is it any good?" "Poetry," unlike other generic designations, signifies a complex of aesthetic-ethical values (and a process of valuation that is at once aesthetic, ethical, and psychological) that is inconsistent with a conception of culture broader than *high* culture. This is the legacy of, in the first instance, the age of Kant and the romantics, and, in the twentieth century, the institutionalization of the materialist poetics: the poem is an object because it is the object of judgment. As Golding remarks, "The significance of the New Critics' status as poet-professors, then, lies in their effort to import the role of the evaluative poet-critic into the academy" ("Poet-Critics" 19). That role grew to include other genres but remained, in historical terms, associated in the first instance with poetry.

In other words, poetry's social form in the academy represents the very idea of literature that historicists and cultural critics reject. Modern poetry, especially, still appears as a preserve of "unchangeable forms" that appeals only to an elite—and, to be sure, the "elite" poetry of the canonized modernist avant-garde predominates poetry studies. Given the traditional representations of poetry, it is not surprising that poetry was the raison d'être of and vehicle for New Critical formalism as well as the last genre to become a focus of historical analysis. Concomitantly, since modernism staged itself as a cosmopolitan rather than national movement, and since the principal New Critics identified with high modernism, "American poetry" came to sound like an oxymoron.[4] In the meantime, the disposition of Mikhail Bakhtin and British Marxist critics in favor of the novel and against lyric poetry as the object of analysis influenced cultural studies in the United States. These legacies, along with sheer institutional inertia, served to discourage cultural critics and Americanists from engaging poetry.[5]

In the professional imaginary, the corollary of poetry's hypostatization is the notion that fiction provides a privileged access to "the social." Accordingly, in U.S. criticism from the 1950s to the 1990s, the emerging field of "American literature" came to be defined preeminently by prose narrative.[6] The most influential studies of American literature have created narratives—about the growth of the American character, about a flight from Eden or from women, about the building of imaginary worlds —from other narratives, particularly nineteenth-century novels. We may have moved, as Fisher (1991) holds, from myths to (historical) rhetorics, but Americanists remained in the business of relating narratives about narratives (including slave narratives, captivity narratives, and conversion narratives). Now that "time, place, circumstance, cause and effect" bear more interest for critics, "a poem," it would seem, bears less, and "a story," more.

Despite the trend toward more genre-specific studies during the last decade of the twentieth century, many astute and valuable works on American narrative and expository prose continued to present themselves as studies of American literature or culture per se. For instance, Michael Newbury does not treat poetry writing or the figure of the poet(ess) in the otherwise very fine social-formalist study *Figuring Authorship in Antebellum America* (1997), though poetry played a central role in the construction of writing in the period (and despite the claim to "aggressively and actively" cross "traditional divisions of genre," [14]); more often than not, "writing" turns out to mean fiction writing.[7] Lois Tyson's *Psychological Politics of the American Dream: The Commodification of Subjectivity in Twentieth-Century American Literature* (1994) includes no discussion of poets of this century, notwithstanding the concern many of them had with the issue under discussion. Bonnie TuSmith, in *All My Relatives: Community in Contemporary Ethnic American Literatures* (1993) quotes lines from Rodolfo Gonzales's epic poem *I Am Joaquin,* "a key literary text during this period," but only as "a jumping-off place" for a discussion of novels by Tomás Rivera and Sandra Cisneros (138).[8]

Likewise, Dana Nelson, in *The Word in Black and White: Reading "Race" in American Literature, 1638–1867* (1992), tells us that "[w]hile our culture, education and experience teach us to accept race as a *fact,* it is important— if we hope productively to analyze 'race'—to study it as a *fiction,*" that is, as something "invented, described, promulgated, and legislated" (ix). However, there is a slippage in the book between this meaning of fiction and fiction as a literary genre, and this slippage is quite common in the field of American literature. *The Word in Black and White* includes chapters on Catherine Maria Sedgwick's *Hope Leslie* and Robert Montgomery Bird's *Nick of the Woods;* however, the book does not address the large body of poems representing racial "others" in the eighteenth century by Philip Freneau, Theodore Dwight, and Sarah Wentworth Morton, or in the nineteenth by William Cullen Bryant, Harriet Beecher Stowe, or William Gilmore Simms. In fact, Nelson includes chapters on fiction by Simms, Poe, and Melville without addressing the substantial poetic output of any of these authors. These choices may be due to fiction's greater popularity. But poetry sold well in the period; indeed, it is hard to believe that "Benito Cereno" was more widely read and quoted than Longfellow's *Evangeline*—or than *Mardi* or *Typee,* for that matter.[9]

In any event, that is not the argument. Rather, the focus on the novel seems to be epistemologically motivated. Nelson, in explaining this generic focus, quotes as a premise William C. Dowling's statement that narrative is "a contentless form that our perception imposes on the raw flux of reality, giving it, even as we perceive, the comprehensible order we call experience" (41). However, this observation didn't stop Dowling from writing *Poetry and Ideology in Revolutionary Connecticut* (1990). Debby Applegate also attempted a rationale for the concentration on fiction in historicist criticism when she wrote that novels came to dominate antebellum literary culture because "fictional representations of recognizable human life are always books with a key. To invoke Hayden White's axiom, while biographical sketches offer the pedestrian truth of correspondence, fiction seems to reveal the truth of coherence" (158). But to argue, following White, for the acceptance of narrativization in the writing of history is not the same thing as writing a history of (or based on) other narratives. And even if "representations of recognizable human life" for antebellum readers of literature *had* occurred only in fiction, it is instructive that Applegate makes precisely the same case for fiction over biography that the New Critics made for poetry over prose: that it gives an aesthetic coherence to the prosaic or chaotic facts of life.

Indeed, the critics come by this predisposition honestly. New Americanists and cultural critics alike in the 1990s perpetuated a centuries-old ideology of poetry, and Golding is right to comment that the exclusion of poetry from "New Americanist work" is a "surprising contradiction of its own principles" ("Dissensus" 6). I take one of these principles to be that all art, including poetry, finds itself embedded within a larger cultural matrix—that all writing is a form of discourse. But if poetry resides outside of (or above) "America," "literature," or "culture," then the integrity of those categories depends upon other generic forms. If the exclusion of poems reveals itself as rhetorically constructed, so too does the inclusion of fiction.

To the extent that critics reflexively turn to the content of fiction, their enterprise becomes as textual-formalist as the New Critics' privileging of the structure of poetry. Modernist and New Critical poetics' problematizing of representational strategies and insistence on the materiality of the text resist a methodology premised upon the reflective, referential, or "documentary" quality of literary texts. If it is easier to make a narrative from another narrative, it is also easier, it would seem, to represent a representation. Indeed, experimental prose rarely fares better than poetry within theories of American literature.[10] Yet by taking the characters, tropes, or topoi of novels to be more indicative of the

Zeitgeist than those of poems, or by using narrative devices as semiotic gene splices from which a larger culture can be cloned, Americanists have transferred "authenticity" from the literary work as autonomous object to the literary work as narrative content. Or rather, they have not considered these works under the social form of their genres. We go to novels to find historical reality because novelists represent historical reality—this premise not only puts a lot of faith in novelists, it also reifies field boundaries by producing a dichotomy between prose narrative as the bearer of "historical value" on the one hand and poetry (understood as non-narrative lyric) as the repository of "aesthetic value" on the other. This assumption means that "American literature" turns on the same axiomatic logic as "poetry."

In effect, then, like the populist critics of the 1910s, the Americanists of the 1990s typically based American literature on works that are relatively "accessible" and through which a national psyche can be discerned. The irony here is that the popular poetry of yesteryear was forgotten, precisely because poetry is an unknown country. Though much of the poetry of the first part of the century was popular, narrative, accessible, and conventional in its representational strategies, it remained invisible within the academy because critics read poems (*if* they read them) through the social form of "poetry" institutionalized fifty years before.

Americanists of the late twentieth century thereby slighted a notion that, as we have seen, critics of the early twentieth century took for granted and even celebrated—namely, that poetry does cultural work. The absenting, during the postwar period, of popular ideas of poetry from the academy facilitated the immunity of poetry from and suitability of prose narrative for cultural critique. But it is precisely this elision that points up poetry's importance for U.S. literary histories and, by the same token, the need to apply cultural critique to poetry. Poetry's perceived abilities—in genteel, modernist, radical, and popular/populist poetics alike—to effect equilibrium and ordering, to preserve or transmit aesthetic and ethical values, and to (de)sacralize twentieth-century capitalist society have made it a perennial battleground in the struggle to define the subject of national culture. That is, critics and poets of the early twentieth century understood poetry as inherently practical and social (and in many cases political) due to the putative transcendence that rendered poetry asocial in the post–New Critical academy. Accordingly, the exclusion of American poetry from American literature and the identification of the latter as prose narrative has more to do with institutional history than with any inherent generic or national characteristics. By the same token, an interest in the institutional history of genres provides the only valid rationale for considering them separately in the context of American literary history. As a result, attempts to integrate American poetry into the field of American literature challenge methodological and formal generic traditions of scholarship in both.

Moreover, even as the enthusiasm for poetry declined in the academy, poetry continued to be produced, distributed, and used via extra-institutional avenues in the rest of U.S. society. Poets and enthusiasts trained and untrained in the 1990s attempted once again, for better or worse, to gain control of the art for themselves. Since the 1950s, when Beat poetry events gained widespread attention, the number of open readings and poetry festivals grew steadily; by the early 1990s a variety of publics participated in newer poetic events, such as poetry slams and performances and open readings through video teleconferencing and interactive poetry, as well as older institutions such as poetry societies and workshops. The creation of poetry films and CDs (or CD-ROMs), poetry on the sides of buildings and buses, and poetry in political movements decenters and decentralizes art-writing from the norms and sites of literary authority. These new and revived social forms constituted an attempt to transform "poetry" as radically as did the avant-garde of the 1910s and 1920s—though "new" poetries often have as much to do with nostalgia as rebellion.

The popularity of such figures as Sharon Olds, Robert Bly, and Patricia Smith and their association with survivor poetry, the men's movement, and poetry slams respectively (and the suspicion of them within English departments) indicate that the "poetry scene" of the 1990s was the scene of an impure assortment of different sorts of values for different sizes, types, and sites of audiences. Unitary definitions of poetry are particularly unstable in such a situation. Neither a definition of poetry as divorced from the public nor one that has determinate and identifiable effects or uses will do. Poetry in the United States in the late twentieth century, like the country itself, included multiple, difficult negotiations between normative standards, equality, community, subjectivity, and competing conceptions of and reactions to "the public."

In 1991, the *Atlantic Monthly* published Dana Gioia's now famous essay "Can Poetry Matter?" in which the poet-critic-businessman lashed out at what he saw as a moribund poetry culture and an American society that rejected poetry. This piece elicited a flood of responses from readers: it seemed as though, while Gioia may have been correct in saying that people didn't read poetry, they certainly loved to argue about it.

This is not necessarily a contradiction. We can view poetry not only as a classification of textual forms but also as an institution, a practice, a manner of reading—as what I have been calling a social form. Confusion about what constitutes a poem—George Steiner's "modal difficulty" (27)—must be understood in the context of related cultural practices, such as the writing of poetic theory. Writers compete to seize the title "Poetry" for the writing they wish to validate; this conflict has shifted the cultural meaning of poetry in this century and has altered the types of texts valued as poems and the types of value poems are seen to instantiate.

In the modern era, avant-gardists have deliberately rendered the meaning of poetry unclear by unmooring the field designation "poetry" from texts previously recognizable as poems. At the same time, traditionalists have sought to conserve already-existing generic boundaries. These orientations represent not positions in a debate, but irreconcilable premises. What is at stake is more than accuracy: "poetry" functions, in a way that "the novel" does not, as what Barbara Herrnstein Smith calls an "honorific labeling of cultural productions" (35). This function indicates the scope and importance of this competition for poetry, which is a synecdoche of broader cultural, ethical, and political competitions.

As I have suggested, to those of us in the U.S. academy, it may seem that poetry, at the turn of the century, is "out." Titles in the 1990s asked "Is Poetry Dead?" "Who Killed Poetry?" or "Can Poetry Matter?" and to many poets and scholars, it seemed that institutional support for poetry, within both academe and publishing, had largely evaporated and that poetry was indeed both dead and irrelevant.

But readers of *Time, Newsweek,* or *People* magazine knew better. Poetry, according to the popular press, was experiencing a boom in the early 1990s. *Vanity Fair,* in its January 1993 issue, ran a list entitled, "They're Back," on which "poetry" appeared right after Oliver North and Sylvester Stallone. This apparent comeback for poetry extended beyond the appointment of an "activist" poet laureate in Rita Dove or the very public appearance of the poetry of Maya Angelou at a presidential inauguration. The new poetry scene largely emerged outside of the traditional institutions of literature, such as universities, literary journals, or academic and commercial presses. Rather, much new work by poets appeared, at least in the first instance, in other social settings: on the sides of buildings, in performance spaces, in poetry films, open readings in coffeehouses, poetry slams in bars or community centers, workshops in homes or in libraries. *Poetry Flash,* a San Francisco Bay Area poetry review and calendar of events, listed eleven open readings in March of 1983 and forty-six at the end of 1993; twenty-eight workshops posted notices in 1983, ninety-six advertised for members ten years later. Gary Glazner, organizer of the National Poetry Slam in 1993, claimed in that year that open readings in San Francisco typically drew fifty or sixty people where ten years previously they drew twenty; and, he added, the poetry slam in Johnson City, Tennessee, regularly drew over two hundred people.[11] All of this led theorist of poetic relevance Dana Gioia to claim that "the physical audience listening to live poetry vastly outnumbers the people who read it in books" ("Notes" 7). In any event, there exists considerable reason to believe that more people listened to, read, and wrote poetry than did so ten years earlier; that people were producing, disseminating, and using poetry in more places and in a less centralized fashion; that the poetry scene in the United States existed largely in informal settings; and that poetry writers increasingly were combining their written texts with other media. These developments suggest that the cultural meaning and uses of poetry shifted in the early 1990s as profoundly as they had in the 1820s or 1920s.

While such a shift does not presuppose either a numinous character for poetry or a populist cultural politics, it does suggest the need to look at the various forms and functions poetry assumes among U.S. readers who do not work in literature departments. That is, there is no reason for academic critics to take popular tastes in poetry less seriously than popular tastes in novels or other media. Yet, as Suzanne Clark points out, "pleasures we are growing used to talking about in studies of the cinema . . . we reject as a 'proper' reaction to poetry" (95). Part of the problem may be that the new developments in poetry defy textualist methods of analysis, insofar as printed or written texts constitute only one aspect of these forms—performance, conversation, music, fiber optics, and context of presentation play equally important roles.

Consequently, any useful critique of this later poetic revival in the United States will focus on process as well as product; in order fully to understand contemporary poetry as it exists, one must do so in terms of the meanings, uses, and effects of poetry in the lives and communities of readers and writers. This orientation would shift our focus away from the textual form and content of poems to the social form of "poetry" as a practice and as a category of understanding. From this perspective, the "poetry scene" redefines both literary authority and poetic value.

So why did poetry experience a revival of sorts in the 1990s? Joyce Jenkins, editor of *Poetry Flash,* attributed the emergence of the early 1990s poetry scene to economics:

In the seventies we had a tremendous influx of NEA money for . . . small press printing, and small press printing went crazy again . . . and people published and published . . . then that dried up. And the economy got very tough.... It became... much more "professionalized"... Meanwhile, there'd been a sort of historical evolution of the reading, and different purposes the reading could be for... somehow, because it's so much harder to publish,... people started putting open readings at small series, weekly series, people put an open reading with a featured poet to draw an audience, so that the experience of going to a featured reading... becomes a participatory experience. It's a participatory art form.... You write a poem and you get up there and read it.... Suddenly, you become an audience that appreciates what they're hearing... and that audience is a much more resilient, much more caring audience.[12]

In this version of the development of a "grassroots" poetry scene, the imposition of a corporate culture of centralized arts funding produces a reaction in the form of new, low-budget institutions of poetry that in turn stimulate poetry as an art. The do-it-yourself poetry of the turn of the century returns and, in Jenkins's version, this collapsing of the roles of writer and reader produces great (and enduring) audiences (if not great poets). Ironically, then, the institutionalization of poetry funding in the late 1970s and 1980s may have contributed to the production, outside universities and other institutions, of alternative grassroots sites of poetic production and uses that later ran on their own steam and gained momentum. And these sites and uses tended to subvert a special status for either artist or critic.

The participatory character that Jenkins identified formed a salient feature of this new "scene." In an open reading, writers who wish to read sign up to do so shortly before the event. Each person is allotted a short time, usually five or ten minutes, to read their work. Typically, a large proportion of the audience turns out to be the poets who read their work. In other words, an open reading series tends to maintain open access and formal equality and tends to collapse or at least blur the binary distinction between artist and audience.

Moreover, open readings in the Bay Area were and are numerous, and they cover a wide geographical area, thereby giving large numbers of people access to them. Whether or not the Bay Area poetry scene or any part of it could or can be termed "democratic" (as in Louis Untermeyer's use of the word in the 1910s), one thing is clear: it is diverse—in its forms, its participants, in the texts that comprise it, and in the standards of judgment brought to bear by its participants. Likewise, Jenkins summarized *Flash* editorial policy as being "to have an eclectic forum-type publication," because "it's easy to get lost as a writer, and . . . the idea is to try to give people some compass so that they can find themselves a way to get into writing." At the same time, however, this democratic intent is potentially at odds with aesthetic value: "Hopefully we're recognizing quality as best we can, and really trying to get at some kind of poetic essence, and not lose that; it's very important to me that it not just become a social rag, that there be aesthetic value to it and that that be honored, not just set aside for what's fast and easy and loud." Jenkins, like many U.S. poets and critics over the course of the last 175 years, represented poetry as an "essence" that is opposed to the "social rag" or political or journalistic criticism; her disavowal of "what's fast and easy and loud" accords with Tate's opposition of "the quick career" to "disciplined craftsmanship." But in Jenkins's account, the *Flash* accords with the participatory nature of the poetry scene by helping poets find a way into *writing* as well as by filling the more traditional pastoral role of book evaluator. The publication attempts to embody both eclecticism and quality through, on the one hand, its listing of events, which manifests the heterogeneity of Bay Area poets, and, on the other, in its reviews and articles, which do indeed attempt to put forth standards for evaluating quality. But the presence of the listings section in the early 1990s located any standard of aesthetic judgment as one out of many within a broad geographical and demographic space, and it marked aesthetic judgment itself as but one form of the judgment of a work of art. Many of the events and workshops it listed did in fact privilege what in the 1930s was called "social poetry," and, easy or not, some audiences in the Bay Area scene favored poetry that is fast and loud.

Perhaps none of the new poetry institutions received as much media hype as the "poetry slam." The initial round of a poetry slam may begin in much the same way as an open reading, with one crucial difference: the writer/performers are judged. For instance, in the National Poetry Slam in the United States, each poet reads (or recites or performs) their work; the judges, who are selected randomly from the audience, then assign the readers scores between one and ten. The two highest-scoring participants hold a final read-off that determines who goes on to the next round. In the quarterfinals, semifinals, and finals, of course, only those who have made the grade may participate, until a slam champion is crowned. In other words, although anyone may participate by reading their poetry in initial rounds, poetry slams nevertheless reinforce the distinction between artist and audience through a very palpable form of the institutionalization of judgment.

Slam organizers instruct judges by asking them to take into account both words and performance; after that, they are on their own. Yet, although judges may also be audience members, slams are famous for the gap between the determinations of the judges and those of the audience. At one round of 1993's National Poetry Slam finals in San Francisco, one judge resigned in the middle of a round due to crowd displeasure in the form of loud hisses, boos, and catcalls. This abdication created minor civil unrest within the auditorium, as some auditors called for the show to go on, while others demanded new judges, or even demanded that the process of judging be dropped altogether. "Let anyone who has a poem read a poem!" one woman called out from the balcony; one noncontestant leapt on stage in an apparent attempt to do so, and it seemed for a moment that a sort of storming of the aesthetic Bastille might be underway. Although dissent subsided, the slam truism that "it's the poems, not the points" became a refrain with rather immediate importance. Meanwhile, in a smaller room of the same building, anyone who had a poem could indeed read it to people in Los Angeles on a videophone teleconference, and those in San Francisco could hear and see poets in L.A. A few slam finalists, poet Francisco Alarcón, and assorted members of the "public" (including this one) did just that and, in the smaller space with fewer people, could enter into dialogue with one another (and their southern California counterparts) as well.[13]

Both slams and open readings lend themselves as media to hybrid textual forms, so that the distinctions between spoken-word performance, stand-up comedy, scat singing, poetry reading, and oratory begin to fade. Many performers' delivery is often indistinguishable from that of stand-up comics; such poems may or may not receive high scores. At the same time, many of the most warmly received poems at the 1993 championship also dealt directly with cultural-political issues; National Slam finalists Patricia Smith and Lisa Buscani (a.k.a. "La Buscani") presented poems dealing with AIDS, the relation between race and taste, homophobia, and street violence. While many poems adhere to one or another standard of aesthetic value, many also supply entertainment value, as evidenced by enthusiastic laughter, cheers, whoops, or intermittent applause of audiences.

Thus, although slam participants often attract or bring their own supporters, it also seems to be the case that multiple standards of judgment account for dissonance between audiences and judges, or rather that each judge employs a different aesthetic or unique mix of different types of value. The dream of a common poetic culture is given the lie — or rather, to the extent that it exists, it has more to do with television or popular music than it does with Aristotle, Donne, or Harold Bloom. As Christopher Beach writes (quoting Jostein Gripsrud), "we increasingly find sites and situations [in slams] in which 'the audiences of [different] cultural spheres overlap'"; these audiences bring "different forms of taste" and judgment to the performance (127). In any event, although the slam reproduces the structure of academic criticism, in which designated authorities pronounce upon works of art and disagree among themselves while a theoretical audience (whether large or small) looks on, in the slam the audience cannot be represented because it is present. Procedural norms do not necessarily account for or accommodate very public divergences between individuals and groups. And judges, in this case, have little claim to aesthetic authority based on training or acculturation.

Beach suggests that "[u]nlike traditional poetry readings, which reify the 'poet' as a distinct and lofty figure and the spectator as a silent and respectful listener . . . everyone in the audience is simultaneously a potential poet, a 'fan,' and an 'expert'" (129). The slam format, in other words, makes the public judge, makes judgment public, and publicizes the diversity of judgments within a public.

Writing workshops have existed longer than open readings and have pervaded the writing scene more thoroughly than have slams. Between August and December of 1993, I interviewed members of writing workshops; I selected the workshops to be interviewed (from listings in *Poetry Flash*) in a way that would provide a representative sample of workshops with regard to race, gender, age, and locality.[14] In these conversations, I found that participants in the burgeoning poetry scene in the San Francisco Bay Area not only derived different sorts of value from poems, but that poetry writing and workshops provided participants with value that exceeded the norms of either classical or modernist aesthetic theory. Put another way, participants in the new poetry scene seemed less interested in disinterestedness than have critics. Although workshops serve, in one way or another, to improve writing, poetry serves a function in the lives of writers at the grassroots beyond that of an autotelic objet d'art. As one writer from an African American arts organization put it, poetry "should enlighten, and it can be therapeutic or inspirational." A participant in an Asian American writer's workshop matter-of-factly addressed the issue of audience, saying: "It all depends on your purpose. I mean, that's what the purpose of a writer is, whether he's interested in teaching others how to do a better job, or to entertain others and make them feel good, or doing propaganda." In any event, the poets I spoke with for the most part represented themselves as writing with a purpose; poetry for them, as for U.S. poets of the pre–World War I era, served a function and did not exist as pure text or as pure, self-contained, self-referential form.

Indeed, the poetry workshop often serves as a medium of communication and cultural interaction, in addition to providing critique. Poetry for some represented a medium of community formation, as workshops either became communities or strengthened existing communities. A writer in a woman's writing group said this: "For me, I think the real function that writing serves is to just forge connections. . . . When I was growing up . . . I really had a very strong sense of community . . . once I left that, I really just felt so disoriented. And I think just the process of poetry helps me to draw connections, through metaphor and just through my own free-associative process. And I think that the purpose of this group for me is the same thing in that it gives me much more of a sense of community and a sense that I am also connected to other people who are doing this, this process." For this writer, as for Gene Stratton-Porter in the 1920s, poetry represents communal connections and purposes remembered from childhood and sought in maturity. The speaker invokes textual technique, process, and form (drawing connections, metaphor, free-association) as metonyms for the social form of poetry in her life. And, indeed, craft provides the grounds for a group identity; in this sense, it is almost as though this poet has attempted to reconcile the positions of Tate with that of Stratton-Porter. Another member of this workshop echoed the previous speaker's sentiments: "Writing is so lonely to do. And in a big city like San Francisco, it's easy to feel lonely in general. . . . When there's a group to come to of other people struggling . . . it really helps to ward away the loneliness." A member of a group of mostly senior citizens reported that "I belong to four or five different [writing] groups, and it's a big part of my social life." While for some the aspect of sharing a craft may be paramount, for others the process and product of writing may be a vehicle for or indistinguishable from a hobby, a social activity in the narrow sense, or a form of therapy.

At the same time, such groups, while existing within a larger poetry scene, can (like *Poetry Flash*) serve a crucial role in communication between often decentralized points within that scene. In many cases, writers belonged to more than one group and shared information from one with the others. "We get suggestions of what's going on in the area," one poet told me. "It's an information sharing. We get references to good articles and essays . . . and readings." Poetry can also serve as a medium of community-formation outside the formal setting of a workshop. Darlene Roberts, president of the International Black Writers and Artists support group's San Francisco local, told me, "Sometimes we get together just to read each other's poems" either over the phone or in person. Likewise, a white writer from a suburban community said, "I get great satisfaction from sharing with a neighbor or friend or what have you on the phone, and they really enjoy that too, and many people feel it's a bit of a lift or a breather in their day." In this sense, a network of poetry workshops and their participants could serve as an informal and ephemeral means of disseminating or "publishing" poems.

The sharing of poetry in person, on the phone, or at a coffeehouse reading forms a trend that Joyce Jenkins called "publishing with the voice." And the new poetry scene in the early 1990s was changing the ways in which poems were made public. Moreover, many poets had ambitions for their poetry as modest as those of amateur poets of the 1910s and 1920s. As a poet and retired secretary put it: "I personally am not looking for the commercial venue of the *New Yorker* or the *New York Times Magazine* or something like that. . . . There is a small group, it's like an artists' coalition . . . and I feel fortunate being invited to join that group and stand up once a month and read two poems of my own before the group, and I feel that they are giving me more reception than I would have ever had, and that to me . . . is right where I want to be." This writer opposes prestigious, for-profit "professional" publications in New York to a small, local face-to-face group in a working-class city in the Bay Area. The speaker does not want to be in the metaphorical "venue" of the commercial press but rather before a local group that provides "more reception." This nonprofessional poetry production and disdain of elite literary institutions reflects a similar conflict in Wilkins's "A Poetess" or in weekly magazines of the 1930s.

I also found that many poetry workshops and circles published their own books, journals, or yearbooks. The Ina Coolbrith writing circle published a yearbook for its members and held an awards dinner that formed a major part of the writing lives of its members. In fact, few poets I spoke with expressed an ambition to appear in glossy large-circulation monthlies or prestigious academic publications; often writers wished to have their poems appear in publications geared toward their geographical area or the micromarket of a particular artist-audience of which they formed a part. As the writer quoted above put it, "We make our own clothes, bake our own bread, and write our own poems."

This spirit of self-sufficiency and of personal and community empowerment appeared to be the most salient aspect of poets' evaluation of their own poetry practices. A member of a workshop in a low-income neighborhood in San Francisco called writing a "survival mechanism." "It makes me feel good about myself," she told me. "I have to write. It's the only thing I know how to do well." Another poet, who was also a secretary, echoed that sentiment, saying, "It's sometimes what makes me get through the drudgery of my work. Anything to do with poetry, whether it's a reading or a workshop, just really helps carry me through life"; a member of the same workshop affirmed that "I'm happy if one person reads my poem and feels better about themselves because they know that someone else feels the same way." A writer/retiree expressed something similar: "I'll be feeling down and I'll sit down and start writing something, and four hours later I get up and I feel great: I've done something. Washing the dishes doesn't accomplish a damn thing!" Sometimes poetry takes on a therapeutic value; one woman with a history of struggling with mental illness told me, "When I found poetry . . . that was it, I had to have that." Or poetry can offer a means of responding to political events; in one workshop after the 1991 bombing of Iraq had begun, every poet brought a poem on that topic—not, as one member put it, "because we're going to try to change the world with our poetry," but rather, "because we're feeling something deeply." In many of these statements, as in those from critics of the 1910s, poetry once again emerges as efficacious, as providing a service beyond its textual form.

Many workshops and writers' organizations serve people with the same ethnicity, gender, age, or sexual orientation; for writers in these communities, the empowerment and self-sufficiency of a grassroots poetry scene becomes particularly important. Members of African American writing groups explained that such groups are important to the community because "[t]he only way we've ever made it is to make it on our own"; it is "a way to be heard," and "if you don't do it for yourself, nobody will." A number of writers in both African American and Asian American communities recommended writing as a way to counter negative media images of people of color. Members of an Asian American writers' group emphasized the importance of the workshop as "a space for ourselves, for our own writing, that will not constantly be setting up to be compared by the same criteria that have been handed to us, that force us to fit a mold we may not fit into." Another writer distinguished between different yet overlapping aspects of value in his writing: "For the immediate gratification of increasing my own self-esteem: like, hey, people like my stuff or see value in my stuff . . . then I guess there's the political goals . . . because I feel that I'm very active within the Asian American community. . . . Maybe I can get published if I water this down or change this . . . but I don't want to jeopardize what my messages are." In addition to workshops, community presses such as Black Angels Press or Mother's Hen Press in Oakland afforded a community-based space for original poetry to appear. As Richard Moore, president of the International Black Writers and Artists local in Oakland, told me, "There's great grassroots talent in Oakland." That talent, however, has had to rely on self-generated spaces and institutions to make its poetry visible both among writers and to a broader public. Moreover, poets use poetry to support other institutions, such as schools and youth guidance programs. Wanda Sabir, organizer of the West Oakland Poetry Celebration, reported that the poetry events she organized helped boost circulation at the West Oakland branch library where the celebrations were held and provided support for those attempting to keep the library's hours from being cut.

But why poetry? Writing workshops also frequently welcome writers in genres other than poetry; indeed, one of the characteristics of the Bay Area poetry scene is that it's not strictly limited to poetry. So why are there no *Autobiography Flash* or literary criticism slams (the MLA convention notwithstanding)? Is there anything about poetry per se that lends itself to a participatory literary culture? Joyce Jenkins of the *Flash* thought so: "When you go to a play . . . you don't start reading the dialogue with the actors. . . . When you go to a traditional gallery, it's not interactive. . . . You might say, 'Well, I can do as well as that,' and that's considered déclassé, that's gauche. . . . Poetry is uniquely suited to act as a vehicle for that and a medium for that . . . because you can hold an open reading, and it works." Poetry, which has existed for many writers as the preeminent generic mark of distinction (or which, as Kant says, "holds first rank among all the arts" [191]), here provides a medium for collapsing the distinction between producer and consumer of art and with it the classed distinction between different ranks of art. Indeed, several poets I spoke with held the opinion that because poems historically have varied in length from lyrics to epics, the form allows enough flexibility to accommodate many poems by many poets in the short period of time allowed by an open reading. Moreover, the lack of expensive materials (the so-called bricks and mortar of the art world) that limits grant funding for poetry also makes it cheaper and more accessible to produce; as one poet put it, "No matter how bad things get, no matter how low you sink, you can always afford a piece of paper and a pencil."

Poetry-slam organizer Gary Glazner suggested that poetry is an especially accessible form of artistic expression. Though much of the newfound interest in poetry was spurred by rap or spoken-word music, one doesn't need amplifiers to present poetry; you can, as Glazner said, "develop a local following" of listeners who will buy your poetry at events. Moreover, Glazner went on to suggest, although the broadcasting and recording industries began promoting some poetry, poetry presents an alternative to television and mass entertainment; not only is the new poetry self-made, but people like to hear about "other people's lives and feelings" in "a language that's heard in the streets and that people use when they're speaking to each other." The success of singer Jewel's poetry suggests that this was still the case in 1999. This preference for accessible, colloquial, or conventional language that recommended the New Poets to many readers in the 1910s still held appeal in the 1990s that an "academic" poetry lacked. At the same time, I found that participants in community workshops often feel alienated from both academic literary institutions and the self-styled avant-garde. One writer said of a local university literature department, "If you don't have a Ph.D., they don't take you seriously." A member of a local writers' club averred that "if you sent some of our kind of stuff to the language poets in the New York state area, they would be less than crumbs on the floor." The war between avant-garde, elite, or established poetry and more popular conceptions of the art has survived from the days of William Rose Benet.

While high modernism succeeded in impressing its version of poetry on universities (even on its enemies), in the rest of U.S. society the cultural meaning of poetry at the end of the twentieth century may have had more in common with its meaning for magazine writers in the 1910s. At that time, in the United States and Britain, critics writing in popular periodicals typically represented poetry as a spiritual quintessence of literature that provided a refuge from a materialist culture, that elevated and ennobled one, and that expanded sympathies. In my interviews with members of community-based writing workshops, I often heard poets of different ages, ethnicities, and areas characterize poetry as possessing a similarly transformative power. Poetry "seems more like the soul talking" than does prose; "poetry is the essence," said another; "poetry has so much salvation in it"; "it's so soul-enriching, and just gives you a spiritual feeling . . . you develop yourself spiritually"; and the Bay Area boasts so many writers because it is "a very spiritual place." Jenkins's contact with reporters provided her with a different angle on the same phenomenon: "I guess the media has decided the eighties were about image and the surfaces of things," she said, "and now the nineties are about content . . . and poetry represents content." And while poetry in the academy may represent material form, poetry to a general audience may provide some spiritual content to life.

And outside the academy, poetry in the 1990s was "in." If poetry was in during the First World War, it may be no surprise that it was back during a period of economic globalization, ecological deterioration, and what many media outlets portrayed as mounting civil violence. Poetry, in its historical function as a medium of idealization, may provide either solace for individuals or, especially in its performance aspect, an idealizing aura for political responses to crises. For instance, at the 1994 Petaluma, California, funeral of murder victim Polly Klaas, several family friends (including the chief of police) recited elegies they had written. One reporter commented: "Nobody much reads poetry these days, but people still turn to it when ordinary language doesn't get you where you want to go" (Carroll). Once again, poetry is spiritual and impractical (practical people like police chiefs turn to it only on extraordinary public occasions), but it is, by the same token, instrumental (it gets them where they want to go in extra-ordinary circumstances).

At the current turn of the century, poetry anthologies continue to proliferate, even as *101 Famous Poems* (1924), the best-selling poetry book in U.S. history, continues to sell in its subsequent (and numerous) editions. Garrison Keillor read a poem from Charles Webb's *Poetry That Heals* on his popular "Writer's Almanac" program on National Public Radio (26 April 1995), and a San Francisco outlet of the chain bookstore Borders carried a shelf devoted to "popular poetry." Moreover, there is more than one context for canonical poetry: as Willis Buckingham notes, "today inexpensive editions in bookstores and cardshops testify to a Dickinson constituency not represented in the academic community" (177), as in the case of *The Love Poems of Emily Dickinson*. And it is not hard to find advertisements for gold-embossed, hide-bound sets of the classics that embody as much cultural capital now as they did in the 1930s. Even so, many poets in community-based workshops read canonical modernist and contemporary poets whose aesthetic philosophies differ markedly from their own.

One response to all of these developments was, predictably, a call for the recentralization of poetry. Gioia, for instance, in "Can Poetry Matter?" lamented the way that contemporary society has "fragmented audiences into specialized subcultures that share no common frame of reference" (246–47). "A common cultural tradition" (246) was for him necessary for poetry to "again become a part of American public culture" (22).[15] For Jonathan Galassi, vice president and executive editor at Farrar, Straus and Giroux, the question was this: "[H]ow do you go from the margins where what's new is always created, to the center? How do you really reach an audience that is not just your own local audience?" ("Who Will" 29). Galassi and Gioia here voice the recurrent liberal anxiety shared by Bryant, Stevens, Tate, and many other poet-theorists over the nature, fate, and role of U.S. poetry. Poetry takes one from the local and particular to the universal, from the outside space of the untutored to the inside of disinterested concern with the common good. As we have seen, however, this anxiety is not necessarily shared by writers who do not represent universities or publishing firms, and the "recentralizers" may be flogging an imaginary dead horse.

Edmund Wilson responded to what he saw as a similar situation in the 1930s by seeking to rid the world of poetry altogether: "It is time, it seems to me, to discard, or to define more carefully, the word 'poetry' which has come to serve for so many ambiguities" (459). But the (de)legitimating power of "the word 'poetry,'" its power as a "coup de gout," we might say, makes such a poetry moratorium doubtful of success. The utility of poetry for various poetics resides precisely in the undecidability that Wilson identifies—the availability of "poetry" as prize. And since, for the same reason, poetry is defined in many ways simultaneously, a "more careful" definition begs the question.

But what if poetry were not the prize but the contest itself? The indeterminacy of "poetry" also may open the possibility of a sustained and inevitable modal difficulty or of a "mode" that is never defined but always coming into being. Such a notion might provide more than a sort of bird's-eye pluralism—it might also provide more rhetorical room for mutation, hybridity, contamination. In other words, it may be possible (to use Chantal Mouffe's terms) to understand and to express not an antagonistic relation between poetries, but an agonistic one. "Poetry" can be a sentence, or it could be a mode of verbal creativity and contestation where one could imagine something other than blows coming down.

Critics have frequently labeled new American poetry scenes "democratic," usually as a positive value. When used in this normative sense, democracy takes on a populist tinge, as in the case of defenders and promoters of poetry in the 1930s. But thinking of a poetry scene in terms of democracy may bear useful explanatory power from a historical point of view as well. Claude Lefort, for instance, thinks of democracy as "the historical society par excellence, a society which, in its very form, welcomes and preserves indeterminacy" (16); in Lefort's democracy, the very grounds for the meaning of the political shift, so that "the meaning of what is coming into being remains in suspense." Accordingly, "the locus of power becomes an empty place" that "cannot be represented" (17): here is a conception that brings poststructuralist thought to bear on Habermas's model of the public sphere.

Seen in this light, our poetry scene becomes a proscenium, the stage on which any number of people with different types of poems—or writings that resist genrefication—can read their work in any number of places. It might be useful, in other words, to consider a poetry or art scene, in a metropolis especially, as a cultural space consisting of a variety of smaller public spheres within which communities may thrive and, just maybe, speak to one another in ways they wouldn't otherwise. Democracy in this case ceases to be a set of either normative values or value-neutral procedures. Rather, it is an institutionalization and acceptance of modal difficulty, a discursive space in which multiple loci of authority and authorization can compete and coexist, however uneasily, without feeling the necessity of imagining a violent or zero-sum ending. Whether or not publicity surrounding an increasingly "public" poetry is or will be a manifestation of or catalyst of a broader cultural-political change is another question altogether. Yet if one considers the role that literary performance and critique played in the development of modern democratic political critique, and if one considers the role that the physical and social spaces of the coffeehouse and the salon played in creating modernity, it may not seem too outlandish to think that something like a "poetry (or writing) scene" might play a role in preserving or revitalizing whatever is left of public culture in the United States.

Now it would be easy to dismiss participants in the extra-academic poetry scene as being either poetasters, as sincere people with "untutored and crude" talent, or simply to ignore the question of the value of the writing process itself. But where would such a response place academic criticism? As access to official culture, such as grant funding and university professorships, declines, and as a grassroots poetry culture continues to thrive, one wonders if poetry studies and its object of study aren't going in opposite directions. Precisely what, we might ask, distinguishes the academic writing scene from the community writing scene, and how is this distinction bound up with the aesthetic educations of poets and poetry critics? As much of poetry criticism continues in canonical, textualist, and evaluative modes, and as the rest of the profession becomes more interested in cultural history, it becomes apparent that poetry studies is at a crossroads. On the one hand, poetry in the academy may continue to be on the outs, marginalized within the profession, even as poetry as an art is in. On the other hand, the new developments in poetry may intimate the future of literary art in the United States; in that case, those interested in what they call poetry might be in a unique position to develop new methods and a new orientation that will help us understand the nature of art-writing in the twenty-first century.

Notes

Introduction

1. Excellent examples of such studies are too numerous to list exhaustively here. In addition to Tompkins, one has only to think of studies by Janice Radway, Michael Newbury, Lawrence Levine, Tony Bennett, or James D. Hart. Among other notable works that deal with the social history of literature are Q. D. Leavis, *Fiction and the Reading Public;* Ian Watt, *The Rise of the Novel: Studies in Defoe, Richardson, and Fielding;* Cathy Davidson, *Revolution and the Word: The Rise of the Novel in America;* Joan Shelley Rubin, *The Making of Middlebrow Culture;* and Adrian Johns, *The Nature of the Book: Print and Knowledge in the Making.* A study of intermedia forms in social context that I have found particularly provocative is Douglas Crimp and Adam Rolston, *AIDS DemoGraphics.*

2. For an excellent exposition of this history, see Alan Golding, "The New Criticism and American Poetry in the Academy," chap. 3 of *From Outlaw to Classic: Canons in American Poetry,* 70–113. And, as I suggest in chapter 6, the institutional history of poetry in the United States also suggests the genealogy of the relative absence of American poetry from studies of American literature.

3. Thus I would designate a study of social form "social-formalist" as opposed to either textual-formalist (whether New Critical or poststructuralist) or historicist (on the "representations of *x* in *y*" model). Sociologists will occasionally use the term "social form" to mean any institution or social practice. Rarely, literary critics will employ the term. Michael Levenson, in *Modernism and the Fate of Individuality,* evokes the problem of "the relation of character . . . to social form" in the modern British novel, by which he means "the portrayal of a dense web of social constraints followed by the effort to wrest an image

Notes to Introduction

of autonomous subjectivity from intractable communal norms" (xii). "Portrayal" and "image of" alert us to the fact that Levenson's study deals with representations of social forms (in the sociological sense) in novels, rather than with the social form of the novel itself, which would be closer to my project at present.

4. For instance, in addition to those discussed here, I would include, among others, works by Jerome McGann, Marjorie Perloff, Frank Ninkovich, Nina Baym (on Lydia Huntley Sigourney), as well as Lawrence Rainey, *Institutions of Modernism: Literary Elites and Public Culture*. Kevin Dettmar and Stephen Watt, *Marketing Modernisms: Self-Promotion, Canonization, and Rereading,* and Claire Badaracco, *Trading Words: Poetry, Typography, and Illustrated Books in the Modern Literary Economy.*

5. In addition to these, for instance, other works that have informed mine are Alan Golding, *From Outlaw to Classic;* Suzanne Clark, *Sentimental Modernism: Women Writers and the Revolution of the Word;* Russell Nye, *The Unembarrassed Muse: The Popular Arts in America;* and Cheryl Walker, *Masks Outrageous and Austere: Culture, Psyche, and Persona in Modern Women Poets.*

6. I use the awkward term "publicness" throughout to approximate the German *Öffentlichkeit,* usually translated as "public sphere," but which also includes, as Miriam Hansen points out, "a spatial concept, the social sites or arenas where meanings are articulated, distributed, and negotiated, as well as the collective body constituted by and in this process, 'the public.'" The term literally means "openness," and, Hansen continues, "the English word 'publicity' grasps this sense only in its historically alienated form" (Negt and Kluge, ix n. 1). Oskar Negt and Alexander Kluge expand *Öffentlichkeit* to mean the "general horizon of social experience." I argue in chapter 5 that Anna Louise Strong's verses, for instance, are alive to and play off all of these senses of "the public."

7. It should go without saying that my holding the populist position up for study does not imply that I hold it up for admiration: poetic populists could frequently be anti-intellectual and defensive, especially when confronted with the avant-garde poetics that dismissed or attacked them.

8. See, for instance, Fredric Jameson, *Fables of Aggression: Wyndham Lewis, the Modernist as Fascist;* Andrew Hewitt, *Fascist Modernism: Aesthetics, Politics, and the Avant-Garde;* Paul Morrison, *The Poetics of Fascism: Ezra Pound, T. S. Eliot, Paul de*

Man; and Erin G. Carlston, *Thinking Fascism: Sapphic Modernism and Fascist Modernity.*

9. Accordingly, my account diverges in important particulars from those influential works that focus on the historical context of canonical modernist poets, such as those by Alan Filreis, James Longenbach, Michael North, Frank Lentricchia, Cary Wolfe, Tim Redman, and many others.

Chapter One

1. By focusing on U.S. periodicals, I do not mean to imply that there existed a self-contained, purely "American" culture in the United States. For example, many articles in U.S. periodicals originally appeared in Britain, and British poets such as Alfred Noyes and John Maesfield were among the most celebrated on this side of the Atlantic. My interest at present concerns the versions of "poetry" available to U.S. readers, regardless of the origins of those versions or those readers.

2. My thanks to Carla Hesse for calling my attention to this aspect of the story.

3. I use "conservative" to describe a position that would conserve the dominant tradition of nineteenth-century poetics, which in turn celebrated and conserved dominant values.

4. I borrow "intransitive" from 1950s New Critic Eliseo Vivas: "By this word I mean that attention is aesthetic when it is so controlled by the object that it does not fly away from it to meanings and values not present immanently in the object; or in other words that attention is so controlled that the object specifies concretely and immediately through reflexive cross-references its meanings and objective characters" (96).

5. John Crowe Ransom likewise wrote that contemplation of an object under "the form of art" is what "Schopenhauer praised as 'knowledge without desire'" ("A Poem" 459). Ransom (chillingly, given his historical moment) calls this type of knowledge "innocence."

6. Tate's accusation is not without merit. Left critics in the 1930s did not necessarily attempt to theorize an identifiable effect of poetry upon its readers. Although, as Stanley Burnshaw says in a letter to *Poetry,* the Marxist poet's work "will be a weapon fighting on the side of the revolutionary proletariat," it will do so primarily by being "the best record of his sense of values" (353).

7. See Hammer's review of *Cleanth Brooks and Allen Tate: Collected Letters, 1933–1976*. For instance, one finds what we might call a "conflation of contempts" (for popular poets of the prewar era and for 1930s Marxist poetry) in Brooks's remark that "[Stephen] Spender's interest in Communism is essentially a sentimental one" (Brooks 281).

8. It is this part of the New Critical program that Gerald Graff refers to when he writes that their "insistence on the disinterested nature of poetic experience was an implicit rejection of a utilitarian culture and thus a powerfully 'utilitarian' and 'interested' gesture" (149). However, as I will argue in the next chapter, Tate's poetics is politically interested in a much less implicit and more obviously contradictory sense.

9. Or, as Benet put it, "I do not see why the same obligation should not rest upon poets that rests upon all prose writers except Gertrude Stein . . . That obligation is to *be clear*. . . . the ego of the poet is so inflated that he considers his public beneath him" ("Round About" 536). If Hemingway was, as Stein declared, "90 percent Rotarian," some Rotarians yearned for a Hemingwayesque simplicity in verse.

10. Not coincidentally, "The Petrified Forest" was originally written as a play by that former Algonquin round table habitué Robert Sherwood.

11. It should be noted that what counted as impossible for Monroe underwent considerable revision over the years. Joyce Kilmer, after all, was one of *Poetry*'s early stars.

12. For instance, Jancovich's bibliography records no appearances of essays after this date by Tate in monthly or weekly magazines other than the *American Review*, by then largely dominated by Agrarian and New-Critical arguments. The *Reader's Guide* confirms Tate's absence from popular periodicals in the late 1930s, though Ashley Brown and Frances Neal Cheney's anthology of Tate's reviews contains two (from the *Nation* and the *New Republic*) published in the early 1940s.

13. David Perkins records that, in the 1900s and 1910s, "[t]he stream of verse in America was swollen from a source that was much less noticeable in England—the 'handyman' or 'do-it-yourselfer'" (89). Ransom's desire for "professionalization" of criticism is a response to the old poetry as much as it is to the old criticism.

14. For fuller treatments of New Criticism in the academy of the 1940s and

1950s, see Jancovich; Graff, *Professing Literature: An Institutional History;* and Richard Ohmann, *English in America: A Radical View of the Profession.* Alan Golding notes that the New Critics would institutionalize, in the academy, "the acts of evaluation that had historically been the preserve of public criticism" ("Poet-Critics" 19). He attributes this shift to "the demise of literary journalism in the Depression." But there was, in fact, an outpouring of criticism in monthlies and weeklies in the 1930s. Peter Brooks is probably closer to the mark when he speculates that "[i]t's not certain that the 'general reader' who sustained and responded to the quarterlies (*Partisan Review, Hudson Review*) and even the monthlies (*Harper's, Atlantic Monthly*) from the 1930s through the 1950s still exists or still is interested—or has turned instead to 'Masterpiece Theater' and McNeil-Lehrer" (523). This account would provide an even stronger basis for Golding's thesis that the institutional routinization of criticism eventually betrayed the larger goals of Tate, Ransom, and company.

15. Pound is, in fact, a shadowy presence in literary debates in U.S. periodicals from the 1920s through the 1960s; he, like Eliot, became a floating signifier rather than a participant in the conversation. Indeed, as K. K. Ruthven points out, academic Pound criticism was rather spotty before Kenner's *The Pound Era* (1972) offered young critics an alternative to Eliotic modernism (Ruthven 167ff).

16. As Brett Cox points out, New Critics spread this sublimated happiness through their later educational endeavors. Cox quotes Brooks and Warren as writing, in their textbook *Understanding Poetry* (1936), that "a successful poem confirms us in the faith that the experiences of life itself may have meaning" and comments, "The function of literature, even formally complex, ambiguous, and ironic literature, is, finally, to make us feel better" (232). Cox suggests that the New Critics introduced this combination of practicality and idealism, but, as we have seen, that combination had been present in U.S. poetics for over a century.

Chapter Two

1. I follow my subject here in the use of "he" to refer to a putatively ungendered antecedent; this pronoun use is, of course, bound up with Tate's political premises.

2. Ezra Pound might seem the more likely (or fashionable) subject in this

respect. I have chosen to focus on Tate because, in addition to his influence on the academic study of literature in the United States, after the mid-1920s, his writings also appeared more frequently in the U.S. popular press than did Pound's. Tate developed what might be called a domestic version of high modernism, one that would have more immediate and far-reaching institutional influence on the construction of poetry in the United States than would Pound's; Tate as much as anyone was responsible for the institutionalization of a self-consciously "Eliotic" poetics.

3. As Mark Jancovich notes, a similar current can be found in Ransom's thought, where the "dilemma for modern writers is that while their traditional function did not distinguish between ethics and aesthetics, or the public and the private, in the modern world, the two are isolated from one another and even come to oppose one another" (40).

4. A reference to Rufus Putnam (1738–1824), Revolutionary War general and early settler of the Ohio Valley.

5. For more on the gendering of political poetry as "hysterical" and "hagridden," see Susan Schweik's discussion of negative responses to Edna Millay and Muriel Rukeyser in *A Gulf So Deeply Cut*.

6. "Aeneas at New York" was published in the *New Republic* to second Archibald MacLeish's rejection of social poetry, "Invocation to the Social Muse," which had appeared in the same venue (and which MacLeish himself was soon to reject in favor of mass poetry).

7. In one strain, this increasing individuation of private life leads to a postromantic antipolitical stance that Rosenblum identifies with aestheticism: "Aestheticism involves cultivating certain exquisite sensations and tastes, but more importantly bringing artistic criteria to bear on every experience. By submitting every action and relation to this imperative aestheticism privatizes experience, or at least does not respect the conventional division among pluralist spheres with distinct attitudes, obligations, and norms" (98).

8. Ernesto Laclau and Chantal Mouffe (1989) describe this contradiction: "We are thus witnessing the emergence of a new hegemonic project, that of liberal-conservative discourse, which seeks to articulate the neo-liberal defence of the free market economy with the profoundly anti-egalitarian cultural and social traditionalism of conservatism" (175). My only disagreement with this description is the adjective "new." This is a mixture of opposites that have been

around since the beginning of liberalism. What was, in fact, new in the 1980s was the political hegemony of this "liberal conservatism."

9. It should be borne in mind that neither Federalists nor Antifederalists argued for what today goes by the name of pluralism; what was at stake in terms of political culture was the *geographical extent* of the unified political community.

10. Marcuse draws a parallel between liberal reliance on natural law and fascist organicism. Regardless of the validity of such a move, my point here is that liberals often posit a certain level of cultural, if not organic, concurrence that preexists and underwrites the existence of the state. For Locke, men living in a state of nature are already "the community" and, in banding together to form the state, form a "political community."

11. Sheldon Wolin sees a similar tension between Mill's opposition to the "despotism of society over the individual" on the one hand, and his acceptance of open ballots and "social disapproval of large families" on the other (349). The key factor is what individuality is to be used for; for Mill, it would seem to be some idea of the common good. Wolin associates the tendency toward social conformity even more powerfully with the Adam Smith of the *Theory of Moral Sentiments* who says that "'of all things,' the individual has the 'greatest desire' to conform" (345).

12. Accordingly, in 1927 the poet wrote his father for a "full list of woiks [*sic*] included in Doc. Eliot's 'bookshelf'" of "essential" literature in the Harvard Classics (Carpenter 468).

13. Letter from Tate to Stevens, 4 Oct. 1941. This item is reproduced by permission of the Huntington Library, San Marino, California.

14. Letter from Stevens to Tate, 6 July 1943. This item is reproduced by permission of the Huntington Library, San Marino, California.

Chapter Three

1. For background on and first-person accounts of this address, see Brazeau, 161ff. Stevens would, of course, go on to deliver numerous lectures during the Second World War and the Cold War that followed; in these lectures, the poet became increasingly committed to describing the relationship of poetry to politics.

2. Further references to this edition in this chapter will be noted parenthetically in the text without the title of the work.

3. Brazeau quotes Stevens as saying, "I suffer like a child with something 'coming on' as the time approaches and it all grows worse when the time actually arrives. Accordingly, I had rather not. It isn't worth reading in public unless one reads as one reads to oneself, and I can't imagine doing that" (162).

4. See Harvey Teres, "Notes toward the Supreme Soviet: Stevens and Doctrinaire Marxism"; Melita Schaum, "Lyric Resistance: Views of the Political in the Poetics of Wallace Stevens and H.D."; and James Longenbach, *Wallace Stevens: The Plain Sense of Things*.

5. See Burnshaw's "Turmoil in the Middle Ground," a review of Stevens's book *Ideas of Order*.

6. Wallace Stevens, "Insurance and Social Change," which originally appeared in the *Hartford Agent*, is collected in *Opus Posthumous*, 233–37; I have used the latter in citing the article.

7. H. G. Wells was not uninterested in the subject at hand, nor unwilling to make it "his field." In *Marxism v. Liberalism, an Interview between Joseph Stalin and H. G. Wells*, conducted in July of 1934, Wells asks, "But is there not a relation in ideas, a kinship of ideas, between Washington and Moscow? In Washington I was struck by the same thing I see going on here; they are building offices, they are creating a number of new state regulation bodies, they are organizing a long-needed Civil Service. Their need, like yours, is directive ability" (4). Stalin replies, predictably, that the New Dealers are leaving "the economic basis" of capitalism untouched, despite reforms. Nonetheless, Wells keeps trying to articulate Soviet communism to "socialism, in the Anglo-Saxon meaning of the word" (5). "Organization, and the regulation of individual action," he claims, "have become mechanical necessities, irrespective of social theories" (7). These comments offer a glimpse into the mechanistic overtones of what many took to be the "social engineering" project of both public insurance and the New Deal; many in this country agreed that what was going on in Moscow was indeed going on in Washington.

8. Thus, Stevens does not claim here that "'perfect insurance' needed to take an unmistakably public form," as one critic has argued (Szalay 51). Quite the contrary: Stevens attempts to downplay the threat of Social Security to the insurance industry by reminding his colleagues that perfect insurance is an impossibility, even for the nation-state. "Risk" does not represent the elimination of chance so much as its description; hence private insurance is necessary in the 1930s just as it was in the 1830s, and for the same reason. It is this notion

of risk on which Stevens's poetics, as well as his anxieties about subjectivity, are based, as I will show.

9. Most of "Surety and Fidelity Claims" is taken up by an extended presentation of seemingly undecidable claims on surety bonds—an object lesson in the need for the imaginative claims man (or, perhaps, poet-critic) to bring interpretive order out of indeterminacy (at least temporarily).

10. See Wallace Stevens, "The Noble Rider and the Sound of Words" (1942): "The mind . . . is a violence from within that protects us from a violence without. It is the imagination pressing back against the pressure of reality. . . . [T]he expression of it, the sound of its words, helps us to live our lives" (*Necessary* 36). In "Sunday Morning" (from *Harmonium*, 1923; reprinted in *Wallace Stevens: The Collected Poems*, 66–70), Stevens writes, "Death is the mother of beauty, mystical / Within whose burning bosom we devise / Our earthly mothers waiting, sleeplessly" (69).

11. Another 1910s version of an insured utopia, one that may have influenced the young Stevens more directly, was that described in Josiah Royce's *War and Insurance* (1914). In this work, Royce posits a "Community of Insurance" bound together by the interpretive powers of the agent. I am grateful to Sandra Gustafson for alerting me to the connection between Royce's writings on insurance and Stevens's. Longenbach discusses this connection in more detail (194).

12. See Alan Filreis, *Wallace Stevens and the Actual World*, xviii.

13. Robert Emmett Monroe, in a very useful reading of "Owl's Clover," also marks this "method of transforming political realities into abstract figures, a method that will become habitual" in Stevens's later work (128). Here, once again, Stevens's style refuses to be "imprisoned by the tyranny of habitual social forms" as the poem "works through central problems of American individualism" (147). In my view, the poem reinscribes those problems and is indeed built around them. Monroe seeks a "justification" of Stevens's style; I am more concerned at present with analyzing the poet's own rationale in the 1930s. Stevens represents his poems not as resisting tyranny or performing a public service but as sublimating the public altogether—precisely because it seems to threaten the integrity of an individual subject that is constituted as private.

14. See Gerald Bruns's comment: "It is not, as Hugh Kenner once remarked, that there are no people in Stevens' poetry (Stevens critics are testy about hav-

ing their man called a solipsist); it is that people in Stevens' poetry never answer back" (26). As Bruns points out, one of the *Adagia* says, "Life is an affair of people not of places. But for me life is an affair of places and that is the trouble" (Stevens, *Opus* 185).

15. The surety bond, taken out by a contractor, indemnifies the issuer of that bond for the successful completion of the contract. So if, for instance, the Hartford bonds a plumber who has a contract to install pipes in a new office building, and the plumber defaults, the Hartford must either finish the job or pay off the builders. Or vice versa, if the builders are bonded and fail to pay.

16. For more on changes in the role of separation of spheres in the political and literary life of liberal societies between the eighteenth and twentieth centuries, see Jürgen Habermas, *The Structural Transformation of the Public Sphere: An Inquiry into a Category of Bourgeois Society;* Reinhart Koselleck, *Critique and Crisis: Enlightenment and the Pathogenesis of Modern Society;* Carole Pateman, "The Fraternal Social Contract," in *The Disorder of Women: Democracy, Feminism, and Political Theory,* 33–57; and Nancy Fraser, "Rethinking the Public Sphere: A Contribution to the Critique of Actually Existing Democracy."

Chapter Four

1. "The arts of SPEECH," Kant writes, in *The Critique of Judgment,* "are *rhetoric* and *poetry*" (184). These arts are defined as opposites: "Thus the *orator* announces a serious business, and for the purpose of entertaining his audience conducts it as if it were a mere *play* with ideas. The *poet* promises merely an entertaining *play* with ideas, and yet for the understanding there enures as much as if the promotion of its business had been his one intention" (185).

2. Compare lines from "Owl's Clover": "Green is the path we take / Between chimeras, and garlanded the way / The down-descent into November's void" (Stevens, *Opus* 97). At this level of abstraction, Edwardians and modernists alike take the long view.

3. And, indeed, Giovannitti's implicit equation of (and ventriloquizing through) the ancient world, biblical times, the Middle Ages, and the eighteenth century harks back to William Cullen Bryant's poems of historical romance, in which the age of chivalry, Indian lore, the American Revolution and the Greeks are all described in the same general terms and speak with the voice of the 1820s.

4. It is difficult to establish a definitive biography of Giovannitti. My account here is composed of those features where the literary critics, propaganda pamphlets (such as *Ettor and Giovannitti before the Jury*), Helen Keller's introduction to *Arrows,* and historians seem to agree. There are many accounts of the Lawrence strike and many details on which they agree; see, for instance Kornbluh, 158–96, for a documentary history, or Philip S. Foner, 306–28, for a more narrative development.

5. Hester Furey makes a similar point about Keller's preface. Furey explains this "contradiction" by ascribing it to "the combination of an obligatory gesture towards the poetry establishment of the time with the American left's own untheorized practices with regard to poetry" (45). As I have attempted to show, however, critics of "the poetry establishment" follow the same pattern of thought with regard to Giovannitti.

6. Letter from Giovannitti to Anton Johannson, 28 March 1917. Wood Collection, WD Box 142 (32). This item is reproduced by permission of the Huntington Library, San Marino, California.

7. At the same time, Giovannitti wrote more overtly political poems in later years. Consider, for example, "The Revolution" (1916): "Arise, then, / Ye men of the plow and hammer . . . Peace shall reign forever! / And this shall be called the revolution." While this poem, like many others by the same poet, deals in abstract nouns, here it takes on a more specific political cast, as it both echoes the "Internationale" and moves more in the direction of proletarian poetry of the next two decades.

8. As James Kloppenberg puts it, progressives "turned the old liberalism into a new liberalism," one "free from the idea of a self-guiding market economy and the negative conception of liberty associated with variations on the theme of liberalism" (299–300). Rather, both progressives and social democrats "replaced their liberal ancestors' model of an atomistic society with an ideal incorporating positive as well as negative liberty, duties as well as rights" (7).

9. Kloppenberg quotes John Dewey's statement that "the non-social individual is an abstraction arrived at by imagining what man would be if all his human qualities were taken away" (329). Dewey is, of course, critiquing the laissez-faire contractual liberalism that he and his "new" liberal colleagues attempted to transcend.

10. Poetry, writes Kant, must have "the appearance of being undesigned and a spontaneous occurrence—otherwise it is not *fine* art . . . For fine art must be free art" (185).

11. Heaton says of Giovannitti's speech that "[h]is final sentences choked up some of the reporters, busy as they were trying to take them down" and quotes a reporter as saying, "In twenty years of reporting I have never heard the equal of that speech" (304). It was precisely these literary-critical and reportorial responses that translated Giovannitti's utterances in both verse and prose into a mode of discourse that is personal expression and public oratory at once.

12. Kant continues, "I must confess to the pure delight which I have ever been afforded by a beautiful poem" as opposed to "oratory (*ars oratoria*), being the art of playing for one's own purpose upon the weaknesses of men . . . [which] merits no *respect* whatever" (193n).

13. The poem "The Revolution" (1916), for instance, carries the subscript, "Written for the Labor Pageant, held by the Rand School of Social Science, New York, in commemoration of its tenth anniversary, April 28 to May 1." For an illuminating discussion of Giovannitti's religious influence, see Donald E. Winters Jr., *The Soul of the Wobblies: The I.W.W., Religion, and American Culture in the Progressive Era, 1905–1917*, 93–100.

14. For more on Untermeyer's shifting assessment of modernism over the years, see Craig Abbot, "Untermeyer on Eliot," 105–19.

Chapter Five

1. Strong is best known as a journalist and propagandist, first for Stalin and later for Mao. In the 1910s, however, her affiliations, like her writing and much of her contemporaries', was more indeterminate, improvised, and independent than during and after the 1930s.

2. I borrow the term "romantico-modernist" from Philip Barnard's and Cheryl Lester's introduction to *The Literary Absolute;* they use it to describe the persistence of the view of literature that Philippe Lacoue-Labarthe and Jean-Luc Nancy see epitomized in the exalted and "indefinable character" the Jena Romantics attribute to "Poetry." As Lacoue-Labarthe and Nancy write: "A veritable romantic *unconscious* is discernable today, in most of the central motifs of our 'modernity' " (15). The aspect that interests me here is the notion of

Poetry as pure literature, a sublimated realm apart from and set in opposition to historical contingency.

3. I use Miriam Hansen's description of Negt and Kluge's revision of Habermas's notion of a unitary pubic sphere (Negt and Kluge xxix). By contrast, Negt and Kluge believe that the bourgeois public sphere was always accompanied and opposed at various times by "counter-publics." Indeed, even in the twentieth century, they see a rump version of the classical bourgeois public sphere as existing alongside industrial-commercial "public spheres of production," as well as a potential proletarian public sphere. In any event, their model for understanding multiple public spheres has obviously informed my understanding of Strong, just as her own work illustrates that model.

4. As a high-school senior, "She wanted to be 'a North Pole explorer, and an airman, and a great writer, and a mother of ten—one child wasn't worth the time'" (Strong and Keyssar 24). By the late 1910s, she seems to have settled upon writing. Unless otherwise noted, biographical information comes from the Tracy Strong and Helene Keyssar biography, *Right in Her Soul*.

5. It is useful to bear in mind some of the chronology of what we now call modernism: *Poetry* began publication in 1912, *Des Imagistes* was published in 1914, "Sunday Morning" in 1915, *Prufrock and Other Poems* in 1917. 1917 also marks the beginning of the widespread use of the term "modernism." And while the avant-garde in poetry may have lacked widespread influence in the prewar years, it was certainly widely known.

6. Typescript, Anna Louise Strong papers, Manuscripts, Special Collections, University Archives Division, University of Washington Libraries, Seattle. I date this poem 1917, given other stylistically similar pieces from the same year, as well as the fact that Strong had watched her friend Louise Olivereau tried for sedition in 1917. The poem may well have been written for publication in the socialist *Seattle Daily Call*, a short-lived newspaper for which Strong wrote under the pen-name "Gale."

7. Anna Louise Strong papers, Manuscripts, Special Collections, University Archives Division, University of Washington Libraries, Seattle.

8. The adjectives "bourgeois" or "classical" describe the historically dominant notion of the public sphere as described by Habermas, namely, a very delimited and abstract space both in terms of activities and participants. I will use Negt and Kluge's term "proletarian public sphere" to denote not only pro-

letarian in the strict Marxian sense of the word, but also any attempt to establish social space that is not limited to the parameters of the classical public sphere or based solely in the structure of production, but which envisions a horizon of experience for human liberation more generally.

9. For poems and articles not included in *Ragged Verse,* dates in parentheses indicate an edition of the *Seattle Union Record.*

10. Typescript history of the Seattle Union Record, written c. 1923. Harry Ault papers, Manuscripts, Special Collections, University Archives Division, University of Washington Libraries, Seattle.

11. Holograph letter (in rhyme), n.d., to the editor of the *Union Record,* signed "a Friend." Harry Ault papers.

12. While it seems unlikely that Strong's ambitions were ever primarily literary, the fact that her self-published book ended up in the hands of reviewers in the East bespeaks a certain concern with their visibility.

13. Letter from Anna Louise Strong to Harry Ault, 31 May 1921. Harry Ault papers, Manuscripts, Special Collections, University Archives Division, University of Washington Libraries, Seattle.

14. Indeed, Strong recognized the power of modern media; as part of her child welfare work in 1910 and 1911, she commissioned several one-reel films for use in hygiene exhibits (Strong and Keyssar 53).

15. There may be a historical connection here. Andreas Huyssen writes that "[a]gainst the codified high modernism of the preceding decades, the postmodernism of the 1960s tried to revitalize the heritage of the European avant-garde and to give it an American form along what one could call in short-hand the Duchamp—Cage—Warhol axis" (Alexander and Seidman 360). In other words, both the poetic style of Strong and the aesthetic of Anderson may have more in common with each other and with the avant-garde tradition (of, say, dadaism), than any of them have with the now-domesticated English-language "modernism." For a fuller exposition of this argument, see Walter Kalaidjian's *American Culture between the Wars.*

16. The editors of the *Union Record* also included verse of the overtly inspirational and sententious variety. Usually these poems decried social wrongs, but on occasion readers would come across a poem whose politics are less explicit, as with "Carry On," by Robert Service: "Carry on. Carry on / Fight the good fight and true; / Believe in your mission, greet dawn with a cheer, / There's big work to do and that's why you're here" (15 Mar. 1919). While this

is a poem designed for a general audience by an extremely popular poet, its valence for unionists who, a month previously, had called off a general strike (that the "kept press" said they had lost) might be different than that for a businessman reading it in a different paper.

17. Letter from Anna Louise Strong to Harry Ault, 18 Mar. 1918. Harry Ault papers, Manuscripts, Special Collections, University Archives Division, University of Washington Libraries, Seattle. Strong also suggests that she be paid "not a certain salary to cover certain hours work per day, but a certain sum to cover the entire department."

18. Letter from Clara H. Waller to Anna Louise Strong, 12 May 1921; letter from N. F. Newcomb to Anna Louise Strong, 29 May 1921. Tracy Strong papers, Manuscripts, Special Collections, University Archives Division, University of Washington Libraries, Seattle. I have retained the authors' punctuation.

Chapter Six

1. Although Mattheissen's book dehistoricized the narrative of American literature, it also marked off that narrative from modernism and from poetry. Mattheissen had already devoted a separate book to *The Achievement of T. S. Eliot* (1935).

2. Likewise, Frank Lentricchia notes the congruence between Francis Palgrave's nineteenth-century poetics and Pound's view of "poetry as an alternative, special kind of discourse" that transcends the market (72). Yet Lentricchia does not pursue this point; rather, he goes on to demonstrate that "The Road Not Taken," despite its inclusion in *The Best Loved Poems of the American People,* really is subtle and complex enough to warrant Frost's inclusion in the modernist pantheon. Another critic comments that "the New Criticism recapitulated the literary idealism of the genteel tradition and did so in a fashion that, however subtly, echoes many of the same cultural anxieties troubling writers of the genteel tradition" (Cox 228). Yet while literary idealism is present in both ideologies, genteel critics harbored considerable suspicion of the idea of the poem as craft object; moreover, for older poets and critics, poetry was not so much "outside the concerns" of history, science, or economics, but rather sought to transform these spheres *from* outside, precisely through an ethical influence.

3. For instance, Ransom, in his scurrilous review of Millay, describes his age as that which "has recovered the admirable John Donne; that is the way to identify its literary taste" ("Poet as Woman" 784).

4. Cf. Alan Golding's discussion of the de-Americanization of poetry in *From Outlaw to Classic: Canons in American Poetry* (1995), chap. 3, "The New Criticism and American Poetry in the Academy."

5. There has been a growing realization of this contradiction among poetry scholars since I first published a version of this argument in 1996 ("Why American Poetry Is Not American Literature"). Michael Davidson reported "feeling that in the last decades of the twentieth century poetry has become marginalized in favor of narrative. This is especially the case in Marxist cultural theory," where this neglect "has been based to some extent on a narrow definition of poetry as ideology whose separation from the production and reproduction of social life is a necessary condition for its existence" (xi–xii). Likewise, Maria Damon (1997) correctly pointed out that cultural studies "has written poetry off as a priori high cultural, ergo unrecuperable. Irony of ironies, because, far more than narrative written genres[,] poetry—ritually charged incantation—has been central to the cultural traditions of many subordinate peoples in the United States" ("Postliterary" 38–39). More recently (1999), Christopher Beach pointed out that "because of the persistent perception of poetry as an exclusively 'high cultural' phenomenon . . . the methods of cultural studies that have been used to interrogate modes of 'popular culture' (film, television, popular music, novels) have not yet been applied in any systematic way to poetry" (2).

6. Accordingly, Marjorie Perloff's essay "Modernist Studies" in *Redrawing the Boundaries,* unlike Tichi's or Fisher's, focuses primarily on poetry criticism. While some influential Americanists have addressed poets in discussions of American literature (one thinks of Charles Fiedelson's inclusion of Poe and Eliot, or R. W. B. Lewis's use of Holmes to represent the immature period of American literature), characterizations of Richard Chase's and Leslie Fiedler's studies of the American novel as theories of American literature are more symptomatic of the general tendency.

7. Newbury does deal with a stanza from a poem by a mill worker in the *Lowell Offering* (72) but does not treat widely read writers such as Lydia Huntley Sigourney or William Cullen Bryant, both of whose poetic careers arguably contributed to the notion of "the authorial profession as something more than a mere commercial trade" (6). Indeed, highlighting the fact that the *Offering* published poetry by workers (and not only fiction or essays) would only strengthen

Newbury's account of the role of this magazine and of authorship more generally, for all the historical reasons I have adduced.

8. Likewise, Rafia Zafar's *We Wear the Mask: African Americans Write American Literature*, despite taking its name from Paul Lawrence Dunbar's 1896 sonnet (and despite the book's comprehensive breadth), does not discuss poems later than Joel Barlow's *Columbiad* (1807). Among many other examples, see Lori Merish, *Sentimental Materialism: Gender, Commodity Culture, and Nineteenth-Century American Literature;* Philip Fisher, *Still the New World: American Literature in a Culture of Creative Destruction;* Nancy Ruttenberg, *Democratic Personality: Popular Voice and the Trial of American Authorship;* Christopher Looby, *Voicing America: Language, Literary Form, and the Origins of the United States;* Sandra Gunning, *Race, Rape, and Lynching: The Red Record of American Literature, 1890–1912;* or Sacvan Bercovich's *Rites of Assent: Transformations in the Symbolic Construction of America.*

9. James D. Hart, in *The Popular Book,* reports that "[t]he mid-century was the great era of poetry" (138); he records twenty-four volumes of poetry published between 1838 and 1870 on his "list of the books most widely read in America in the years immediately following publication" (301). The stock in one New York bookstore in 1840–41 included 479 books of poems, 668 novels, 3,283 religious titles, and 5,401 general educational books (cited in Zboray 141); were sales the sole rationale for critical attention, it is not clear why it should settle on narrative rather than didactic prose. In fact, Nicholas Zill and Marianne Winglee used a 1985 NEA/Census Bureau survey to conclude that 19 percent of adults and 22 percent of all readers in the United States at that time were "poetry readers" (27).

10. I am grateful to Marjorie Perloff for calling my attention to this point.

11. Personal interview, Nov. 1993.

12. Personal interview, Sept. 1993.

13. For a detailed account of how slams function at the Nuyorican Poets Cafe in New York City, see Beach 128–32.

14. These interviews, unless otherwise noted, were conducted on condition of anonymity.

15. Gioia since moved away from this position and embraced the heterogeneity of the contemporary scene. See his very lively discussion in "Notes toward a New Bohemia."

Bibliography

Abbot, Craig. "Untermeyer on Eliot," *Journal of Modern Literature* 15, 1 (summer 1988): 105–19.

Abbott, Christabel. "Problems in the School Reading of Poetry." *Education* 34 (May 1914): 555–60.

Alden, Raymond Macdonald. "The New Poetry" (letter). *Nation*, 17 Apr. 1913, 386–87.

Alexander, Jeffrey C., and Steven Seidman, eds. *Culture and Society: Contemporary Debates*. Cambridge: Cambridge University Press, 1990.

Alston, Madeline. "Children and Poetry." *Living Age* 299 (1918): 485–91.

Amfitheatrof, Erik. *The Children of Columbus: An Informal History of the Italians in the New World*. Boston: Little, Brown, 1973.

Applegate, Debby. "Roman à Clef." *American Literary History* 7 (spring 1995): 151–60.

Arbiter, Petronius. "What Is Poetry?" *Art World* 3 (1918): 506–11.

Arnold, Matthew. *Culture and Anarchy*. New Haven, Conn.: Yale University Press, 1994.

Ashleigh, Charles. "The Poetry of Revolt." *Little Review* 1:6 (Sept. 1914): 22–25.

A.W.P. "A Word for Magazine Verse" (letter). *Dial* 52 (1912): 308.

Badaracco, Claire. *Trading Words: Poetry, Typography, and Illustrated Books in the Modern Literary Economy*. Baltimore, Md.: Johns Hopkins University Press, 1995.

Bates, Milton J. *Wallace Stevens: A Mythology of Self*. Berkeley: University of California Press, 1985.

Baym, Nina. *American Women Writers and the Work of History, 1790–1860*. New Brunswick, N.J.: Rutgers University Press, 1995.

Beach, Christopher. *Poetic Culture: Contemporary American Poetry between Community and Institution.* Evanston, Ill.: Northwestern University Press, 1999.

[Benet, William Rose.] "Poetry and Modern Life." *Saturday Review of Literature* 12 (1935): 8.

Benet, William Rose. "Round about Parnassus." *Saturday Review of Literature* 12 (1935): 536.

Bennett, Tony. *Outside Literature.* London: Routledge, 1990.

Bercovich, Sacvan. *Rites of Assent: Transformations in the Symbolic Construction of America.* New York: Routledge, 1993.

Black, Matthew Wilson. "Boys and Poetry." *Scribner's Magazine* 78 (1925): 538–44.

Bourdieu, Pierre. *Distinction.* Cambridge, Mass.: Harvard University Press, 1984.

Bradley, William Aspenwall. "The New Poetry." *Bookman* 40: 2 (Oct. 1914): 202–10.

Braley, Berton. "People *Do* Read Poetry." *Literary Digest* 117 (1934): 41.

Brazeau, Peter. *Parts of a World: Wallace Stevens Remembered.* San Francisco: North Point Press, 1985.

Breslin, James E. B. *From Modern to Contemporary: American Poetry, 1945–1965.* Chicago: University of Chicago Press, 1983.

Brooks, Cleanth. "Poetry and Political Faith." Review of *The Destructive Element* and *Forward from Liberalism,* by Stephen Spender. *Poetry* 50 (1937): 280–84.

Brooks, Peter. "Aesthetics and Ideology: What Happened to Poetics?" *Critical Inquiry* 20 (spring 1994): 509–23.

Bruns, Gerald. "Stevens without Epistemology." In *Wallace Stevens: The Poetics of Modernism,* edited by Albert Gelpi, 24–40. New York: Cambridge University Press, 1985.

Bryant, William Cullen. "Lectures on Poetry." In *Prose Writings of William Cullen Bryant, Volume First: Essays, Tales, and Orations,* edited by Parke Godwin, 3–44. New York: D. Appleton and Company, 1889.

Buckingham, Willis. "Poetry Readers and Reading in the 1890's: Emily Dickinson's First Reception." In *Readers in History: Nineteenth-Century American Literature and the Contexts of Response,* edited by James L. Machor, 164–79. Baltimore, Md.: Johns Hopkins University Press, 1993.

Burnshaw, Stanley. "Stanley Burnshaw Protests" (letter). *Poetry* 44 (1934): 351–54.

———. "Turmoil in the Middle Ground," *New Masses,* 1 Oct. 1935, 41–42.

"Can You Name These Modern Poets?" (pictorial feature). *Ladies' Home Journal,* Mar. 1928, 22+.

Erin G. Carlston, *Thinking Fascism: Sapphic Modernism and Fascist Modernity*. Stanford, Calif.: Stanford University Press, 1998.

Carpenter, Humphrey. *A Serious Character: The Life of Ezra Pound*. London: Faber and Faber, 1988.

Carroll, Jerry. "Second Act of Polly Klaas Tragedy Plays Out over T.V." (editorial). *San Francisco Examiner*, 11 Dec. 1993.

Clark, Suzanne. *Sentimental Modernism: Women Writers and the Revolution of the Word*. Bloomington: Indiana University Press, 1991.

Crimp, Douglas, and Adam Rolston. *AIDS DemoGraphics*. Seattle: Bay Press, 1990.

Cox, F. Brett. "'What Need, Then, for Poetry?': The Genteel Tradition and the Continuity of American Literature." *New England Quarterly* 67 (1994): 212–33.

Damon, Maria. "Postliterary Poetry, Counterperformance, and Micropoetries." In *Class Issues: Pedagogy, Cultural Studies, and the Public Sphere*, edited by Amitava Kumar, 33–47. New York: New York University Press, 1997.

———. *The Dark End of the Street: Margins in American Vanguard Poetry*. Minneapolis: University of Minnesota Press, 1993.

Davidson, Cathy. *Revolution and the Word: The Rise of the Novel in America*. Oxford: Oxford University Press, 1984.

Davidson, Michael. *Ghostlier Demarcations: Modern Poetry and the Material Word*. Berkeley: University of California Press, 1997.

Dettmar, Kevin, and Stephen Watt, eds., *Marketing Modernisms: Self-Promotion, Canonization, and Rereading*. Ann Arbor: University of Michigan Press, 1996.

"Do You Know Your Poetry?" *Ladies' Home Journal*, June 1938, 63+.

Dolan, Frederick M. *Allegories of America: Narratives, Metaphysics, Politics*. Ithaca, N.Y.: Cornell University Press, 1994.

Dowling, William C. *Poetry and Ideology in Revolutionary Connecticut*. Athens: University of Georgia Press, 1990.

Dresner, Zita. "Heterodite Humor: Alice Duer Miller and Florence Guy Seabury." *Journal of American Culture* 10:3 (fall 1987): 33–38.

Drew, Elizabeth. "The Poet and His Audience." *Forum* 103:5 (May 1940): 270–71.

Drinkwater, John. "Poetry and Conduct." *Living Age* 286 (1915): 98–106.

Ebert, Justus. "Who Arturo Giovannitti Is: A Short Sketch of His Life." *Industrial Worker*, 30 May 1912.

Ettor and Giovannitti before the Jury at Salem, Massachusetts, November 23, 1912. Chicago: Industrial Workers of the World, n.d.

Ficke, Arthur Davison. "The Present State of Poetry." *North American Review* 194 (Sept. 1911): 429–41.

Filreis, Alan. *Modernism from Right to Left: Wallace Stevens, the Thirties, and Literary Radicalism*. Cambridge: Cambridge University Press, 1994.

———. *Wallace Stevens and the Actual World*. Princeton, N.J.: Princeton University Press, 1991.

Fisher, Philip. "American Literary and Cultural Studies since the Civil War." In Greenblatt and Gunn 1992, 232–50.

———. *The New American Studies: Essays from* Representations. Berkeley: University of California Press, 1991.

———. *Still the New World: American Literature in a Culture of Creative Destruction*. Cambridge, Mass.: Harvard University Press, 1999.

Flynn, Elizabeth Gurley. *I Speak My Own Piece*. New York: Masses & Mainstream, 1955.

Foner, Philip S. *History of the Labor Movement in the United States*. Vol. 1, *The Industrial Workers of the World, 1905–1917*. New York: International Publishers, 1965.

Fraser, Nancy. "Rethinking the Public Sphere: A Contribution to the Critique of Actually Existing Democracy," *Social Text 25/26* (1990): 56–80.

[Freeman], Mary E. Wilkins. "A Poetess" (story). *Harper's New Monthly Magazine* 81 (1890): 197–204.

Furey, Hester L. "The Reception of Arturo Giovannitti's Poetry and the Trial of a New Society." *left history* 2:1 (spring 1994): 27–50.

Gallagher, Catherine. "Formalism and Time." *MLQ: Modern Language Quarterly* 61:1 (2000): 229–51.

Gilbert, Roger. *Walks in the World: Representation and Experience in Modern American Poetry*. Princeton, N.J.: Princeton University Press, 1991.

Gioia, Dana. "Notes toward a New Bohemia." *Poetry Flash* 248 (mid-Nov.–Dec. 1993): 7+.

———. *Can Poetry Matter: Essays on Poetry and American Culture*. Saint Paul, Minn.: Graywolf Press, 1992.

———. "Can Poetry Matter?" *Atlantic Monthly*, May 1991, 94–106.

Giovannitti, Arturo. *Arrows in the Gale*. Introduction by Helen Keller. Riverside, Conn.: Hillacre Bookhouse, 1914.

———. "The Cage" (poem). *Atlantic Monthly*, June 1913, 751–55.

———. Letter to Anton Johannson, 28 March 1917. Erskine Scott Wood Collection, WD Box 142 (32). Huntington Library, San Marino, Calif..

———. "The Revolution" (poem). *Survey* 36:13 (24 June 1916): 335.

Giovannitti's Address to the Jury. Boston: Boston School of Social Science, 1913.

Golding, Alan. *From Outlaw to Classic: Canons in American Poetry*. Madison: University of Wisconsin Press, 1995.

———. "Dissensus and Evaluation: Issues in the Wri(gh)ting of American Literary History." Paper given at the MLA Convention, Toronto, 27 Dec. 1993. Quoted by permission of the author.

———. "Poet-Critics and Professionalism in the 1930s." *Sagetrieb* 10 (winter 1991): 17–26.

Graff, Gerald. *Professing Literature: An Institutional History*. Chicago: University of Chicago Press, 1987.

Greenblatt, Stephen, and Giles Gunn, eds. *Redrawing the Boundaries: The Transformation of English and American Literary Studies*. New York: MLA, 1992.

Gunning, Sandra. *Race, Rape, and Lynching: The Red Record of American Literature, 1890–1912*. New York: Oxford University Press, 1996.

Habermas, Jürgen. *The Structural Transformation of the Public Sphere: An Inquiry into a Category of Bourgeois Society*. Translated by Thomas Burger with Frederick Lawrence. Cambridge, Mass.: MIT Press, 1991. Originally published as *Strukturwandel der Öffentlicheit*, 1962.

Hagedorn, Hermann. "A Note on Contemporary Poetry." *North American Review* 196 (1912): 772–79.

Hamilton, Alexander, James Madison, and John Jay. *The Federalist Papers*. New York: Bantam Books, 1982.

Hammer, Langdon. Review of *Cleanth Brooks and Robert Penn Warren: A Literary Correspondence* and *Cleanth Brooks and Allen Tate: Collected Letters, 1933–1976*. *Modernism/Modernity* 7:1 (2000): 165–68.

———. *Hart Crane & Allen Tate: Janus-Faced Modernism*. Princeton, N.J.: Princeton University Press, 1993.

Harrington, Joseph. "Why American Poetry Is Not American Literature." *American Literary History* 8:3 (1996): 361–72.

Hart, James D. *The Popular Book: A History of America's Literary Taste*. New York: Oxford University Press, 1950.

Haywood, William D. *The Speech of Wm. D. Haywood on the Case of Ettor and Giovannitti*. Lawrence, Mass.: Ettor-Giovannitti Defense Committee, n.d.

Heaton, James P. "The Salem Trial." *Survey*, 7 Dec. 1912, 301–4.

Heller, Scott. "New Life for Modernism." *Chronicle of Higher Education*, 5 Nov. 1999, A21–22.

———. "Beyond the Usual Suspects: Scholars Expand the Modernist Canon." *Chronicle of Higher Education*, 5 Nov. 1999, A23.

Hewitt, Andrew. *Fascist Modernism: Aesthetics, Politics, and the Avant-Garde*. Stanford, Calif.: Stanford University Press, 1993.

Hill, Frank Ernest. "Why We Don't Read Poetry." *New Republic*, 5 Dec. 1923 (supplement), 10+.

History Committee of the General Strike Committee. *The Seattle General Strike*. Seattle: Seattle Union Record Publishing Co., Inc., n.d.

Huyssen, Andreas. "Mass Culture As Woman: Modernism's Other." In *Studies in Entertainment*, edited by Tania Modleski. Bloomington: Indiana University Press, 1986, 188–207.

Jameson, Fredric. *Fables of Aggression: Wyndham Lewis, the Modernist as Fascist*. Berkeley: University of California Press, 1979.

Jancovich, Mark. *The Cultural Politics of the New Criticism*. Cambridge: Cambridge University Press, 1993.

Johns, Adrian. *The Nature of the Book: Print and Knowledge in the Making*. Chicago: University of Chicago Press, 1998.

Johnson, Robert Underwood. "Obstacles to Poetry in America." *Art World* 1 (1916): 176–79.

Kalaidjian, Walter B. *American Culture between the Wars*. New York: Columbia University Press, 1993.

Kant, Immanuel. *Critique of Aesthetic Judgement*, part 1 of *The Critique of Judgement*. 1928. Translated by James Creed Meredith. Oxford: Clarendon Press, 1986.

Kilmer, Joyce. "The Prosperous Poet." *Bookman* 43 (1916): 181–82.

Kloppenberg, James T. *Uncertain Victory: Social Democracy and Progressivism in European and American Thought, 1870–1920*. New York: Oxford University Press, 1986.

Kornbluh, Joyce. *Rebel Voices: An I.W.W. Anthology*. Chicago: Charles H. Kerr, 1988.

Koselleck, Reinhart. *Critique and Crisis: Enlightenment and the Pathogenesis of Modern Society*. Cambridge, Mass.: MIT Press, 1988. Originally published as *Kritik und Krise*, 1959.

Kreymborg, Alfred. *Our Singing Strength*. New York: Coward-McCann, 1929.
Laclau, Ernesto, and Chantal Mouffe. *Hegemony and Socialist Strategy: Towards a Radical Democratic Politics*. London: Verso, 1985.
Lacoue-Labarthe, Philippe, and Jean-Luc Nancy. *The Literary Absolute: The Theory of Literature in German Romanticism*. Translated and introduced by Philip Barnard and Cheryl Lester. Albany: State University of New York Press, 1988.
Lears, T. J. Jackson. *No Place of Grace: Antimodernism and the Transformation of American Culture, 1880–1920*. Chicago: University of Chicago Press, 1981.
Leavis, Q. D. *Fiction and the Reading Public*. London: Chatto and Windus, 1932.
Lefort, Claude. *Democracy and Political Theory*. Translated by David Macey. Minneapolis: University of Minnesota Press, 1988.
"A Legal Status for Poets." *Literary Digest* 59 (1918): 27–28.
Lentricchia, Frank. *Ariel and the Police: Michel Foucault, William James, Wallace Stevens*. Madison: University of Wisconsin Press, 1988.
———. "Lyric in the Culture of Capitalism." *American Literary History* 1 (1989): 302–315.
———. *Modernist Quartet*. Cambridge, Mass.: Harvard University Press, 1994.
Levenson, Michael. *Modernism and the Fate of Individuality*. Cambridge: Cambridge University Press, 1991.
Levine, Lawrence W. *Highbrow/Lowbrow: The Emergence of Cultural Hierarchy in America*. Cambridge, Mass.: Harvard University Press, 1988.
Longenbach, James. *Wallace Stevens: The Plain Sense of Things*. New York: Oxford University Press, 1991.
Looby, Christopher. *Voicing America: Language, Literary Form, and the Origins of the United States*. Chicago: University of Chicago Press, 1996.
Lowell, Amy. "A Consideration of Modern Poetry." *North American Review* 205 (1917): 103–17.
Macgowan, Kenneth. "Giovannitti: Poet of the Wop." *Forum* 52 (1914): 609–11.
MacLeish, Archibald. "Amy Lowell and the Art of Poetry." *North American Review* 221 (1925): 508–21.
Marcuse, Herbert. *Negations: Essays in Critical Theory*. Boston: Beacon, 1968.
Marzolf, Marion. *Up from the Footnote: A History of Women Journalists*. New York: Hastings House, 1977.
Mason, Walt. *Rippling Rhymes*. Chicago: A. C. McClurg, 1914.

———. "A Kansas Poet's Income" (interview). *Literary Digest* 48 (1914): 340–43.
Matthiessen, F. O. *American Renaissance: Art and Expression in the Age of Emerson and Whitman.* New York: Oxford University Press, 1941.
———. *The Achievement of T. S. Eliot: An Essay on the Nature of Poetry.* Boston: Houghton Mifflin, 1935.
McCall, Anne Bryan. "A Girl's Friendship with the Poets." *Woman's Home Companion* 38 (1911): 30.
McClure, John. "The Substance of Poetry." *American Mercury* 2 (1924): 103–8.
McClung, Quantrille. "A Poetry Circle as a Substitute for the Story Hour." *Public Libraries,* Nov. 1924, 453–56.
McGann, Jerome. *Black Riders: The Visible Language of Modernism.* Princeton, N.J.: Princeton University Press, 1993.
———. *The Textual Condition.* Princeton, N.J.: Princeton University Press, 1991.
———. *Social Values and Poetic Acts: The Historical Judgment of Literary Work.* Cambridge, Mass.: Harvard University Press, 1988.
Mencken, H. L. "Market Report: Poetry." *American Mercury* 24 (1931): 151–53.
Merish, Lori. *Sentimental Materialism: Gender, Commodity Culture, and Nineteenth-Century American Literature.* Durham, N.C.: Duke University Press, 2000.
Merquior, J. G. *Liberalism Old and New.* Boston: Twayne, 1991.
Michaels, Walter Benn. "American Modernism and the Poetics of Identity." *Modernism/Modernity* 1 (1994): 38–56.
Mill, John Stuart. *On Liberty.* New York: W. W. Norton, 1975.
Monroe, Harriet. "The Radio and the Poets." *Poetry* 36 (1930): 32–35.
Monroe, Robert Emmett. "Figuration and Society in 'Owl's Clover,'" *Wallace Stevens Journal* 13 (fall 1989): 128.
Morrison, Paul. *The Poetics of Fascism: Ezra Pound, T. S. Eliot, Paul de Man.* New York: Oxford University Press, 1996.
Mouffe, Chantal. *The Return of the Political.* London: Verso, 1993.
Negt, Oskar, and Alexander Kluge. *Public Sphere and Experience: Toward an Analysis of the Bourgeois and Proletarian Public Sphere.* Translated by Peter Labanyi, Jamie Owen Daniel, and Assenka Oksiloff. Minneapolis: University of Minnesota Press, 1993.
Nelson, Cary. *Repression and Recovery: Modern American Poetry and the Politics of Cultural Memory, 1910–1945.* Madison: University of Wisconsin Press, 1989.
Nelson, Dana. *The Word in Black and White: Reading "Race" in American Literature, 1638–1867.* New York: Oxford University Press, 1992.

"The New Poetry." *Independent* 78 (1914): 342–43.

Newbury, Michael. *Figuring Authorship in Antebellum America*. Stanford, Calif.: Stanford University Press, 1997.

Nichols, Lewis. "Talk with Mr. Stevens." *New York Times Book Review,* 3 Oct. 1954.

"Nine and Two." *Time,* 26 Dec. 1938, 41–44.

Ninkovich, Frank A. "The New Criticism and Cold War America." *Southern Quarterly* 20 (fall 1981): 1–24.

North, Michael. *The Political Aesthetic of Yeats, Eliot, and Pound.* Cambridge: Cambridge University Press, 1991.

Northup, Clark S. "The Folk and the Individual as Poets." Review of *Democracy and Poetry,* by Francis Gummere. *Dial,* Dec. 1911, 524–57.

Nye, Russell. *The Unembarrassed Muse: The Popular Arts in America.* New York: Dial Press, 1970.

Ohmann, Richard. *English in America: A Radical View of the Profession.* New York: Oxford University Press, 1976.

Pateman, Carole. *The Disorder of Women: Democracy, Feminism, and Political Theory.* Stanford, Calif.: Stanford University Press, 1989.

Perkins, David. *A History of Modern Poetry: From the 1890s to the High Modernist Mode, vol. 1.* Cambridge, Mass.: Harvard University Press, 1976.

———, ed. *English Romantic Writers.* New York: Harcourt Brace Jovanovich, 1967.

Perloff, Marjorie. *The Futurist Moment: Avant-garde, Avant-guerre, and the Language of Rupture.* Chicago: University of Chicago Press, 1986.

———. "Modernist Studies." In Greenblatt and Gunn 1992, 154–78.

———. *Radical Artifice: Writing Poetry in the Age of Media.* Chicago: University of Chicago Press, 1991.

———. "Revolving in Crystal: The Supreme Fiction and the Impasse of Modernist Lyric." In *Wallace Stevens: The Poetics of Modernism,* edited by Albert Gelpi, 41–64. New York: Cambridge University Press, 1985.

Platt, David. "The Social Muse Replies" (letter). *New Republic,* 14 Dec. 1932, 125.

Pocock, J. G. A. "Conservative Enlightenment and Democratic Revolutions: The American and French Cases in British Perspective." *Government and Opposition* 24 (1989): 81–105.

"Poetry and Modern Life." *Saturday Review of Literature* 12 (1935): 8.

"Poetry and Profits." *Literary Digest* 46 (1913): 14–28.

"Poetry in English: 1945–62." *Time,* 9 Mar. 1962, 92–95.

"The Poetry of Syndicalism" (The Contributors Club). *Atlantic Monthly,* June 1913, 853–54.

Pouget, Emile. *Sabotage.* Translated and introduced by Arturo Giovannitti. Chicago: Charles H. Kerr, 1913.

Pound, Ezra. *ABC of Reading.* New York: New Directions, 1960.

———. "The Audience (I)." *Poetry* 5 (1915): 29–30.

———. *Guide to Kulchur.* New York: New Directions, 1970.

———. *Literary Essays of Ezra Pound.* New York: New Directions, 1968.

———. "The Renaissance (II)." *Poetry* 5 (1915): 283–87.

———. *Selected Letters, 1907–1941.* London: Faber and Faber, 1950.

Pratt, William, ed. *The Fugitive Poets: Modern Southern Poetry in Perspective.* New York: E. P. Dutton, 1965.

Radway, Janice. *A Feeling for Books: The Book-of-the-Month Club, Literary Taste, and Middle-Class Desire.* Chapel Hill: University of North Carolina Press, 1997.

———. "Mail-Order Culture and Its Critics: The Book-of-the-Month Club, Commodification and Consumption, and the Problem of Cultural Authority." In *Cultural Studies,* edited by Lawrence Grossberg, Cary Nelson, and Paula A. Treichler, 512–30. New York: Routledge, 1992.

———. *Reading the Romance: Women, Patriarchy, and Popular Literature.* Chapel Hill: University of North Carolina Press, 1984.

Rainey, Lawrence. "The Creation of the Avant-Garde: F. T. Marinetti and Ezra Pound." *Modernism/Modernity* 1 (1994): 195–219.

———. *Institutions of Modernism: Literary Elites and Public Culture.* New Haven, Conn.: Yale University Press, 1998.

Ransom, John Crowe. "Criticism, Inc." *Virginia Quarterly Review* 13 (autumn 1937): 586–602.

———. "The Poet as Woman." *Southern Review* 2 (1937): 783–806.

———. "Poets without Laurels." *Yale Review* (spring 1935): 503–18.

———. "A Poem Nearly Anonymous, II: The Poet and His Formal Tradition." *American Review* 1 (1933): 444–67.

Redman, Tim. *Ezra Pound and Italian Fascism.* Cambridge: Cambridge University Press, 1991.

Rice, Wallace. "Mr. Ezra Pound and 'Poetry'" (letter). *Dial* 54 (1913): 370–71.

Richards, I. A. "Science and Poetry." *Atlantic Monthly,* Oct. 1925, 481–91.

Ritchey, John. "Today's Faith, Tomorrow's Reality." *Christian Science Monitor Weekly Magazine,* 11 Jan. 1939, 15.

Rosenblum, Nancy L. *Another Liberalism: Romanticism and the Reconstruction of Liberal Thought.* Cambridge, Mass.: Harvard University Press, 1987.

Rowe, John Carlos. *At Emerson's Tomb: The Politics of Classic American Literature.* New York: Columbia University Press, 1997.

Royce, Josiah. *War and Insurance.* New York: Macmillan, 1914.

Rubin, Joan Shelley. *The Making of Middlebrow Culture.* Chapel Hill: University of North Carolina Press, 1992.

Ruthven, K. K. *Ezra Pound as Literary Critic.* London: Routledge, 1990.

Ruttenberg, Nancy. *Democratic Personality: Popular Voice and the Trial of American Authorship.* Stanford, Calif.: Stanford University Press, 1998.

Schauffler, Robert Haven. "The Poetry Cure: A Novel Remedy for Weary Hearts." *Good Housekeeping,* Oct. 1925, 37+.

Schaum, Melita. "Lyric Resistance: Views of the Political in the Poetics of Wallace Stevens and H.D." *Wallace Stevens Journal* 13 (fall 1989): 191–205.

Schweik, Susan. *A Gulf So Deeply Cut: American Women Poets and the Second World War.* Madison: University of Wisconsin Press, 1991.

Shelley, Percy Bysshe. "A Defence of Poetry." In Perkins 1967, 1072–87.

Smith, Barbara Herrnstein. *Contingencies of Value: Alternative Perspectives for Critical Theory.* Cambridge, Mass.: Harvard University Press, 1988.

"The Social Significance of Arturo Giovannitti, the Dreamer Who Did Not Turn Out a Murderer." *Current Opinion* 54 (Jan. 1913): 24–26.

Sorby, Angela. "Performing Class: James Whitcomb Riley's Poetry of Distinction." *MLQ: Modern Language Quarterly* 60:2 (1999): 197–222.

Steiner, George. *On Difficulty and Other Essays.* New York: Oxford University Press, 1978.

Stevens, Wallace. *The Collected Poems.* New York: Vintage, 1982.

———. "Insurance and Social Change," *Hartford Agent* 29 (1937): 49–50.

———. Letter to Allen Tate. 6 July 1943. Wallace Stevens Collection #WAS 2390. Huntington Library, San Marino, Calif.

———. *Letters of Wallace Stevens,* edited by Holly Stevens. New York: Knopf, 1977.

———. *The Necessary Angel.* New York: Vintage, 1951.

———. *Opus Posthumous: Poems, Plays, Prose*, edited by Milton J. Bates. New York: Alfred A. Knopf, 1989.

Stone, Eliot Kays. "We Are All Poets." *Forum* 98:3 (Sept. 1937): 144–45.

Stork, Charles Wharton. "The Writing of Social Poetry." *Survey*, 6 June 1914, 283–84.

Strong, Anna Louise. *I Change Worlds: The Remaking of an American*. New York: Henry Holt, 1935.

———. *Ragged Verse by Anise*. Seattle: Seattle Union Record Publishing Company, Inc., n.d. [1918].

———. *The Song of the City*. Oak Park, Ill.: self-published, 1907.

———. "Tenement Back Yards" (poem). *Current Literature* 42 (Feb. 1907): 199–200.

———. "The Woman Speaks" (poem). "Selected Poems of the Month." *Current Opinion* 63 (Aug. 1917): 123.

Strong, Tracy B., and Helene Keyssar. *Right in Her Soul: The Life of Anna Louise Strong*. New York: Random House, 1983.

Stratton-Porter, Gene. "Let Us Go Back to Poetry." *Good Housekeeping*, Apr. 1925, 34–35+.

"The Substance of Poetry." Review of the *Poetry Review*, edited by William S. Braithwaite and Joseph Lebowich. *American Review of Reviews* 54 (1916): 113–14.

Sumner, Mary Brown. "Arturo Giovannitti." *Survey* 2 Nov. 1912, 163–66.

Szalay, Michael. "Wallace Stevens and the Invention of Social Security." *Modernism/Modernity* 5, 1 (1998): 49–74.

Tate, Allen. "Aeneas at New York" (poem). *New Republic*, 14 Dec. 1932, 125.

———. "American Poetry since 1920." In *The Poetry Reviews of Allen Tate, 1924–1944*. Ed. Ashley Brown and Frances Neel Cheney, 78–88. Baton Rouge: Louisiana State University Press, 1983.

———. *Collected Essays*. Denver, Colo.: Alan Swallow, 1959.

———. Letter to Wallace Stevens. 4 Oct. 1941. Wallace Stevens Collection #WAS 2344. Huntington Library, San Marino, Calif.

———. *Poems, 1922–1947*. New York: Charles Scribner's Sons, 1948.

———. "Poetry and Politics." *New Republic* 75 (1933): 308–11.

———. *Reactionary Essays On Poetry and Ideas*. New York: Charles Scribner's Sons, 1936.

———. "Three Types of Poetry: III." *New Republic*, 11 Apr. 1934, 237–40.

———. "Three Types of Poetry: II." *New Republic*, 28 Mar. 1934, 180–82.

———. "T. S. Eliot." In *The Poetry Reviews of Allen Tate, 1924–1944*. Ed. Ashley Brown and Frances Neel Cheney, 105–12. Baton Rouge: Louisiana State University Press, 1983.

Teres, Harvey. "Notes toward the Supreme Soviet: Stevens and Doctrinaire Marxism." *Wallace Stevens Journal* 13 (fall 1989): 150–67.

Tichi, Cecelia. "American Literary Studies to the Civil War." In Greenblatt and Gunn 1992, 209–31.

Todorov, Tzvetan. *Genres in Discourse*. Translated by Catherine Porter. Cambridge: Cambridge University Press, 1990.

Tompkins, Jane. *Sensational Designs: The Cultural Work of American Fiction, 1790–1860*. New York: Oxford University Press, 1985.

Tuan, Kailin, ed. *Modern Insurance Theory and Education*. Vol. 1, *A Social History of Insurance Evolution in the United States during the Twentieth Century*. Orange, N.J.: Varsity, 1972.

TuSmith, Bonnie. *All My Relatives: Community in Contemporary Ethnic American Literatures*. Ann Arbor: University of Michigan Press, 1993.

Twelve Southerners. *I'll Take My Stand*. New York: Harper and Brothers, 1930.

Tyson, Lois. *Psychological Politics of the American Dream: The Commodification of Subjectivity in Twentieth-Century American Literature*. Columbus: Ohio State University Press, 1994.

Untermeyer, Louis. *American Poetry since 1900*. New York: Henry Holt, 1923.

———. *Modern American Poetry and Modern British Poetry: A Critical Anthology*. New York: Harcourt Brace, 1936.

———. *The New Era in American Poetry*. New York: Henry Holt and Company, 1919.

———. "Poetry and the Common Man." *Rotarian* 46 (1935): 13+.

Van Wienen, Mark. *Partisans and Poets: The Political Work of American Poetry in the Great War*. New York: Cambridge University Press, 1997.

Vinh, Alphonse. *Cleanth Brooks and Allen Tate: Collected Letters, 1933–1976*. Columbia: University of Missouri Press, 1998.

Vivas, Eliseo. *Essays in Criticism and Aesthetics*. New York: Noonday Press, 1955.

"Voices of the Living Poets." *Current Opinion* 57 (July–Dec. 1914): 54–56.

Walker, Cheryl. *Masks Outrageous and Austere: Culture, Psyche, and Persona in Modern Women Poets*. Bloomington: University of Indiana Press, 1991.

Watt, Ian. *The Rise of the Novel: Studies in Defoe, Richardson, and Fielding*. Berkeley: University of California Press, 1957.

Wells, H. G. *Marxism v. Liberalism, an Interview Between Joseph Stalin and H. G. Wells.* New York: New Century Publishers Marxist Pamphlet no. 2, 1945.

"Who Will Hear Us? Musing on the Future at Poets House." *Poetry Flash: A Poetry Review and Literary Calendar for the West* 248 (mid-Nov.–Dec. 1993): 1+.

"Why All Should Enjoy Poetry." Review of *The Enjoyment of Poetry*, by Max Eastman. *Literary Digest* 46 (1913): 1060–61.

Wilkinson, Marguerite. "Poets of the People No. V: Robert Frost." *Touchstone* 3 (1918): 71–74.

Wilson, Edmund. "The Canons of Poetry." *Atlantic Monthly,* Apr. 1934, 455–62.

Winters, Donald E., Jr. *The Soul of the Wobblies: The I.W.W., Religion, and American Culture in the Progressive Era, 1905–1917.* Westwood, Conn.: Greenwood Press, 1985.

Wolfe, Cary. *The Limits of American Literary Ideology in Pound and Emerson.* Cambridge: Cambridge University Press, 1993.

Wolin, Sheldon S. *Politics and Vision: Continuity and Innovation in Western Political Thought.* Boston: Little, Brown, 1960.

Zafar, Rafia. *We Wear the Mask: African Americans Write American Literature.* New York: Columbia University Press, 1997.

Zboray, Ronald J. *A Fictive People: Antebellum Economic Development and the American Reading Public.* New York: Oxford University Press, 1993.

Zill, Nicholas, and Marianne Winglee. "Literature Reading in the United States: Data from National Surveys and Their Policy Implications." *Book Research Quarterly* 5, 1 (spring 1989): 24–58.

Index

Note: Page references in *italics* are to illustrations.

abstraction, 82, 93–103, 196n2
academic institutions, 19, 34, 50–52, 159–69, 182; American literary studies, 14–16, 19, 23, 159–61, 164–69, 202n5, 202n6; literary criticism, 17, 22, 162–63, 186, 190–91n14; modernist poetry, 15, 38, 160, 190–91n14
activism: Giovannitti, 113–14; Strong ("Anise"), 132–33, 136–37. *See also* political contexts of poetry
advertising, 32–33, 140–42, *142–43*
Agrarian movement, 40, 58, 70, 71, 190n12
alienation, 82–83, 109
America, 61–63, 71–77
American literary studies, 14–16, 201n1; poetry, 23, 159–61, 164–69; prose, 19, 202n5, 202n6. *See also* academic institutions
Anise, 128, 134–36, 139, 144–45. *See also* Strong, Anna Louise
appearance of poetry, 137–44

"Are Women People?" (Miller), 145
Arnold, Matthew, 48, 68, 75
Arrows in the Gale (Giovannitti), 107–25; "The Cage," 109–11, 114, 121–22, 131–32; introduction, 112–13; "The Prisoner's Bench," 110–11; "Proem," 113, 114; "The Stranger at the Gate," 122–23; "The Walker," 107–9, 111, 115–16, 121, 125
artistic integrity: liberalism, 58; public affairs, 67–70
Atlantic Monthly, 19, 53, 107, 109, 111, 115, 169
audience, 8, 16, 27–35, 47–48, 52, 181–82, 190–91n14; modernism, 38–41, 48–51, 66–68; narrative prose, 167–68; participation, 172–76; performance poetry, 11, 183; poetry in the 1990s, 168–86; popular poetry, 23–24, 27–35, 170–86; proletarian poetry, 106, 129–31, 133, 148, 157, 199–200n8, 199n3, 200–201n16; Strong ("Anise"), 129, 144–45, 150–51. *See also* poetry events
Ault, Harry, 150–51

authority, 26–27, 34–35, 40; gender, 41–43; public, 57–60, 113–14
autonomy, 29–30, 57–63, 82–83, 113. *See also* individualism

Beach, Christopher, 3–4, 8–9, 10, 175–76, 202n5, 203n13
Beat poetry, 13, 51–52, 168
Benet, William Rose, 18, 40–41, 182, 190n9
Bennett, Tony, 5–6, 187n1
Best Loved Poems of the American People, 49, 201n2
Biblical references, 108–9, 122–24
Bollingen Prize, 51, 65
Book-of-the-Month Club, 39–40, 51
Bourdieu, Pierre, 9, 22
Brooks, Cleanth, 38, 53–54, 60, 190n7, 191n16
Brooks, Van Wyck, 38, 60, 70
Bruns, Gerald, 82, 195–96n14
Bryan, William Jennings, 33
Bryant, William Cullen, 11, 92, 165, 184, 196n3, 202–3n7; audience, 13, 31, 54; function of poetry, 34, 39; "Lectures on Poetry," 29, 34, 54; role of poetry, 29
Buckingham, Willis, 24, 183
Burnshaw, Stanley, 18, 82, 189n6, 194n5

"The Cage" (Giovannitti), 109–11, 114, 121–22, 131–32
Capra, Frank, 46–48
censorship, 57–60
civil society, 69, 73–74
Clark, Suzanne, 171, 188n5
classical liberalism, 14, 55, 97–98, 113, 129, 199–200n8; personal autonomy, 29–30, 60–63; Tate, 58–79; universality, 115–16
Coleridge, Samuel Taylor, 5, 54
Communism, 87–93, 156–57
community functions. *See* social role of poetry
conservative liberalism, 59–60, 189n3. *See also* classical liberalism
contexts of poetry, 14–17, 170, 175–83; cultural issues, 9–10, 22, 61–63, 71–77, 163, 201n2; historical events, 82, 107, 114–15, 122–23, 157. *See also* political contexts of poetry; social role of poetry
Cooper, Gary, 47–48
Cox, F. Brett, 191n16, 201n2
critical writing. *See* literary criticism
"Criticism, Inc." (Ransom), 50
cultural contexts of poetry, 9, 10, 163, 175, 201n2; America, 61–63, 71–77; social rankings, 22. *See also* labor movements; political contexts of poetry
cultural studies. *See* American literary studies
Culture and Anarchy (Arnold), 68
current events. *See* political contexts of poetry
Current Opinion, 107–9, 113

Daily Worker, 49
Damon, Maria, 8, 10, 202n5
Davidson, Michael, 202n5
Declaration of Independence, 72
democracy, 10, 14, 33–35, 173–76, 185–86, 193n9
Depression, 81–82, 102–3
Dewey, John, 14, 58, 59, 197n9

Dial, 32, 33, 48
Dickinson, Emily, 24, 67–68, 74, 159, 183
Dowling, William C., 165

Eastman, Max, 31, 137
economic aspects of poetry. *See* audience; political contexts of poetry
Eliot, T. S., 2, 5, 32–33, 42, 49, 78, 191n15
Emerson, Ralph Waldo, 92–93, 159
entertainment, 146–51, 181–82. *See also* popular poetry
equality, 116–18
Ettor, Joe, 110–11, 123

Fascism, 14, 44, 87–88
features journalism, 128, 150–57
Federalists, 72–73, 75
Ficke, Arthur Davison, 11, 28, 29–30, 33, 35
fiction, 159–60, 164–68
Filreis, Alan, 82
Fisher, Philip, 159, 164, 202n6, 203n8
Flynn, Elizabeth Gurley, 123
Foner, Philip S., 145, 197n4
form, 170; punctuation, 139–48, 153–54; Strong ("Anise"), 130–32, 137–44, 146–49; Tate, 76, 191–92n2
Foucault, Michel, 75
Fraser, Nancy, 13, 196n16
Freeman, Mary E. *See* Wilkins, Mary E.
Freneau, Philip, 11, 13, 165
Frost, Robert, 2, 33, 51–52, 162, 201n2
Fugitives 40, 58, 71. *See also* Agrarian movement
function of poetry, 22–55, 169–86, 189n5, 189n6, 191n16. *See also* political contexts of poetry; social role of poetry
Furey, Hester L., 115, 197n5

Gallagher, Catherine, 161
gender issues, 41, 42, 63–64, 168; newspaper writing, 150–57; politicized writing, 134–35, 192n5
Gilbert, Roger, 162
Gioia, Dana, 169, 170, 184, 203n15
Giovannitti, Arturo, 6–19, 105–25, *118*, 197n4; *Address to the Jury*, 120–23, 198n11; *Arrows in the Gale*, 107–25; equality, 116–18; historical contexts, 107, 114–15, 122–23, 196n3; political activities, 113–14; political contexts of poetry, 111–20, 197n7; propaganda, 117–20, 124–25; "The Revolution," 198n13; rhetorical style, 120–24, 198n11; sabotage, 114, 119; trial and imprisonment, 110–11, 114–18, 120–23
"Giovannitti: Poet of the Wop" (Macgowan), 119–20
Glazner, Gary, 170, 181–82
Golding, Alan, 160, 163, 166, 187n2, 188n5, 190–91n14
Good Housekeeping, 42–44, 54
Graff, Gerald, 190–91n14, 190n8
grassroots poetry scene, 169–86

H. D. (Hilda Doolittle), 2, 138
Habermas, Jürgen, 11–13, 113, 114, 185, 196n16, 199–200n8, 199n3
Hagedorn, Hermann, 161
Hammer, Langdon, 7, 33, 38, 58, 157, 190n7

Hansen, Miriam, 188n6, 199n3
Hart, James D., 27, 187n1, 203n9
Hegemony and Socialist Strategy: Towards a Radical Democratic Politics (Laclau and Mouffe), 12
Hill, Joe, 117
Hirsch, E. D., 78–79
historical analyses of poetics, 7, 16, 18–19, 163–64
historical contexts of poetry, 82, 107, 114–15, 122–23, 157
historical time periods, 7, 18–19, 22; nineteenth century, 29, 31; 1900–1920s, 27–35, 124–25, 127, 157; 1930–1940s, 35–52, 83–84, 157; 1950–1960s, 51–52, 83–84; 1990s, 169–86
Hobhouse, L. T., 59
Hull House, 130
humor, 128, 135–36, 144–49, 175
Huyssen, Andreas, 38, 200n15
hybrid forms, 19–20, 127–32, 138–39, 144–48, 198–99n2

I Change Worlds: The Remaking of an American (Strong), 148–49, 151, 156
idealism, 117, 191n16, 198n10, 198n12, 201n2
Ideas of Order (Stevens), 94–97
I'll Take My Stand (Twelve Southerners), 60, 69, 76–78
"Imagination as Value" (Stevens), 94
"In Court" (Strong), 131–32, 199n6
individualism, 29–30, 65, 71–80, 193n11; abstraction, 99–100; aristocracy, 74–77; Emily Dickinson, 67–68, 74; imagination, 87–92; personal autonomy, 29–30, 57–63, 82–83, 113; public concerns, 113–14; Stevens, 195n13. *See also* privacy
Industrial Workers of the World (I. W. W.), 19, 106, 110–11, 114, 119–20, 122
insurance, 84–92, 101, 194–95n8, 195n10, 195n11, 196n15
International Black Writers and Artists, 178, 180
"Invocation to the Social Muse" (Tate), 192n6
"The Irrational Element in Poetry" (Stevens), 81–83, 93–94, 103–4

Jameson, Fredric, 188–89n8
Jancovich, Mark, 50–51, 57–58, 75, 190–91n14, 190n12, 192n3
Jefferson, Thomas, 60, 76–77
Jenkins, Joyce, 171–73, 178, 181, 182
Jewel, 182
Johnson, Robert Underwood, 11, 28, 31, 162–63
journalistic genres, 162–63, 190–91n14; features, 128, 150–57; Strong ("Anise"), 128, 144–45, 150–57, 198n1. *See also* newspaper poets

Kalaidjian, Walter B., 200n15
Kant, Immanuel, 36, 58, 75, 114, 124, 163, 196n1, 198n10, 198n12
"Keep the Girls off the Cars," 145
Keller, Helen, 112–13, 115, 119, 197n4, 197n5
Keyssar, Helene, 128, 133, 199n4
Kilmer, Joyce, 27–28, 190n11
Kloppenberg, James T., 59, 197n8, 197n9

Kluge, Alexander, 13, 157, 188n6, 199–200n8, 199n3
Koselleck, Reinhart, 113, 196n16
Kreymborg, Alfred, 111

labor movements, 15–16, 19, 200–201n16, 202–3n7; Giovannitti, 105–25; Strong ("Anise"), 128, 132–33, 136–37
Laclau, Ernesto, 12, 35, 192–93n8
Lacoue-Labarthe, Philippe, 198–99n2
Ladies' Home Journal, 21, 48–49
Lawrence, Mass. textile strike, 107, 197n4
Lears, T. J. Jackson, 55
Leavis, Q. D., 187n1
Lefort, Claude, 185
leftist politics, 38, 83–84, 93, 102, 164, 189n6, 190n7, 194n7. *See also* Giovannitti, Arturo; Strong, Anna Louise
Lentricchia, Frank, 52, 82, 201n2
"Let Us Go Back to Poetry" (Stratton-Porter), 42–44
Levenson, Michael, 59, 187–88n3
Levine, Lawrence, 187n1
liberalism, 14, 58–60, 192–93n8, 193n10, 197n8, 197n9. *See also* classical liberalism; social liberalism
Library of Congress, 51, 65, 79
Lindsay, Vachel, 21–22, 34
literary criticism, 11, 22–23, 26–27, 74–75, 106, 190n13; academic institutions, 17, 159–69, 186, 190–91n14; modernist poetry, 18, 58, 161–62, 186; political commentary, 111–13; prose, 164–68
Literary Digest, 29, 41, 49

literary journals, 16, 48–52
Locke, John, 14, 60, 193n10
"Locksley Hall" (Tennyson), 91
Longenbach, James, 82, 84, 194n4
Lowell, Amy, 21, 33, 35, 134, 160

Macgowan, Kenneth, 119–20
MacLeish, Archibald, 35–36, 38, 160; liberalism, 40, 60, 70–71; New Criticism, 84; popular appeal, 50
magazine poetry. *See* periodicals
The Man with the Blue Guitar and Other Poems (Stevens), 94–95
"The Man with the Hoe" (Markham), 30, 33, 54
Marcuse, Herbert, 75, 193n10
Marxist poetics, 38, 164, 189n6, 190n7, 194n7
Marzolf, Marion, 150, 155
Mason, Walt, 31–34, 49, 53, 68, 144
The Masses, 34
Matthiessen, F. O., 159, 201n1
McGann, Jerome, 188n4
media, 48–50, 140, 168–69, 200n14. *See also* audience
Mencken, H. L., 41–42, 49–50
Merquior, J. G., 59–60
Mill, John Stuart, 14, 75, 193n11
Millay, Edna St. Vincent, 41, 192n5, 201n3
Miller, Alice Duer, 145
modernist poetry, 21–52, 125, 127–28, 169–70, 182–83, 190–91n14, 199n5; abstraction, 82, 93–103, 196n2; academic institutions, 15, 38, 159–69, 190–91n14; audience, 13–14, 17–18, 21–52, 66–68; Fascism, 14, 44, 87–88; hybrid forms, 144–48;

223

modernist poetry, *continued*
  personal autonomy, 57–63, 82–83; political contexts, 58, 63–67, 71–78, 82, 88–90, 92–103; privacy, 103–4; social role of poetry, 23, 27, 52–55, 201n2; Strong ("Anise"), 128, 137–44; techniques, 137–44; textualism, 27, 35–40, 48–50, 64, 93, 160–61, 170, 176, 189n4, 189n6. *See also* individualism
Modernist Studies Association, 2
Modern Language Association (MLA), 51, 159, 181
Monroe, Harriet, 44, 50, 190n11
Monroe, Robert Emmett, 195n13
Moore, Marianne Craig, 2, 114
Moore, Richard, 180
Mouffe, Chantal, 12, 35, 45, 185, 192–93n8
"The Mountain That Was God: Mount Rainier at Sunset" (Waite), 148
"Mozart 1935" (Stevens), 96
"Mr. Burnshaw and the Statue," 87–90, 93
Mr. Deeds Goes to Town (film), 17, 46–48

Nancy, Jean-Luc, 198–99n2
Nation, 27, 34, 48
National Endowment for the Arts, 171–72, 203n9
national insurance. *See* Social Security
nationalism, 34. *See also* Fascism
National Poetry Slam, 170, 174–76
Negt, Oskar, 13, 157, 188n6, 199–200n8, 199n3
Nelson, Cary, 6–8, 10, 31, 128, 139
Nelson, Dana, 165

Newbury, Michael, 164, 187n1, 202–3n7
New Criticism, 2–11, 51–52, 124, 191n16; academic institutions, 17, 22, 162–63, 186, 190–91n14; modernist poetry, 58, 84, 161–64; political contexts, 6–7, 71, 190n8; Strong ("Anise"), 157. *See also* modernist poetry
New Deal, 66–67, 92, 194n7
New Journalism, 107, 150
New Masses, 18, 67, 82
New Poetry, 130–32, 169–86, 182
New Republic, 18, 27, 36, 39, 49, 71, 192n6
newspaper poets, 11, 13, 31–34, 46; Mason, Walt, 31–34, 49, 53, 68, 144; Strong ("Anise"), 128, 144–45, 150–57
1990s poetry scene, 169–86
Ninkovich, Frank A., 51, 65, 188n4
Noyes, Alfred, 32–33, 34, 189n1
Nuyorican Poets Cafe, 203n13
Nye, Russell, 49, 188n5

objectification of poetry, 35–40, 163, 176, 189n5, 189n6, 201n2
101 Famous Poems, 183
oratory, 106–7, 120–24, 137, 196n1, 198n11

Parrington, V. L., 14
Pateman, Carole, 13, 45, 196n16
performance poets, 11, 183
periodicals, 21, 24, 27–35, 50, 130, 189n1
Perkins, David, 27, 147, 190n13
Perloff, Marjorie, 82, 188n4, 202n6

"The Petrified Forest" (Sherwood), 48, 190n10
physical benefits of poetry, 28, 53–54
"The Pleasures of Merely Circulating" (Stevens), 100
Poetry (magazine), 21, 34, 163, 189n6, 190n11, 199n5
poetry events: festivals, 168; readings, 51–52, 168, 172; slams, 19–20, 168–69, 174–76, 203n13; writing workshops, 19–20, 168, 176–81
Poetry Flash, 170–78, 181
poetry groups, 13, 41, 168
poetry recordings, 51–52
poetry studies. *See* academic institutions
poetry workshops, 19–20, 168, 176–81
political contexts of poetry, 9–19, 82, 103–4, 175, 179–80, 196n16; abstraction, 93–103; gender, 63–64; Giovannitti, 106–7, 111–20; leftist politics, 38, 83–84, 93, 102, 164, 189n6, 190n7, 194n7; liberalism, 14, 30–35, 58–60, 192–93n8, 193n10, 197n8, 197n9; market forces, 29, 32–35, 66–68; modernist poetry, 58, 63–67, 71–78, 82, 88–90, 92–103; New Criticism, 6–7, 71, 190n8; personal autonomy, 29–30, 57–63, 82–83, 113; satire and humor, 144–49; southern writers, 58, 66–68, 77; Stevens, 82, 88–103; Strong ("Anise"), 144–57; Tate, 58, 63–67, 71–78. *See also* classical liberalism; labor movements; social liberalism
political correctness, 67, 71, 97, 157
popular poetry, 13–18, 21–52, 67, 188n6, 188n7; audience, 23–24, 27–35, 170–86; entertainment, 146–51, 181–82; newspaper poets, 11, 13, 31–34, 46, 49, 53, 68, 144; 1990s poetry scene, 169–86; Strong ("Anise"), 128, 144–45, 150–57. *See also* audience; proletarian poetry
post-modernism, 142, 200n15
Pouget, Emile, 114, 119
Pound, Ezra, 2, 27, 157, 191–92n2, 191n15; *ABC of Reading*, 78, 163; antipopulism, 34, 39, 42, 44–45, 201n2; Bollingen Prize, 51, 65; *Des Imagistes*, 199n5; "How to Read," 44–45, 77–78; technique, 77–79
privacy, 15, 192n7; Giovannitti, 101–2, 106–7, 113–14, 125; Stevens, 83, 94–95; Strong ("Anise"), 129, 137; Tate, 68–70, 83
"The Profession of Letters in the South" (Tate), 63–67
proletarian poetry, 106, 129–31, 133, 148, 157, 199–200n8, 200–201n16
propaganda: Giovannitti, 117–20, 124–25; Strong ("Anise"), 128, 151, 198n1
prose fiction, 159–60, 164–68
publicity, 106–7, 113–20, 129, 188n6
publishing of poetry, 16, 27–28, 39–40, 49, 50, 178–79, 183; nineteenth century, 203n9; Strong ("Anise"), 130, 200n12
Pulitzer, Joseph, 150
punctuation, 139–48, 153–54

radicalism, 83–84, 93, 102
radio, 49–50
Radway, Janice, 39–40, 187n1

Ragged Verse by Anise (Strong), 19, 128–30, 133–57
Rainey, Lawrence, 22, 188n4
Ransom, John Crowe, 6–7, 60; audience, 39, 41, 50, 201n3; "Criticism, Inc.", 50–51; "The Poet as Woman," 41, 201n3; "Poets without Laurels," 38, 39, 44, 52–53; privacy, 192n3; role of poetry, 37–41, 52–55, 79–80, 189n5; role of the academy, 50–51, 190n13
Reactionary Essays on Poetry and Ideas (Tate), 61–68, 77
readers. *See* audience
"Remarks on the Southern Religion" (Tate), 69, 78
rhetoric, 106–7, 120–24, 137, 196n1, 198n11
Richards, I. A., 53–55
Riley, James Whitcomb, 46
Roberts, Darlene, 178
romanticism, 161, 163, 196n3. *See also* Bryant, William Cullen
romantico-modernism, 128, 198–99n2
Rosenblum, Nancy L., 69, 101–2, 192n7
Royce, Josiah, 195n11
Ruthven, K. K., 191n15
Ruttenberg, Nancy, 203n8

Sabir, Wanda, 180
Sabotage (Emile Pouget), 114, 119
"Sad Strains of a Gay Waltz" (Stevens), 96
Sandburg, Carl, 33
San Francisco Bay Area, 170–83
satire, 144–47
Saturday Review of Literature, 38, 40–41, 48, 51, 52, 67

Schaum, Melita, 194n4
Scherman, Harry, 39–40
Schlegel, Friedrich, 5
Schopenhauer, Arthur, 37
Schweik, Susan, 4, 192n5
Seattle Daily Call, 132–33, 199n6
Seattle General Strike of 1919, 156–57
Seattle Union Record, 19, 128, 133–49, *142–43*, 200–201n16
Service, Robert, 200–201n16
Sewanee Review, 49
Shelley, Percy Bysshe, 92, 161, 163
Shimmons, Earl, 137
Smith, Barbara Herrnstein, 169–70
Smith, Patricia, 11, 168, 175
social liberalism, 14, 30–35, 55, 58, 115–16, 125, 129, 192–93n8; 197n8; Giovannitti, 113–14; popular poetry, 30–35. *See also* classical liberalism
social role of poetry, 4–27, 45–46, 124, 187–88n3; entertainment, 146–51, 181–82; Giovannitti, 106–7, 119–20, 124–25; modernists, 52–55, 65, 68–77, 197n9; moral concerns, 44–45; 1990s, 169–86; *vs.* narrative prose, 164–68. *See also* poetry events
Social Security, 84–92, 194–95n8
Sorby, Angela, 46
southern writers, 58, 66–68, 77
Stalin, Joseph, 194n7, 198n1
Steiner, George, 44, 169
Stevens, Wallace, 2–18, 37, 52–53, 68, 71, 79–80, 81–103, 184; abstraction, 93–103; alienation, 82–83, 109; insurance, 84–92; "Insurance and Social Change," 84–85, 194n6; *The Necessary Angel*, 53, 79, 94; "The

Noble Rider and the Sound of Words," 79–80, 195n10; "Owl's Clover," 18, 71, 81–82, 86–103, 195n13; insurance, 87–92, 194–95n8, 195n10; political contexts of poetry, 82, 88–103, 195n13; privacy, 83, 94–95, 101–2; "Sea Surface Full of Clouds," 38, 52–53; "Sunday Morning," 195n10, 199n5; "Surety and Fidelity Claims," 90, 101, 195n9
Stratton-Porter, Gene, 42–44, 45, 46, 177
Strong, Anna Louise, 6–19, 127–57, *129*, 188n6, 199n4; appearance of poetry, 137–44; current events, 144–57; entertainment value of poetry, 146–51; features journalism, 150–57; political activity, 132–33, 136–37, 156–57; political poetry, 134–37; propaganda, 128, 151, 198n1; prose, 148–51; publishing, 130, 200n12; punctuation, 139–48, 153–54; *Ragged Verse by Anise*, 19, 128–30, 133–57; satire, 135–36, 144–47
Strong, Tracy B., 128, 133, 199n4
style. *See* form
"The Swimmers" (Tate), 75–76
syndicalism, 106–7, 113–14, 122

Tate, Allen, 6–18, 27, 57–79, 84, 184, 191–92n2; "American Poetry since 1920," 38–40, 72; aristocratic views, 74–77; audience, 50, 66–68; Bollingen Prize, 51, 65; conservative liberalism, 59–60; critical authority, 57–58; letter to *New Republic,* 71; Library of Congress, 51, 65, 79;

New Deal, 66–67; "Poetry and Politics," 45; politics and poetry, 63–67, 71–78, 190n8, 191n1; prose publications, 190n12; role of poetry, 36–40, 53–55, 189n4, 189n6; role of the academy, 51; "Three Types of Poetry," 36–37, 45, 53–54, 57; views on Jefferson, 76–77
Taylor, Charles, 65
teaching poetry. *See* academic institutions
Teasdale, Sara, 33, 107–8
Teres, Harvey, 82, 194n4
textualism, 35–40, 160–61, 170, 176, 189n4, 189n6; function, 27, 64, 93; media, 48–50. *See also* modernist poetry
Tichi, Cecelia, 159, 202n6
Time, 41, 51–52
Tocqueville, Alexis de, 72, 75
Todorov, Tzvetan, 5
Tompkins, Jane, 3
transcendence, 160–62, 182–86
Tuan, Kailin, 87, 91, 92

Union Record. *See Seattle Union Record*
unions. *See* labor movements
universality, 45–46, 109–10, 115–16
universities. *See* academic institutions
Untermeyer, Louis, 21, 173, 198n14; political contexts of poetry, 111–12, 114, 119, 125; popular poetry, 18, 33, 38–39, 42; publishing, 49
utopia, 85–92, 108–9, 148, 195n11

Van Wienen, Mark, 4, 9–10
Vinh, Alphonse, 53–54, 60
Vivas, Eliseo, 189n4

Walker, Cheryl, 188n5
"The Walker" (Giovannitti), 107–9, 111, 115–16, 121, 125
Warren, Robert Penn, 191n16
Wells, H. G., 194n7
"We Want Bread—and Roses, Too!", 114
White, Hayden, 166
Whitman, Walt, 29, 159
Wilkins, Mary E. [Freeman], 23–27, 44–46, 178
Williams, William Carlos, 2, 27
Wilson, Edmund, 36, 184

Winglee, Marianne, 203n9
Wolin, Sheldon S., 60, 73–75, 79, 193n11
"The Woman Speaks" (Strong), 130–31, 133–34
Women's Home Companion, 23, 48
Wordsworth, William, 22, 54
World War I, 9–10, 28–29, 128–29, 183
writing workshops, 19–20, 168, 176–81

Zboray, Ronald J., 203n9
Zill, Nicholas, 203n9

Library of Congress Cataloging-in-Publication Data
Harrington, Joseph, 1962–
Poetry and the public : the social form of modern
U.S. poetics / Joseph Harrington.
   p. cm.
Includes bibliographical references (p.) and index.
ISBN 0-8195-6537-7 (cloth : alk. paper) —
ISBN 0-8195-6538-5 (pbk. : alk. paper)
1. American poetry—20th century—History
and criticism. 2. Social problems in literature.
3. Poetry—Social aspects—United States—History
—20th century. 4. Poetry—Appreciation—United
States—History—20th century. 5. Literature and
society—United States—History—20th century.
6. Books and reading—United States—History—
20th century. 7. Public opinion—United States—
History—20th century. 8. Poetry—Public opinion
—History—20th century. 9. Poetics. I. Title.
PS310.S7 H37 2002
811'.509—dc21   2001056763

www.ingramcontent.com/pod-product-compliance
Lightning Source LLC
Chambersburg PA
CBHW032249150426
43195CB00008BA/382